Harold Stassen

HAROLD STASSEN

Eisenhower, the Cold War, and the Pursuit of Nuclear Disarmament

LAWRENCE S. KAPLAN

UNIVERSITY PRESS OF KENTUCKY

Scholarly publisher for the Commonwealth,
serving Bellarmine University, Berea College, Centre College of Kentucky, Eastern Kentucky University, The Filson Historical Society, Georgetown College, Kentucky Historical Society, Kentucky State University, Morehead State University, Murray State University, Northern Kentucky University, Transylvania University, University of Kentucky, University of Louisville, and Western Kentucky University.

Editorial and Sales Offices: The University Press of Kentucky
663 South Limestone Street, Lexington, Kentucky 40508-4008
www.kentuckypress.com

Library of Congress Cataloging-in-Publication Data

Names: Kaplan, Lawrence S., author.
Title: Harold Stassen : Eisenhower, the Cold War, and the pursuit of nuclear disarmament / Lawrence S. Kaplan.
Other titles: Harold Stassen, Eisenhower, the Cold War, and the pursuit of nuclear disarmament
Description: Lexington, Kentucky : The University Press of Kentucky, [2018] | Series: Studies in conflict, diplomacy, and peace | Includes bibliographical references and index.
Identifiers: LCCN 2017042890| ISBN 9780813174860 (hardcover : alk. paper) | ISBN 9780813174884 (pdf) | ISBN 9780813174891 (epub)
Subjects: LCSH: Stassen, Harold E. (Harold Edward), 1907-2001. | Statesmen—United States—Biography. | Nuclear disarmament—United States—History. | Eisenhower, Dwight D. (Dwight David), 1890-1969. | Cold War—Political aspects—United States—History—20th century. | United States—Politics and government—1945-1989. | United States—Foreign relations--1945-1989.
Classification: LCC E748.S784 K37 2018 | DDC 973.921092 [B] — dc23
LC record available at https://lccn.loc.gov/2017042890

This book is printed on acid-free paper meeting the requirements of the American National Standard for Permanence in Paper for Printed Library Materials.

Manufactured in the United States of America.

Member of the Association of
American University Presses

To Phil Cantelon,
distinguished historian and loyal friend,

and to Steve Rearden,
who has read and improved
every NATO manuscript I have written.

Contents

Introduction

There are few figures in the American political firmament whose long career began so early and so auspiciously and then faded gradually but steadily into obscurity. Bursting into fame toward the end of the Great Depression, Harold Stassen, Minnesota's "boy governor"—elected at age thirty-one in 1938 and reelected in 1940 and 1942—excited a new generation of Republicans to support him enthusiastically for president. After failing to win the nomination in 1948, a goal he believed his early successes merited, he chased after the nomination over the next generation. It made him a figure of mockery as a perennial also-ran on the margins of the history of the twentieth century. He sought the nomination of the Republican Party for president of the United States twelve times between 1944 and 1992.

Arguably, his persistent quest for high office devolved from his early successes as district attorney of his native Dakota County in his twenties, his spectacular popularity as governor of Minnesota in his early thirties, and his prominence as a US delegate to the San Francisco Conference on the United Nations Charter in 1945. His sense of entitlement was enhanced by the reactions he aroused in young Republicans, who saw in him a liberal internationalist who would return the party to the White House. Stassen was keynote speaker at the 1940 Republican National Convention before he was old enough to be a presidential candidate. He redeemed a promise to his constituents in 1942 that he would leave the governor's office the following year. He joined the US Navy in 1943, serving as a lieutenant commander in the Pacific on Admiral William H. (Bull) Halsey's staff.

Small wonder, then, that he believed he would achieve the presidency after leaving the navy in 1945. Stassen's path to distinction seemed destined from the time he graduated from the University of Minnesota Law School in 1929. As an undergraduate, he had been a masterful intercollegiate debater and captain of the university's rifle team. It was a logical step from a law office in South St. Paul, Minnesota, in 1929 to election

Governor Harold E. Stassen, circa 1940. (Harris & Ewing, photographer; Library of Congress)

as district attorney of Dakota County in 1934 and 1936 and then to the governor's office two years later.

At the cusp of what was anticipated to be a brilliant career, his trajectory began to fall with missteps in a debate with Governor Thomas E. Dewey of New York in the Oregon presidential primary campaign in 1948 and spiraled downward from there. He did not win the nomination that year, despite impressive grassroots support from young Republicans in the face of opposition from party leaders. His 1948 campaign was the closest he would come to realizing his dream in politics. Thereafter, he campaigned for governor of Pennsylvania in 1958 and 1966 and mayor of Philadelphia in 1969, seeking to capitalize on his prestige as president of the University of Pennsylvania from 1948 to 1952. After moving back to Minnesota in 1982, he ran for a congressional seat in 1985, failing once again. In the midst of these activities he continued to seek the presidency without success. His was a tale of continual rejection, yet continual perseverance, in politics at every level.

The objective of this study is not to revise Stassen's record as a politician. Rather, it is to look closely at his activities as an administrator and a diplomatist, to which he brought the same energy and talent that had been so conspicuous in his service as governor of Minnesota, as administrative aide to Halsey, as delegate at the San Francisco Conference on the United Nations Charter, and as a leading contributor to the framing of President Eisenhower's foreign policies.

Inevitably, he made enemies along the way. Notwithstanding serial failures in the political arena, his overweening self-confidence led to efforts to dominate whatever gathering he attended. He gladly entered combat with Secretary of State John Foster Dulles, even though Dulles's experience and connections outmatched the younger man's resources. Stassen's reputation, however, was distinguished enough to pose a threat to Dulles's management of foreign affairs in the Eisenhower administration. His performance at the San Francisco Conference in 1945 in expressing and defending American objectives in the UN Charter won him sufficient recognition in North Atlantic Treaty Organization (NATO) circles to be cited as a potential secretary-general of that organization.

Consequently, Stassen met resistance from members of any team he joined. His early successes in politics aroused envy, and his sense of entitlement led to resentment. His goal as a young reformer was to infuse the Republican Party with liberal programs that could lure partisans of the New Deal away from the Democrats. Most importantly, he embodied a new vision of American leadership in the world that emerged after World War II.

Given his youth and enthusiasm, it was not surprising that he attracted supporters of college age and younger. He broke with Republican Party leadership to engage in grassroots campaigning, bringing a corps of youthful admirers into his fold. He was a vigorous and articulate spokesman for a new generation ready to take over a demoralized party in the wake of Roosevelt's election to an unprecedented third term in the White House. His keynote address to the Republican National Convention in 1940 affirmed candidate Wendell Willkie's rejection of isolationism at a time when Europe was coming under the control of Nazi Germany. As temporary chairman of the 1940 convention, Stassen's voice on Willkie's behalf was a factor in the latter's winning the nomination.

It was his appointment five years later as one of three Republican delegates to the San Francisco Conference that solidified his attachment to the objectives of the United Nations. President Roosevelt chose wisely in making a conscious effort to ensure that the United Nations would avoid the fate of Woodrow Wilson's League of Nations. The presence of two influential Republican enthusiasts—Lieutenant Commander Stassen and Senator Arthur H. Vandenberg—was a critical factor in winning the Senate's support for the UN Charter.

Like Vandenberg's, Stassen's voice was audible in the deliberations at San Francisco. He was no callow discussant; rather, he was a persuasive figure in framing the American conception of the United Nations. His identification in the minutes of the conference proceedings as "Governor" and more often as "Commander" implied respect for his credentials as a former governor of Minnesota and for his military experience, which added weight to his presence in San Francisco. He left the navy as a captain in November 1945. The head of Canada's delegation, Lester B. Pearson, judged that the young Stassen and Vandenberg were the most influential members of the US delegation.

World War II convinced Stassen which direction the United States should take in the postwar world. Perhaps more importantly, it confirmed his belief that he could be the one to lead the nation in that world. Even though this did not happen, as one failed political effort followed another, his important role in the Eisenhower administration has often been overlooked. Recognizing that he would not win the nomination in 1952, Stassen felt it was imperative that Eisenhower, as spokesman for the new Republican internationalism, defeat the most powerful conservative contender—Ohio senator Robert A. Taft. Stassen used his waning political authority to set up a scenario in which he would throw his votes to

Eisenhower on the floor of the convention. The plan succeeded, even as his enemies were never fully convinced that the Minnesotan had given up hope of ultimately being the party's choice.

President Eisenhower probably appreciated Stassen's empathy with his own internationalist predilections more than his political alignment. To Stassen's disappointment, the president did not name him secretary of state. John Foster Dulles, with his long and distinguished career in international law and diplomacy, was Eisenhower's choice. Nevertheless, Stassen's positions in the administration enabled him to establish the parameters of Eisenhower's foreign policies. As director of the Mutual Security Agency (MSA) in 1953, Stassen was not only in charge of military and economic aid to the European allies but also a member of the cabinet and the National Security Council with direct access to the president. In addition, he was appointed special assistant to the president for disarmament in 1955. In both these positions, Stassen would expand his authority as far as he could manage. Not incidentally, this guaranteed friction between Dulles and Stassen as competitors for leadership in framing US foreign policy. Dulles was especially annoyed with a *New York Times* editorial dubbing Stassen the "Secretary of Peace."

Stassen lost the leadership contest in part because he stretched his mandate too far, but not before his persistent efforts to limit nuclear armaments became the hallmark of the Eisenhower administration's national security policy. Even though his most ambitious project, the nuclear test ban treaty of 1957, failed, he left a legacy that his successors in both the Eisenhower and subsequent administrations pursued.

He represented a strain in the Republican Party that the president valued and advanced. Stassen remained optimistic that the nuclear demon could be tamed, and his ultimate goal was the Wilsonian dream of global disarmament. Even if this could not be realized, he urged lesser measures, such as the abandonment of nuclear testing and transparent reciprocal exposure of armaments. He feared that the Cold War—unchecked—could lead to a nuclear holocaust. If nuclear weapons could not be eliminated, Stassen, like Eisenhower, hoped that at least they could be controlled. His political convictions were undergirded by a religious faith that impelled him to leadership in the American Baptist Convention and in such organizations as the International Council on Religious Education and the US Inter-Religious Committee on Peace. Overall, Stassen was not unaware that success in such activities would promote his long-standing ambition to become president of the United States.

Given the Minnesotan's prominence in the generation following World War II, the absence of any serious academic consideration of his contributions to American history deserves an explanation. The one offered most often is the folly of his increasingly futile pursuit of the presidency. This perception may have distorted the reality of his role. His positions on foreign policy in the 1940s, which repudiated the Republican Party's isolationism of the 1930s; his incisive commentaries on the importance of the American stake in the United Nations in the 1940s; and his impact on the foreign policies of the Eisenhower administration in the 1950s all paled in light of his diminished presence in the later years of the twentieth century.

As a consequence, Stassen is virtually absent from the historical scholarship of the Truman and Eisenhower years. Occasional references appear in many books on that era, but these are marginal to the more significant figures of the time. Recently, three scholars collaborated to produce a Stassen biography: Alec Kirby, David G. Dalin, and John F. Rothmann, *Harold Stassen: The Life and Perennial Candidacy of the Liberal Progressive Republican* (Jefferson, NC: McFarland, 2013). The principal author met with and interviewed the governor and was starstruck along with his coauthors. They succeeded in crafting a credible study of his long life, emphasizing his progressive background without excessive deference to his persona. Less objective is the reverent monograph by Robert E. Matteson: *Harold Stassen: His Career, the Man, and the 1957 Arms Control Negotiations* (Inver Grove Heights, MN: Desk Top, 1991). A devoted aide to Stassen in his many positions, Matteson concentrated on the one key issue in his career.

Stassen's campaign biography prepared for the 1948 presidential race—*Where I Stand* (New York: Doubleday, 1947)—set out his political objectives in conventional fashion. Written late in life, his biography of Eisenhower coauthored with Marshall Houts—*Eisenhower: Turning the World toward Peace* (St. Paul, MN: Merrill/Magnus, 1990)—was essentially a justification of Stassen's role in the Eisenhower administration. All told, the list of publications is thin, with major publishing houses notably absent.

For further insights into Stassen's contributions to arms control in the

Eisenhower administration, scholars have to rely on biographies of Eisenhower and Dulles that touch on Stassen's positions. Additionally, major monographs such as David Tal's *The American Nuclear Disarmament Dilemma, 1945–1963* (Syracuse, NY: Syracuse University Press, 2008) focus on the differing approaches of Stassen and Dulles. Arguably, Tal's perceptive "The Secretary of State vs. the Secretary of Peace: The Dulles-Stassen-Dulles Controversy and US Disarmament Policy, 1955–1958," *Journal of Contemporary History* 41, no. 4 (2006): 721–82, does not take into sufficient account the responsibilities of the secretary of state in the management of foreign affairs in a global arena.

This study examines the sources of Stassen's ideas about international affairs and how they manifested in his meteoric rise to national attention. Its emphasis is on his roles in the Eisenhower administration as director of the MSA and as the president's special assistant for disarmament. Among the questions raised is the effect of his seminal experience at the San Francisco Conference in 1945 on refining and expanding his judgments on foreign relations. Did his insatiable appetite for high political office affect his positions on foreign policy goals? Did his constant intrusion into the spaces of cognate offices, reflected in his voluminous commentaries on every issue connected with foreign policy, impair his effectiveness as a diplomatist? These are the issues discussed in this book.

In striking contrast to the paucity of academic studies of Stassen's career are the rich resources available in archives and libraries that illuminate the most significant facts of his life. Primary among them are the Stassen Papers at the Minnesota Historical Society in St. Paul—214 boxes relating to his career before 1958. Given the importance of Eisenhower and Dulles in Stassen's life, the Eisenhower Papers at the Eisenhower Presidential Library in Abilene, Kansas, and the Dulles Papers at Princeton, New Jersey, are the most significant supplementary sources. Photocopies of the Dulles collections are located in the Manuscripts Division of the Library of Congress. Useful supplementary material can also be found among the papers and memoirs of Dewey, Taft, and Vandenberg and of the European statesmen Harold Macmillan and Jules Moch.

Robert E. Matteson, Stassen's most influential colleague, also deposited his papers at the Minnesota Historical Society. They are particularly significant in revealing Stassen's role as director of the White House disarmament staff in the Eisenhower administration. Because Stassen figured prominently at NATO meetings in the 1950s, the NATO archives in Brussels are useful to researchers. The National Archives in College Park, Maryland, contain State Department correspondence in Record Group 59 and Defense Department documents in Record Group 330, which frequently involved Stassen. The *New York Times* is particularly valuable as a newspaper of record. Secondary accounts in articles and newspapers are available in abundance.

In summary, this project seeks to explain Stassen's role in the foreign policies of the Eisenhower administration and to judge whether it merits a more important place in American history than it is usually given.

1

The Preparatory Years, 1938–1945

Young Stassen had many of the qualifications that aspiring American politicians find so valuable in the nation's presidential tradition. Prominent among them was a "log cabin" origin, which William Henry Harrison used successfully in the presidential campaign of 1840. It did not matter that Harrison was a member of Virginia's gentry or that his father was a signer of the Declaration of Independence. What it signified was an individual's ability to rise from obscurity through the image of an imagined past.

Stassen capitalized on his rural background, which included managing a forty-two-acre farm at age fifteen when his father was ill. Immigrant origins in northern Europe, widely shared in Minnesota and enhanced by his mother's Norwegian ancestry, served him especially well. His paternal grandfather had emigrated from Austria.[1] Stassen's home was hardly a log cabin. Nor did the Dakota County farmstead, not many miles from the state capital of St. Paul, qualify as a frontier. His father served several terms as mayor of West St. Paul. These deviations mattered no more than the myth of Harrison's humble origins.

Stassen's spectacular rise derived from his intelligence, ambitions, good looks—and good luck. The fourth of five children, he was born on April 13, 1907, and was identified as a golden boy early in his youth. Though not quite a boy wonder in his teens, he was a visible presence at the University of Minnesota. Tall and burly, he was aware of his gifts at a young age. There was little doubt in most people's minds, least of all his, that he was destined for great things in life.

Success came early. He graduated from St. Paul's Humboldt High School at age fifteen and from the University of Minnesota Law School in 1929. Everything he encountered as an undergraduate pointed in the same direction—early success and fame. Journalist John Gunther was impressed by the range of Stassen's undergraduate activities and noted that his record—"he practically ran the campus—is unmatched to this day."[2] He was not only a sharpshooter and captain of the university's rifle team but also a star on the debating team. While spreading his name around campus, he worked his way through college with jobs ranging from bakery flunky to Pullman car conductor. A lifelong Baptist, he also immersed himself in religious affairs during his college years. He was later elected president of the American Baptist Convention and was active in the World Council of Churches.[3]

At the University of Minnesota Law School, the gregarious Stassen made friends who would become loyal supporters in his campaigns for the presidency. He and classmate Elmer J. Ryan opened a law firm in South St. Paul upon their graduation in 1929. Both were young men in a hurry. The law practice was barely under way when Stassen announced his candidacy for district attorney of Dakota County. Ryan, though a Democrat, campaigned for him. Stassen subsequently reciprocated, stumping for Ryan in his successful run for Congress in 1934.[4] As district attorney, Stassen worked to root out corruption in his state, much like his future rival Thomas E. Dewey did in New York. Edward Thye, Stassen's friend and successor as governor of Minnesota, liked to recall how the youthful district attorney faced down a crowd of angry dairy farmers threatening to dump their milk and block highways in an effort to raise milk prices. Stassen told them he would prosecute anyone who broke the law but went on to suggest that they appoint a committee to negotiate for higher prices. He displayed the kind of courage and resourcefulness that Franklin D. Roosevelt admired.[5]

Given the attention his activities as district attorney gave him, it is hardly surprising that Stassen eyed the governor's office as his next goal. His timing was fortunate. For a generation, the Farmer-Labor Party, founded in 1920 as a populist movement to promote the interests of farmers and urban laborers, had dominated politics in Minnesota. Led by popular governor Floyd B. Olsen in the 1930s, it suffered from his premature death as well as from Roosevelt's New Deal, which co-opted many of the party's issues. Olsen's immediate successor, Elmer A. Benson, lacked charisma and was plagued by the recession of 1937 and the strikes that followed. These circumstances provided an opportunity for the Young Republican League, organized by Stassen, to restore a Republican to the governor's office. As president of the County District Attorney Association in 1935 and delegate to the Republican National Convention in 1936, Stassen had positioned himself to become the Republican favorite son.[6]

Stassen had only the Republican Old Guard, veterans of continual defeat, to contend with in his own party. He managed this with ease and was, in fact, his own campaign manager. Business leaders, discouraged by past failures, rallied to him after eight years of Farmer-Labor dominance, providing the necessary financial backing for his campaign. But it was the enthusiasm of young volunteers that assured him victory in the primary.

The election itself proved to be no more difficult than the primary. Governor Benson was an inept campaigner. When stung by the charge that the Farmer-Labor administration was a corrupt city-slicker machine, Benson's only riposte was to label his strapping young opponent "a drugstore cowboy." Furthermore, Benson was not helped by divisions within his party.[7]

The Boy Governor

The young governor faced more than his share of problems in a Depression year, but his youthful team (the lieutenant governor was only twenty-eight years old)—patronizingly dubbed the "Diaper Brigade"—was equal to the challenge. His immediate problem was how to deal with labor strikes sponsored by the Teamsters Union. A rural-dominated legislature demanded punitive action from its Republican governor. Instead, Stassen crafted a labor conciliation law, a successful initiative that provided for a thirty-day waiting period before the start of any strike involving a public interest. The governor appointed a three-man board representing the interests of business, labor, and the public to reconcile differences. If the board failed to find a solution, a strike was still an option. But once tempers cooled, strikes were reduced. This brought the governor national attention in his first few months in office. His moderation not only led to some labor support but also opened a popular new approach for Republicans.[8]

Less dramatic yet equally impressive was his success in taming the budget. Responsibility for controlling Minnesota's finances was placed with a commissioner charged with reducing costs and eliminating graft. The commissioner was legally obliged to cut costs if tax receipts declined—a substantial boost to fiscal health. Stassen's reforms continued with the introduction of Minnesota's first civil service law. That accomplishment was important enough for him to consider it first among his attainments as governor.[9]

Reward for this success came quickly, enhanced by the political environment of 1938. Republican victories at the polls reflected the seeming failure of the New Deal and particularly the negative public reaction to President Roosevelt's attack against the Supreme Court. In this context, Minnesota's ambitious young governor was hailed as the face of a rejuvenated Republican Party, and he made the most of the acclaim. Stassen was twice elected chairman of the National Governors' Conference, first in 1938 and again in 1940. As keynote speaker at the Republican National Convention in 1940, he anticipated further political advancement, but not yet the presidency. He was still two years away from meeting the constitutionally mandated age requirement for the White House.

Stassen's ambitions were widely recognized and usually appreciated. "Every move he made, every speech was news. He was the youngest state governor in United States history, he was bold and unpredictable and courageous and marvelous newspaper copy," one journalist gushed.[10] Still, there was an occasional touch of uneasiness about how he would use his influence in the Republican Party. Looking at the array of young Republican politicians in 1938, veteran journalist Erwin Canham praised Stassen as "a very pleasant young man, definitely a mid-westerner, tall and broad of frame, a big head, a first-class platform presence, and [an] unassuming, friendly manner." But Canham cautioned that Stassen "so far is an unproved quantity, mightily promising but still problematical."[11] Although his eye was on the main chance, he could still jump to the side of the Old Guard.

When Stassen entered the presidential campaign five years later, the *New Republic* called him "the product of a successful nation-wide publicity build-up. His press agents have done their work well, aided by the Governor's own acute sense of what will make the front pages." *Time* perceived a whiff of arrogance in his visit to Washington in May 1939. Fresh from his middle-of-the-road reform program as governor of Minnesota, he proceeded to tell John Hamilton, chairman of the Republican National Committee, how to defeat the Roosevelt administration in 1940.[12]

The Election of 1940

Stassen's record as governor generally reflected the liberal Republicanism of Senators George W. Norris of Nebraska, William J. Borah of Idaho, and Hiram Johnson of California, but with a critical difference. He looked at the world from an internationalist perspective, fully supportive of the European democracies' confrontation with fascism. His potential to lead the Republican Party was recognized in December 1939 when he was designated the Republican speaker at Washington's famed Gridiron Club. Its membership comprised representatives of the national press who gathered annually for a ribbing of politicians. This was essentially Stassen's introduction to the national stage, and it was made all the more significant by the presence of President Roosevelt. Although speeches at the club were supposedly off the record, journalist Harold Brayman recorded the event.[13] Referring to his age, Stassen captured the spirit of the occasion by noting, "I am perhaps the only man at this head table who is willing to say 'unequivocally,' I will not run for President in 1940." In keeping with this theme, the Gridiron Cub put on a skit in which President Roosevelt used his authority to change Stassen's birthday (as he had done to alter the date of Thanksgiving), thus making him eligible for the presidency next year.[14]

This playful press attention was enough to turn anyone's head, and Stassen was hardly immune to the praise showered on him. But it was the speech itself that impressed the audience, including Roosevelt. In essence, the young governor outlined a platform that he wanted his party to run on: appreciation for the New Deal's advances in social justice, fair dealing with labor without concomitant attacks against business. He did not miss the opportunity to tout his own success in introducing a mandatory cooling-off period before a strike or a lockout. It was a middle-of-the-road program that incorporated the benefits of the New Deal while correcting its mistakes. He opposed the domination of government by business and, equally, the domination of business by government: "in the separation of the two we see the safeguarding of individual rights and a defense against special privilege, either economic or political."[15]

Governor Harold E. Stassen, circa 1940. (Harris & Ewing, photographer; Library of Congress)

Stassen spoke as a midwesterner, but he became a valued partner of the eastern Republican establishment. It was no coincidence that presidential aspirants would use Minnesota as a launching pad for their campaigns. And the governor was not hesitant about taking advantage of their eagerness to see Minnesota as an appropriate starting point for their presidential ambitions.

Initially, Stassen treated Wendell Willkie much as he treated the other candidates, or perhaps slightly worse, given the candidate's very recent conversion from Democrat to Republican. Senators Arthur H. Vandenberg and Robert A. Taft were old political hands, but Stassen's early inclination was to support the young governor of New York, Thomas E. Dewey, who, at age thirty-seven, was almost as youthful as himself. Stassen showed his hand in December 1939 when he made a point of noting that western states looked positively on the New Yorker's candidacy. Speaking at La Guardia airfield en route to a visit with Rhode Island governor William Vanderbilt, Stassen observed, "There has been a very favorable and friendly reaction since Mr. Dewey spoke out our way" and "a deep interest in what Mr. Dewey's policies will be, and the people of the West are eagerly awaiting their disclosure." The two young governors appeared to be in sync, as Dewey flaunted their youth. A *New York Times* editorial suggested that Dewey had chosen Minnesota to make his debut as a salute to its thirty-two-year-old governor. The emphasis was on Dewey's youth and vigor, in contrast to the other tired old candidates. Dewey would emphasize his maturity by noting that Stassen was five years his junior.[16]

This youthful harmony evaporated in the face of the Willkie phenomenon. "We want Willkie" was the slogan of wildly enthusiastic delegates at the Republican convention in June 1940 for a man who had been a relatively unknown Democrat just six months earlier. He was also a leading spokesman against the New Deal's economic policies as president of Commonwealth and Southern, a powerful utilities company. But Willkie was not a spiritual brother of the Old Guard. Rather, he inclined toward a liberal labor policy and was emotionally supportive of Britain in World War II. Given his internationalist leanings, he attracted the attention of brothers John and Gardner Cowles, the liberal Republican publishers of Minnesota's *Star Journal.* They were figures on the national scene as well, publishing the popular *Look* magazine, which rivaled Henry Luce's *Life* for national influence. The brothers quickly identified Stassen as a future star, but in 1940 they considered Willkie the ideal candidate to restore the Republican brand by jettisoning the isolationism of the Old Guard. They first had to mold the neophyte politician into a viable candidate by giving him lessons in the art of politicking.[17]

A test of Willkie's viability came on May 11, 1940, in St. Paul, where the Cowles brothers bought a half-hour time slot on the CBS network for a major speech. Five hundred prominent Minnesotans gathered at Hotel Lowry to listen to Willkie's address. Initially, it went badly. The candidate bored his audience with a prepared text that struck the right notes without the accompanying music. Recognizing how poorly the speech was being received, Willkie "then took off his coat and glasses, and proceeded to sound the same theses impromptu, condemning Roosevelt's excessive spending and chastising him for insufficient aid to the European allies. The audience awakened with wild applause." At John Cowles's home afterward, Willkie expressed his appreciation for Governor Stassen's hospitality. Possibly carried away by the excitement of the moment, he professed to "have more respect for Stassen than for any other man in American political life."[18]

Stassen's transformation into an influential supporter of Willkie was easily arranged. He shared the candidate's rejection of isolationism. As he moved quickly away from the Dewey camp, the New York governor became bitter about the Minnesotan's desertion, claiming that, before his keynote speech, Stassen had promised to remain neutral in the presidential race.[19] Yet Stassen's action should not have come as a surprise. Stassen's record fitted Willkie's full embrace of Britain's and France's war against the Nazis far more than Dewey's cautious, nuanced stance. Upon stepping down as chairman of the Republican National Convention, Stassen announced his backing of Willkie, pointing out Willkie's clearer views on foreign policy.[20]

There was, however, a competitive element in the new relationship, though it may have been obscured by age and Willkie's sense that 1940 might be his only opportunity. Stassen mentioned that "the time may come when I'll ask you to return the favor." His message could not have been clearer. If Willkie failed to win the presidency, Stassen expected to be his successor as Republican nominee. Willkie, pleased with his success in wooing Stassen to be his floor manager, readily agreed.[21]

As journalist Arthur Krock observed, if there was a problem for Stassen, it would be the unseemly transition from a neutral keynote speaker into a manager of Willkie's campaign. Krock's colleague on the *New York Times,* Turner Catledge, resolved the issue by noting that Stassen would be free to become a partisan after he delivered his speech.[22]

Stassen subsequently applied his energetic personality to the Willkie campaign. He was as indefatigable in promoting Willkie's cause as he had been in his own pursuit of the governorship. He was convinced that by tracking down Alf Landon in a freight elevator, he was responsible for getting the former presidential candidate to deliver the Kansas delegation's votes to Willkie. Landon's version of the conversation did not support Stassen's, although he and his colleagues ultimately joined the Willkie bandwagon.[23]

The excitement Willkie generated among the delegates may have been more important than any substantive contribution by the youthful governor, but the professionalism Stassen brought to the campaign and to the candidate was a factor in Willkie's success. His link to Stassen also gave

Willkie an opportunity to show his supporters that he was not just a Wall Street plutocrat. Willkie exulted: Stassen's presence "kills the story that I'm an eastern seaboard candidate."[24]

The governor's enthusiasm was not just a political ploy. He shared Willkie's progressive views as well as his rejection of isolationism. Specifically, he endorsed Willkie's support for Roosevelt's revision of the Neutrality Act, including the arming of merchant ships. He persuaded three Republican senators to introduce an amendment repealing the entire act. And like Willkie, he braved the wrath of the Old Guard in approving Roosevelt's appointment of Republicans Henry Stimson and Frank Knox to be secretaries of war and navy, respectively, on June 21, 1940, the eve of the Republican convention. Consequently, Willkie failed to convince the majority of his party in either house to rally behind Roosevelt's foreign policies. But he had a strong ally by his side in the person of the governor of Minnesota.[25]

Stassen had his chance to shine when he delivered the keynote speech on June 24 at the Convention Hall of Philadelphia's Benjamin Franklin Hotel. It was not a success. Despite a few crowd-pleasing lines, the audience was restive after listening to the rambling speech for an hour. The acerbic H. L. Mencken, writing in the *Baltimore Sun,* claimed that "Stassen's age appeared to be somewhere between seventeen and thirty-three."[26]

While this judgment may have been correct, the speech did no damage to the governor's prospects. His presentation provided little opportunity to move beyond the usual Republican campaign slogans. He criticized the president for failing to lift the nation out of the prolonged Depression. The speech coincided with the release of the Republican Party platform, which had nonintervention in Europe as a major theme—that is, keeping out of other nations' wars. The *New Republic* mocked Stassen: "Will he go further to say that he wants to discourage our present burgeoning export trade in munitions? Except for the tiny handful of isolationists, no politician of either party will."[27]

But one noteworthy aspect of his speech did not fit the stereotypical campaign rhetoric—namely, his call to place country above party: "Every citizen of this nation, regardless of his station in life, his political party, his nationality, background, his creed or his race faces the responsibility of supporting his government, as now constituted, in every measure for the common good." He specifically asserted that "so long as the now President of the United States is in the White House, national unity must take priority over party differences when it comes to the defense of the nation." The war that was jeopardizing Western democracy had already subjugated France to Nazi domination, and as the Republicans met in Philadelphia, newspaper headlines exposed France's humiliating treaty with Mussolini's Italy. This was the context of the most important part of Stassen's address. He could even rationalize Roosevelt's choice of two prominent Republican leaders as secretaries of war and navy. "Politically timed" as the appointments were, they reflected an eleventh-hour confession of fault in the president's national defense program.[28]

This was not the party line. Most Republicans, unlike Stassen and Willkie, would not forgive Stimson and Knox for their apostasy. On balance, the keynote address was hardly a call to arms against a fourth term for President Roosevelt. It also lacked a clear exposition of Stassen's ambitions within a party that remained wary of involvement in Europe. But the direction of his preferred foreign policies was in tune with the positions of candidate Willkie.

Reward for his loyalty was minimal. Although he was briefly considered for chairman of the Republican National Committee, Willkie chose Representative Joseph W. Martin Jr. of Massachusetts. As compensation, Stassen received the meaningless office of chairman of the Campaign Advisory Committee. This was not a blow to the Minnesota governor's visibility, however. Progress toward his eventual nomination once he came of age was advanced by the campaign—and even by Willkie's failure to win the presidency.

World War II

For Wendell Willkie, the war was an opportunity to maintain leadership in his party while boldly supporting Roosevelt's assistance to Britain in its war with Germany. Almost as a partner with the president, he vigorously opposed isolationists in his own party and became an ardent advocate of postwar international cooperation after the United States entered the war. His most notable activity in public life was to serve as the president's personal envoy on a global trip in September 1942, emphasizing the importance of a postwar international organization in which the United States would exercise leadership. His book *One World,* published in 1943, was an instant best seller, advocating a new world order and celebrating the creation of the United Nations on January 1, 1942. Willkie's book was the climax of his collaboration with the president and the occasion of national acclaim.[29]

It was also the kiss of death for his presidential ambitions as a Republican candidate. Long repudiated by the isolationist wing of his party, Willkie burned his bridges with its majority by his close embrace of Roosevelt. This was painfully evident in his failed efforts to recapture the Republican nomination in 1944. After a humiliating defeat in Wisconsin, he terminated his campaign. A heart attack in August 1944 led to his death in October. The contrast between his spectacular entry into the national scene in 1940 and his rejection by the party four years later was striking.[30]

Stassen's experience was quite different from Willkie's. Pearl Harbor opened new opportunities for public service and for his presidential aspirations. He retained and even enlarged his popularity as governor when he ran for a third term in 1942. He had no trouble being reelected despite giving notice that he intended to join the navy before his term ended. His popularity in 1942 also pulled in a Stassenite as senator, Joseph Ball. More importantly, given his intention to resign his office, he was able to jettison the sitting lieutenant governor, C. Elmer Anderson, in favor of an old friend, Edward J. Thye, who could be counted on to continue his policies. The Anderson camp, of course, felt jilted, but Stassen's eye was on his legacy. Thye would be a more reliable protector of it.[31]

The nation's entry into the war embellished the governor's qualifications for higher office. It vindicated both his rejection of isolationism and his persistent insistence on military aid to the beleaguered Europeans. In case his position on foreign affairs was not sufficiently transparent, he asserted on the eve of the Pearl Harbor attack that he was "one of the Republicans who have been early, consistent, and outspoken in opposition to isolationism and in support of the foreign policy of the present federal Administration."[32]

The prospect of war increased Stassen's political appeal. When he registered for the draft on October 17, 1940, less than a month before the presidential election, it drew the attention of the *New York Times.* So did his induction as a naval officer in April 1942. He joined the staff of Admiral William Halsey in April 1943 as his assistant chief of staff for administration. Few politicians who served in the military received as much attention from the nation's leading newspaper.[33] Stassen was well aware of the political advantages his well-publicized patriotism would give him upon his return to private life.

Service in the far-off Pacific did not mean that Stassen's voice on foreign policy was stilled. He continued his commentaries on the state of America's defense establishment, which he had begun after the Republican defeat in 1940. As a newly appointed member of the Civilian Defense Board in April 1941, he followed a pattern he had set in Minnesota of seeking compromises on important issues. In one instance, he asked Mayor Fiorello LaGuardia of New York and Dean James M. Landis of Harvard Law School to submit a dispute over defense supplies to the Civilian Defense Board for arbitration. He also took the initiative in urging cooperation between Republicans and Democrats as the pace of American participation in the war increased. But his call for support of the president's policies did not prevent him from criticizing delays in building the defense program.[34]

While in uniform in 1943, Stassen continued to make himself visible to the public through his speeches at conferences. Shortly before he entered active service, he used his position as president of the National Governors' Conference to circulate his views on the postwar world. He could not have been surprised when a Gallup poll identified him as a potential Republican presidential candidate in 1944. The former governor was the obvious heir of Wendell Willkie's internationalism, and Willkie certainly recognized this when he cited Stassen in August 1941 as a future leader of the Republican Party.[35]

Lieutenant Commander Stassen took advantage of every opportunity in a variety of venues to advocate his conception of America's role in the postwar world. Typically, he was prepared to offer specific recommendations when he spoke about the importance of a postwar international organization. To the St. Paul–Minneapolis branch of the Foreign Policy Association, he proposed a parliament for the United Nations. He outlined a complete set of government functions for the United Nations in a series of talks just a month before starting his naval duty. Appreciating that his name had been mentioned as a possible Republican presidential nominee, he delivered an elaborate speech at Constitution Hall in Washington on March 8, 1943, not only urging renewal of the Lend-Lease program but also encouraging the nation to prepare for a government of the united nations of the world.[36]

With impeccable timing, his entry into military service took place only three weeks before the publication of an article in the *Saturday Evening Post* in which Stassen summarized the points he had been making since 1942: "The nations of the world must not merely agree that they wish to live together they must establish a mechanism of government to achieve that end. I do not propose that, as Americans, we should place all our eggs in the international basket. But the time certainly has come for us to place some of them there. They may hatch something better than devastating wars."[37]

In 1944 Stassen's concentration on the new league of nations permitted him to deflect questions about his presidential intentions in that election year. It is worth noting that he accompanied his concern for the United Nations with assurances that his postwar objectives included a strong foreign policy within a Republican framework. America's national interests would be protected.[38] As a presidential aspirant, he had to maintain his party credentials. This was to be Stassen's trademark—a bold claim to internationalism within limits that Americans could accept.

The Election of 1944

That Stassen was Willkie's heir was obvious, especially to himself. The former Minnesota governor, now a naval officer on Admiral Halsey's staff, would be thirty-seven in 1944 and eligible for the presidency. Richard Rovere, writing in the *Nation* in June 1944, found Stassen more attractive than his competitors—"brighter than Bricker, more personable than Dewey and less reactionary than Warren." But since Governor Dewey was favored to win the nomination in 1944, Stassen's chances of becoming the vice presidential nominee were dim. Dewey "dislikes the thought of sharing platforms with a noticeably taller man. He has a terrible Mutt and Jeff complex and the thought of a Vice President a half a head taller than himself was not appealing."[39]

In any event, Stassen's eye in 1944 was not on the vice presidency but on another competitor—Wendell Willkie. The informal exchange of mutual support in 1940, as well as Willkie's appreciation of Stassen's foreign policy views in 1941, ended abruptly even before the campaign began. Willkie was anxious for a second run at the presidency, while Stassen, with the enthusiastic backing of his Minnesota friends, inevitably sought the same constituency—the progressive internationalists.

In Willkie's judgment, Stassen initiated the break with his caustic critique of *One World* in the *New York Times* in April 1943. Willkie was justly proud of his triumphant world tour on behalf of the Roosevelt administration. His book had been widely praised and became an instant best seller. Conceivably, it was the contrast between the rave reviews it enjoyed and Stassen's seemingly sour complaint about the author's "overemphasis of the wrongs of the British colonial administration and an understatement of the evils of communism and underestimating the more pressing danger of communism" that disturbed Willkie. While recognizing that much of the book "is an able re-emphasis of the principles which Mr. Willkie had been courageously fighting for in international affairs," Stassen noted that "there is some weakness in a tendency to be dogmatic in the statement of them." The newly commissioned lieutenant commander also felt that "the concrete suggestions of the manner in which the nations of the world will become free and work together are limited." His conclusions, however, were positive. He believed that Willkie rightly emphasized "the interdependence of peoples of all continents . . . and particularly the need of following through in a definite continuing United Nations organization for peace, justice, and progress."[40] It is unlikely that Stassen intended the review to signal a break with the titular head of the Republican Party. Arguably, Willkie was too defensive about his reputation and too suspicious of Stassen's motives in writing the review.

Willkie regarded the review as a personal rejection, made all the more painful because he considered himself instrumental in elevating Stassen's image in Philadelphia in 1940. Their political positions were similar. Before leaving for navy duty, the governor reputedly urged his friends to support Willkie for the presidential nomination in 1944. Only after the war ended would the Minnesotan return to politics.[41] Obviously, this was not Stassen's recollection of events. Rather, he remembered Willkie's promise to support his future candidacy.

The major venue for Stassen's challenge was Wisconsin, where Willkie failed to win a single delegate. Stassen won four delegates, and General Douglas MacArthur won three. Willkie appeared to be less upset about Dewey's victory in the state than he did about Stassen's betrayal by enter-

Commander Harold E. Stassen, circa 1944, while serving as aide to Admiral William F. Halsey, Commander, Third Fleet. (US Navy, National Archives)

ing the race. Stassen's willingness to enter the fray divided the liberal constituency that should have been Willkie's. He subsequently withdrew from the campaign and died in October 1944.[42]

Stassen's intrusion in Wisconsin should not have come as a shock. In some respects, Willkie was still the naïf he had been four years earlier when he was suddenly thrust into prominence. He had alienated potential allies by his aggressive attachment to Roosevelt and by his distance from the remnants of isolationism that persisted in his own party. Stassen, however, was hardly the favorite of the party establishment. His ambition was on display too blatantly and too often, and he would have offended party leaders even if he had not repudiated the Old Guard's isolationism.

Stassen's military status was no obstacle, as evidenced by MacArthur's candidacy. If the commander of the Pacific theater in the midst of a war against Japan was an acceptable candidate for the Republicans, Admiral Halsey's assistant chief of staff for administration could advance under that same cover. The question of the eligibility of a serving officer to run for president was formally settled in March 1944, making it clear that military service was not a barrier to the highest office in the land.

Actually, the absence of both men from the hustings hurt their campaigns, the general's more than the lieutenant commander's. Stassen's loyal cadre in Minnesota did its best to drum up his candidacy in Nebraska and Wisconsin, but it was not enough. Although the war hero MacArthur had attracted the support of such prominent figures as Senator Arthur Vandenberg of Michigan, his lack of familiarity with domestic politics and the mistakes of his sponsors made him a less viable candidate than Stassen.[43]

Although the Republicans had repudiated Willkie for his deviations from the party line, Stassen did not share his fate. He did not become a favorite of the Old Guard, but he always wrapped himself in the Republican brand and made a respectable showing in 1944. His military service was a factor in explaining why the Republican loss in the 1944 election did not diminish his prospects for a successful political future. Countering the inevitable opposition of Colonel Robert R. McCormick's isolationist *Chicago Tribune,* Stassen enjoyed the continued backing of the Cowles brothers and of the followers he had acquired as governor. He was well placed to resume his career when he left the navy in October 1945.

The United Nations Charter

Happily, but not surprisingly, Stassen's outspoken defense of Roosevelt's foreign policies and his frequent favorable references to the United Nations made him a logical choice as one of the US delegates at the upcoming conference on the United Nations in San Francisco. The delegation was appointed to frame a charter for the new organization. By naming Vandenberg and Stassen, the president picked leading internationally minded Republicans to represent the United States. By selecting a veteran and a rising young politician, Roosevelt would rectify a mistake made by Woodrow Wilson in 1919, when he had failed to appoint an active Republican to the Versailles conference. A less flamboyant figure,

Representative Charles Eaton of New Jersey, was the third Republican member of the delegation.

According to pundit John Gunther, Stassen was flabbergasted by the invitation, fearing that acceptance could be a political liability. Yet he announced, "It is as much my duty to take an assignment to work for a successful peace as to work for a successful war."[44] His tone of self-sacrifice did not quite fit either his mood at the time or the public image he had been cultivating since the war began. The naval officer presented himself not as a radical one-worlder in the Willkie model but as a statesman protecting America's national interests by promoting a world organization. He recognized that the San Francisco Conference could be just the vehicle he needed to burnish his qualifications for the presidency.

A week before the first meeting of the US delegation, in his first public address since resigning as governor of Minnesota, Stassen observed, "We realize that neither this nation nor any other nation can be a law unto itself in the modern world, and that we are willing to delegate a limited portion of our national sovereignty to our United Nations organization." He had prepared for this occasion with a six-point program that included police powers under the control of an international organization. He promised that no superstate would develop from his ideas.[45] His was an approach via a middle road.

A more persuasive, though not necessarily more accurate, account of his reaction to the appointment grew out of an interview in 1973. He recalled that the president, on his way back from the Yalta Conference, had cabled Admiral Halsey that he would like his naval aide to be a member of the delegation. Stassen claimed, "It was a complete surprise to me and, of course, I very much wanted to do it, because this was a basic objective, practically, in my life, and I thought I had kind of left this behind when I went on active duty in World War II, and I told the Admiral 'I'd very much like to do it.'" Stassen's memory was sharp with respect to his pleasure at receiving the invitation, yet his recollection of removing himself from politics when he joined the navy was disingenuous. Wearing a naval uniform did not keep him out of the limelight. He allowed himself to be considered a Republican nominee for president in 1944, and he launched a flow of commentary on the future of the nation. These activities had brought him to the attention of the president and accounted for the formal offer on February 21, 1945, before the end of the war and just before FDR died.[46]

Admiral William F. Halsey (left) and Commander Harold E. Stassen under five-inch gun barrels of the USS *New Jersey* en route to the Philippines, December 1944. (US Navy, Admiral Carney Collection, National Archives)

From the outset, Stassen was as visible at US delegation meetings and conference sessions as he had been as governor of Minnesota. As the prospective chairman of the Trusteeship Committee at the San Francisco

Conference, he announced that the American position on colonies would have to be clarified before his committee could formally meet. It is noteworthy that this meeting was recorded in the *New York Times.* Even when there were no results, Commander Stassen found an opportunity to be heard.[47]

His presence in San Francisco was marked by two characteristics that had frequently been evident during his brief career. One was a gift for organization and efficient administration, which had helped make him successful during his two and a half terms as governor and subsequently as Admiral Halsey's aide. The other was a propensity to thrust himself into the center of any activity, regardless of whether his contributions were useful.

This flair for self-promotion generated distrust as well as reluctant admiration. Certainly, his relations with Willkie and Dewey in 1940 and 1944 displayed the negative aspects of his personality. His accomplishments at the conference, in contrast, earned him the votes of thirty-seven correspondents covering the sessions as one of the two most effective delegates in San Francisco (the other was Australian foreign minister Herbert V. Evatt). US delegate Virginia Gildersleeve, the dean of Barnard College, was impressed by his ability to get to the heart of any matter. On one occasion, when Secretary of State Edward R. Stettinius Jr., chairman of the US delegation, "failed to grasp the implications of a complicated question, Stassen got up from his chair at the end of the room, walked quietly along and sat down behind our Chairman to help straighten out the tangle."[48]

His less attractive qualities surfaced at a session on May 5, when the four major powers agreed to France's request for a change in language that involved the wartime bilateral pacts aimed at keeping the Axis countries permanently demilitarized until the new world organization could settle the question. But "our stumbling block," Senator Vandenberg noted in his diary, "is Stassen. He claims that the new language makes some sort of a fatal surrender to European federalism." Vandenberg speculated that "he may be trying to make a political issue of the change in language. In any event, he has put on an amazing (not to say irritating) exhibition of bullheadedness. He is a very fine, very able, industrious young man—but when it comes to his belligerent respect for his own opinion, he makes F.D.R. look like a reed in the wind."[49]

President Franklin Roosevelt, seated, meets American delegates to the San Francisco Conference at the White House, 1945. Standing left to right are Representative Sol Bloom, Dean Virginia Gildersleeve, Senator Tom Connally, Secretary of State Edward R. Stettinius Jr., Commander Harold Stassen, Senator Arthur Vandenberg, and Representative Charles A. Eaton. (Library of Congress)

Stassen's behavior at the San Francisco Conference displayed the range of qualities that impressed so many of his fellow delegates. But he expressed his opinions with a vigor that bordered on arrogance. For example, at the very first meeting of the US delegation in Washington on March 13, he dissented from the judgment of Tom Connally (D-TX), chairman of the Senate Foreign Relations Committee, who opposed opening important subsidiary commissions to the public. Connally's point was that this would excessively lengthen the time required for the United States to seek the annexation of any territory. Stassen responded that time mattered less than the benefits of providing open access to the commission's proceedings.[50]

This exchange set the tone for his role in the US delegation. He was not always abrasive, but he was always assertive. When Vandenberg signaled his approval of the language of the charter's preamble, Stassen quickly expressed his dislike of the term "High Contracting Parties" as too pretentious. The question of the veto in the Security Council also bothered him, and it put him in the midst of the discussion among the US delegates. He declared that if the organization failed to act in the event of a violation of the charter, "we would not spinelessly give up." He recommended including a provision allowing force to be applied on a regional basis if the Security Council refused to respond. "He added that he had always preferred some modification of the veto power."[51]

Stassen's role in San Francisco, however, was not defined by his dissents. He was given the important assignment of chairing the Trusteeship Committee and exercised his considerable talents as administrator to make it effective. While expressing his continuing concern for the rights and needs of the peoples in the trust territories, he maintained that bases in some of these areas were a significant part of America's defense network and must be kept under US control. He was, after all, a US naval officer as well as a member of the US delegation.[52]

He took seriously the temporary nature of a trusteeship, with the understanding that the United States was not seeking to annex any territory. He displayed sensitivity to the concerns of the Arab League, which feared that the trusteeship draft document might prejudice its interests in some way. But Stassen sought to be evenhanded. When the Arab delegates tried to freeze the status quo at the expense of Jewish interests in Palestine, he indicated his opposition to the measure. Asserting that all existing rights would be preserved, he noted that freezing the status quo "would, in effect, constitute legislation on a specific problem, and that such legislation could not be accomplished at this conference." Nevertheless, he was open to changing the wording of the trusteeship working paper. Even if it was "not good form" to include a paragraph from the League of Nations Covenant, he favored its acceptance if it would satisfy the Arabs without materially affecting the document.[53]

By contrast, he only reluctantly condoned the behavior of the French in Syria and Lebanon, who were trying to hold on to their League of Nations mandates. He feared that "if regional arrangements were left entirely free of control by the Security Council, a very dangerous situation would be established." The youthful chairman empathized with the

Syrian prime minister's "anxiety that nothing in the trusteeship system should interfere with the independent states of Syria and Lebanon." The meeting between the Arab delegations and Stassen and his aides concluded with the assurance that Syria and Lebanon could depend on the friendly support of the United States when the appropriate time came to accomplish a de jure liquidation of the mandate. But despite the likelihood of "future headaches," Stassen accepted the French amendment of the trusteeship draft, thus deferring to Anglo-French priorities rather than risk the breakup of the conference. What he refused to accept was any infringement on US defense needs, even if it meant a "grand battle with British and French delegates."[54]

On balance, Stassen steered a steady course in reconciling the interests of the colonial powers and the emerging independent nations and US territorial responsibilities. General Carlos Romulo of the Philippines expressed his "disappointment over the fact that in the trustee deliberations the United States had not supported Russia and China on the point of independence," particularly when "the billion people of Asia . . . looked to America for encouragement and inspiration in the struggle of dependent Asiatic peoples for self-determination and independence." Despite Stassen's professed support for the independence of the Philippines, his hope for its future and for the future of other states emerging from colonialism was "interdependence" along the lines of America's forty-eight states. He trod carefully over the term "independence" and suggested that "progressive development toward self-government" would be sufficient to imply independence. "If one goes beyond that phrase there was danger that we would be interpreted as butting in on colonial affairs." US delegate Representative Sol Bloom (D-NY) was so impressed with Stassen's speech to the committee that he thought it should be distributed to all members of the delegation.[55]

Despite the forcefulness of his presentations, it was usually a middle-of-the-road path that Stassen advocated. In essence, he was no radical reformer; progress toward his goals rested on the art of compromise. He was hopeful that the charter would be reviewed at a future gathering, to be called "A Revisionary Conference of the United Nations," convened by the UN General Assembly. This was the recommendation of Leo Pasvolsky, the State Department's chief adviser to the US delegation, who worried that a provision for revising the present charter might detract from the prestige of the new organization. Stassen disagreed. His point was that changes would strengthen the United Nations by winning over people who might be dissatisfied with the results of the San Francisco Conference. If the smaller states demanded a date for the revisionary conference, he was inclined to accede to their wishes, even if it might be premature. The alternative would be having the conference end on a "sour note." Stassen offered a broader view of the United Nations' future than older advisers to the delegation—Pasvolsky and John Foster Dulles—had in mind. He would like certain rules to be applicable worldwide, not just to members of the United Nations, "so that there would be some things which the Organization would decide would be aided by everyone."[56]

As the proceedings continued, Stassen was increasingly pleased with the prospects for world peace. He gladly joined in a recommendation that the final draft of the UN Charter be accepted. He applauded reasonable compromises that recognized the paramount authority of the world organization in enforcing the peaceful settlement of disputes but also permitted freedom of action in the event the United Nations could not end the violence. This formula, he felt, would fit both national and regional requirements.[57]

When the conference adjourned on June 16, 1945, Stassen was justified in feeling satisfied with his actions in San Francisco. He merited the praise he received from both political parties and believed that the results of the conference confirmed the foreign policy pattern he had followed since the beginning of his career: rejection of isolationism and support for US engagement in world affairs. He had found the instrument to pursue these objectives in the new UN Charter and hoped to entrust his political future to the intimate links between the United States and the United Nations.

2

Toward the 1948 Debacle

Commander Stassen returned to his naval duties after the San Francisco Conference adjourned, but only temporarily. He left the service in November with the rank of captain. The war in Europe had ended. Prospects for victory in the Pacific looked bright after the atom bomb leveled Hiroshima and Nagasaki in August 1945. As a member of Admiral Halsey's staff, Stassen witnessed the surrender of Japan in September and was given responsibility for freeing prisoners of war in a camp near Tokyo. The cheers of grateful Americans on this occasion seemed to portend the reception his political ambitions would inspire. Stassen was prepared to take full advantage of his experience as Minnesota's governor, as a leading contributor to the framing of the UN Charter, and as a battle-tested veteran of World War II.

The UN Impact

Understandably, the United Nations was a major preoccupation in this period, and Stassen used the momentum of the San Francisco Conference to publicize his convictions about the relationship between US foreign policy and the United Nations. Public support for ratification of the UN Charter was only to be expected from one of its most prominent authors. On July 2, the day President Truman presented the charter to the Senate and asked for quick ratification, Commander Stassen, interviewed at the Governors' Conference in Mackinac Island, Michigan, won equal billing on the front page of the *New York Times*. In response to a question about the inevitability of war, he stated that he was confident war could be avoided over the next fifty years. Although war was not inevitable after that time, he observed that fifty years was "about the limit any human should try to anticipate." In his address at the Grand Hotel Commodore, he urged the governors to recognize that the policy of isolationism must be permanently removed from American foreign relations and that American power must be used to help mediate differences among nations: "We occupy a very unusual position in the world. This carries with it great responsibilities. We have great economic and military strength and great powers of ideals. It is our responsibility to use the strength we have for the welfare of the world as a whole."[1] This was an expression of triumphalism modified by the patronizing implication that America's superior station in the world should be employed in the service of lesser nations.

His impending return to naval duties did not prevent him from delivering a major speech extolling the virtues of the United Nations on July 5 at the auditorium of the Department of Commerce in Washington, DC. It was broadcast over national networks. Although recognizing that the UN Charter was not perfect, he predicted that "the cynics of the day who scoff at the United Nations [will] be as wrong as [the] cynics of yesterday who scoffed at the United States." He insisted that the greatness of the UN Charter was not in the wording of its current clauses but "in the fact that it has within it room for growth and adjustment and change under future world transitions and experience."[2]

Then, in his usual well-organized way, he proposed a twelve-point program for American aid to the United Nations. Much of it was commonplace, such as his call for complete victory over Japan. Equally specific but more relevant was number six in his program—namely, that "we enter in agreements for the use of armed forces to support the stability and security of the world."[3] The UN Charter actually did provide for a Military Staff Committee, but it lacked the importance Stassen attached to it. To summarize, his passionate defense of an organization of nations had preceded his participation as a US delegate in San Francisco. He had been reporting on the charter's prospects even before the conference adjourned.[4] His speech in Washington on July 5 was the capstone of these efforts.

Efforts to tweak the UN Charter surfaced periodically throughout his long career. In January 1948, as Stassen was entering the contest for his party's presidential nomination, he used an address to the New York Republican Club to push his recommendations for revising the UN Charter, ideas that had been on his mind since the San Francisco Conference in 1945. He alluded to the presidential race, as he was speaking in Governor Dewey's home state. He also noted, "It is customary in an opening address in a new year to express personal hopes for the new year. May I say, with a smile, that in this instance in 1948, and with your permission, I will dispense with that portion of the custom."[5]

His message was to young Republicans, encouraging them to bring "an expanded vision of the realities of world conditions. The continuing clash with Russia at the UN makes it imperative that our Republican party proposes a positive far-reaching foreign policy in 1948 and seek Democratic agreement upon it as a bipartisan policy and enlist general public approval for it as an American policy."[6] Stassen recognized the necessity of collaborating with Democrats to call for a major UN convention in 1950 to strengthen the organization. This was not a new theme; he had called for a "revisionary conference" when he was a delegate in San Francisco to correct deficiencies in the charter, most notably, the role of the veto power in the Security Council. That the State Department was less than enthusiastic about his proposal obviously did not deter him.[7]

While advocating bipartisanship with the Truman administration, he criticized it for shipping more industrial machinery to the Soviet Union than to either France or England. Given the persistent anti-Western behavior of the Soviets, this made no sense to Stassen. "The fallacious notion that we received most of our manganese and chrome from Russia does not justify this concession." Stassen's memory of the Soviets' behavior at San Francisco remained vivid. At the end of his speech, he reminded the party's youth of the importance of rejecting the "shortsighted, obstructionist, evasive, and narrow policies" of the Republican establishment for the sake of the country and the success of the party in 1948. This was the constituency he was counting on to win him the party's nomination six months later.[8]

Stassen's passion for restructuring the United Nations, to make it a fit vehicle for association with US foreign policy, never dimmed. He participated in conferences in Dublin, New Hampshire, and Princeton, New Jersey, in the fall of 1945 that formulated a petition to the UN General Assembly to revise the UN Charter and facilitate the formation of "a World Federal government."[9] This was not a goal he would long support, however.

A generation later, the fortieth anniversary of the San Francisco Conference provided another occasion to draft revisions of the charter. These were followed by additional revisions in 1987, 1989, and 1990 and a seventh edition with a familiar title—"Restructuring Suggested for the United Nations Organization"—in 1995, the fiftieth anniversary of the framing of the charter.[10]

By the last decade of the twentieth century, Stassen's presidential ambitions were at last extinguished, but not his aspirations for the United Nations. In anticipation of the charter's fiftieth anniversary in 1995, he wrote an extended working paper in 1991 embodying his plans for reconstructing the organization, complete with a ten-point program (reduced from the twelve-point program of 1945). It summed up ideas he had been nurturing for fifty years; for instance, the United Nations must become "more effective in peacemaking, more effective in peacekeeping, more efficient in peacekeeping, and more dynamic in securing the well-being of the children, women, and men of the world." For these purposes, a restructuring was needed. Although the Cold War had ended, the United Nations had failed to intercede in the civil war engulfing the former Yugoslavia, which Stassen cited as a further reason for strengthening the organization.[11]

Among Stassen's many proposals were regular annual meetings of world leaders at the United Nations to seek out and put into effect "nonviolent and just solutions for future relationships of peoples of the world." Chapter 8 of the working paper called for elite legions of volunteers to enforce Security Council decisions about violations of peace. Presumably, this mandate would be broader and its enforcers freer to act than the aborted Military Staff Committee under Article 42 of the UN Charter. It is worth noting that this paper repeated sentiments Stassen had expressed in his first major speech on the United Nations in July 1950. Chapter 5 of the working paper recommended abolishing the single-member veto power, as well as adding Japan and Germany as permanent members of the Security Council. In chapter 4 he called for broadening the membership of the General Assembly to give each member a guaranteed voting power that was commensurate with its size. Noteworthy in these recommendations was an echo of his worry about the Soviet Union's abuse of the veto power. Whether this concern was realistic or not, when it came to devising changes in the UN Charter, Stassen's mind was as fertile in his eighties as it had been in his thirties.[12]

Taming the Atom

In linking his political fortunes in 1945 to his role in writing the UN Charter, Stassen made control of the atom bomb his special interest. It was a way to capitalize on his experience in San Francisco as well as to hone in on an issue that dominated the news in the summer and fall of 1945. The enormous destructive power of the harnessed atom that destroyed Hiroshima and Nagasaki in August could threaten the survival of civilization itself unless it was contained. Stassen envisioned the United Nations as the appropriate entity to take charge of the bomb.

As the issue of controlling the atom bomb was debated in the State Department and among US delegations in UN committees, Stassen delivered a speech in the fall of 1945 that attracted considerable attention in Republican circles looking for possible candidates to take on Truman in 1948. A week before his formal discharge from the navy, Stassen spoke at the Hotel Astor in New York on November 8, 1945, addressing the annual meeting of the Academy of Political Science. He maintained that differences over control of the atom bomb that divided the United States, Great Britain, and the Soviet Union should be resolved by outlawing the production or possession of the weapon. Moreover, research into the development of atomic power should be placed under the authority of a commission that answered to the UN Security Council. Stassen worried that the current policy of secrecy with respect to the bomb could challenge other countries—notably the USSR—to develop their own atomic capability.[13]

In his customary fashion, Stassen proposed specific answers to the problem. As he put it to the political scientists: "I believe the best way to discuss that future course is to take up specifically one of the world's problems. I believe we can best come to grips with the issues of the days ahead by discussing frankly and in great detail our policy on the world's major challenge of the future—atomic energy." One option would be to keep control wholly in American hands, imposing "heavy penalties against anyone who would reveal any part of the information that was not already known." This was not the recommendation of Henry D. Smyth, a Princeton physics professor and a leading member of the Manhattan Project. It would place extraordinary power in the hands of a peacetime government. It could also inspire other nations to develop their own bombs.[14]

An alternative would be to release all information about the bomb. But this, too, was unsatisfactory. It might encourage some nation to build its own bomb, generating fear of a surprise attack. Stassen warned that "all of history says that good faith alone is not sufficient for the peaceful relationship between men. . . . Under the give-away alternative, there would be no guarantee of openness of information. We would, in effect be increasing armament of every other individual United Nation. There is no logical reason why each nation of the world should have the power to destroy other nations. Balancing of power has not proved in the past to be a road to peace, but rather a road to war."[15]

Stassen concluded that only a third alternative was feasible: for nations to manufacture an atomic bomb in the future would be considered "a crime against mankind." The present plants in existence—all American—would manufacture just the number required for the World Stabilization Force he had in mind, and then stop. He proposed that "no one shall engage in any nuclear or atomic research without registering with this United Nations Atomic Commission, and that once having registered, any scientist would be entirely free to carry on scientific research and to publish its results to the world." He countered the expected objections that this idea was impractical and violated the absolute national sovereignty of member nations by stating: "Yes, it will!" But, he observed, the narrow concept of absolute national sovereignty "belongs in the same category as the theory of the divine right of kings." No genuine sovereignty would be lost; a portion of it would be delegated "to a new and higher level of governmental machinery where it can be more effectively administered for the people's welfare."[16] Here was a stirring declaration of his hope for the United Nations.

Taming the atom became an ongoing subject in wake of the devastation of Hiroshima and Nagasaki in 1945, and the politically ambitious Stassen remained in the forefront of the debates. When Harold Urey, a distinguished nuclear scientist, Nobel Prize winner, and collaborator in atomic research at Columbia University and the University of Chicago, spoke to the American Association for the United Nations in New York on December 14, 1945, Stassen objected to his thesis. It was not that he opposed Urey's objective—control of the atom. It was the means of doing so that disturbed him. Urey urged the postponement of any production of atomic energy until control of its manufacture was assured. Stassen agreed with Urey that the United Nations should be the entity that controlled atomic energy. But banning the manufacture of atomic bombs had a dangerous implication: "This course would have the effect of placing a high premium on lawlessness." In place of an unenforceable ban, Stassen recommended the creation of an international police force within the United Nations, armed with atomic weapons and situated at various trouble spots around the world to act as insurance against a lawless aggressor. He cited recent events in the Dutch East Indies, Indochina, and Palestine as indicative of areas in need of stabilization.[17]

Given his own role in chairing the Trusteeship Committee at the San Francisco Conference, he was watchful as the first session of the UN General Assembly convened in January 1946. His conception of the United Nations' role conformed with the middle path he so frequently urged. Production of an atomic bomb could proceed, but under strict regulations, and its use should be confined to the international police force, the equivalent of the "world stabilizing force" mentioned in his September proposals. Like Urey and most of the scientific community, he would have preferred outlawing the bomb. Yet it would have to be done in a way that promoted peaceful relations among the world's nations.

But this was not the Truman administration's approach to the atomic problem. It took time before the administration came to grips with the issue, and when it did, it had to deal with the Joint Congressional Committee on Atomic Energy and the role it wanted to play. There was inevitable American suspicion of Soviet intentions in and out of the United Nations, but no clear-cut strategy. Certainly there was no specific reaction to Stassen's initiatives by either Congress or the administration. Not until March 1946 did Undersecretary of State Dean Acheson and David E. Lilienthal of the Atomic Energy Commission draft a report on US atomic policy for the next two years. It called for the international sharing of atomic secrets and control of the production of atomic weapons, with the ultimate goal of their destruction. This was certainly a position Stassen could endorse, though with some reservations. He saw too many lacunae in the Acheson-Lilienthal report that the Soviets could fill with distortions of the report's intentions. Also, there was no consideration of banning the sale of industrial machinery to the Soviet Union.[18] Stassen's suspicions of Soviet behavior were reinforced by events in the Cold War.

Given Stassen's vivid memory of Soviet tactics at the San Francisco

Conference, it was likely that he found another proposal more acceptable. The report by businessman and statesman Bernard Baruch and financier James M. Hancock recommended the punishment of violators and suspension of the veto in the Security Council. Under the Baruch plan, the United States would retain control of atomic power until it was convinced that its national security interest would be protected under UN authority. This was a harsher document than the Acheson report, and it addressed Stassen's concerns about protecting America's sovereignty. Baruch, dissatisfied with the limited inspections advocated by Acheson and Lilienthal, "emphasized penalizing the violators and preventing them from finding protection in the veto."[19]

Stassen held no public office while the atomic energy debate continued in Washington in 1945 and 1946. The precise terms of the Acheson and Baruch plans were less relevant to him than the projections of a reformed United Nations in the future. He saw its many flaws, as well as the inevitable Soviet rejection of any program that retained America's monopoly in atomic weapons. Yet the vision of a new and better world remained a key element in the image the Minnesotan presented to the world. It marked him not only as a founding framer of the UN Charter but also as a spokesman of invigorated young Republicans who had abandoned isolationism and accepted American leadership in the postwar world. As his record attests, throughout the twentieth century, Stassen's advocacy for the United Nations and for American leadership in that organization was a consistent theme. It may have harmonized with his political aspirations, but it was as deeply felt as his longing for the White House.

The Long Campaign, 1945–1948

It was not coincidental that many of the speeches Stassen gave took place on college campuses around the country. Students were a major component of the enthusiasm he was whipping up for his candidacy in 1948. His energetic campaign against the Republican establishment caught the attention of such influential journalists as the Alsop brothers, who admired his unpretentious headquarters as much as they did his personal courage.[20] Nonetheless, the challenges were formidable. Opposition from the Old Guard was to be expected. The stature of competitors such as Robert Taft and Thomas Dewey further complicated his task. Another obstacle was the accurate perception of Stassen's overzealous pursuit of his goals, which earned questions about his suitability for the presidency.

Stassen left no doubt about his ambitions. He may have been an outlier in the competition for popularity among Republicans in 1947, as the polls suggested. Dewey and Taft were more visible than the former Minnesota governor. As late as March 1947, it was Senator Arthur H. Vandenberg (R-MI), a former isolationist turned leading internationalist, who dominated the survey of county chairmen and district and state committeemen. The approval rate for Vandenberg on foreign policy was 71.8 percent, compared with 35.6 percent for Stassen; both Dewey and Taft had higher percentages than Stassen. In terms of popularity, the Minnesotan ranked fourth after Vandenberg, Taft, and Senator John W. Bricker of Ohio.[21]

These figures hardly slowed Stassen's quest. Ever since his successful runs for governor, he had built up grassroots support among the younger generation of Republicans and had won the loyalty of such future luminaries as Edward J. Thye, his successor as governor in 1943, and Luther Youngdahl, a state supreme court justice. He positioned himself as the person who could best influence the American public's view of the United Nations, despite Vandenberg's prominent role in the Senate. On a slightly lower plane, Stassen believed that his record of facilitating harmony between labor and capital during his governorship would draw former New Dealers into his camp.

Confident of his ability to achieve higher office, Stassen decided not to run for the US Senate in 1946. He certainly would have won that race against isolationist representative Henrik Shipstead, a paragon of the Farmer-Labor Party. Stassen's reasoning was clear and self-serving. He would be only one of ninety-six in the Senate, and as a junior senator, there would be too few opportunities to keep his name in the national papers or bring his ideas to fruition. He had projected a two-year plan, which involved travel to Europe and Latin America, with a special emphasis on Russia, to burnish his internationalist credentials. These visits would be followed by extensive talks in every part of the nation on domestic as well as international issues.[22] A reluctant Governor Thye agreed to accommodate his patron by accepting the Senate nomination Stassen had turned down. Former Minnesota Supreme Court justice Luther Youngdahl was handpicked to serve as governor.

Stassen's decision disappointed his friends and allies. Even Thye thought he had made a mistake. As a presidential aspirant, Stassen could have distinguished himself in the Senate, much as Taft and Vandenberg had done. Instead, unlike his rivals, he would have no office to attract the attention he needed. As a private citizen, he would have to generate excitement on his own. Particularly unhappy was Minnesota congressman Walter Judd. When Stassen visited Judd's office in the Capitol, Stassen naïvely, (in Judd's opinion) said, "Oh, I'm not interested in the Senate. I want to go out and talk about national affairs and debate issues." Judd thought this was Stassen's first major mistake in his presidential campaign. Stassen, however, never admitted error, believing that his talents were better suited to administration than legislation. By debating the issues from a college rostrum or at a party meeting, he would not only identify himself more indelibly with a particular cause but also ensure that his listeners recognized his priorities. The open forums he organized would attract the young enthusiasts he hoped to enlist in the effort to modernize the Republican Party.[23]

Stassen's dominance of Minnesota's politics bred overconfidence. It seemed reasonable that success in his home state could be replicated in another midwestern state, Nebraska. Victory there would propel his campaign. He invaded the state with the intention of helping liberal governor Dwight Griswold unseat another old isolationist, Hugh Butler. His expectations were high, as Nebraska Republicans had supported Stassen in 1944. But his intervention failed badly. The backlash from aroused Nebraskans led to a landslide victory for Butler and a serious setback for the Minnesotan. The *Chicago Tribune* announced that Stassen "is as dead politically as Willkie after the Wisconsin primary in 1944." The stop-Stassen movement was led by the same right-wing forces that had quashed Willkie's hopes in 1944. The Minnesota primary in July, a month after the Nebraska primary, might have validated the obituary that Colonel McCormick's paper published.[24]

Yet the failure in Nebraska did no lasting damage to Stassen's campaign. Thye and Youngdahl won convincingly in the primary, as they did in the fall election. Stassen could put the Nebraska setback behind him, which he quickly did. He was confident enough to use the Mayflower Hotel in New York as the venue for his announcement on December 17, 1946—more than a year and a half before the Republican convention would meet—that he was opening an office in Washington and intended to seek the Republican nomination in 1948: "I intend to develop and present a definite, constructive, and progressive program to our Republican party. And on that basis, I intend to let my supporters present my name in the primaries and to the convention in 1948." It was an unintended bonus for Stassen that Vandenberg, whose foreign policies were similar, renounced a bid for the Republican candidacy at the same time the Minnesotan proclaimed his availability.[25]

Presidential Rivals

Stassen did not need to be an officeholder to make the front page of the *Washington Post.* Given the signals he had been publicly emitting since returning from San Francisco in June 1945, his announcement should have come as no surprise. But since it violated the custom of coyness, his frankness separated him from his competitors. Just the day before, Taft had answered a reporter's question by stating, "No, I don't consider myself to be an active candidate for president." Governor Dewey, a landslide victor for a second term in New York the month before and a leading potential candidate in 1948, remained silent when he heard about Stassen's announcement. His press secretary gave a two-word answer: "No comment."[26]

Soon Stassen's future rivals for the nomination recognized the threat he posed to their candidacies. Dewey tried unsuccessfully to keep Stassen away from the National Republican Club's annual Lincoln Day dinner in New York City. Dewey presumably did not want any avowed candidate to be a speaker at the dinner. Stassen used the occasion to bridge the gap between Republicans and Democrats on tariff policy. His speech was carefully crafted to appeal to a new Republican constituency without stepping outside party boundaries, as Willkie had done. Before an audience of 900 at the Waldorf-Astoria Hotel, he railed against the party's traditional high tariff policies and gave his backing to the reciprocal trade program developed under the New Deal. But he took pains to note that reciprocal trade had been a hallmark of Republican secretary of state James G. Blaine in the Garfield and Harrison administrations in the nineteenth century. Europe was now in desperate straits, and the Republican response would not be merely an echo of the Truman administration's;

rather, it would recognize that a retreat to isolationism would be disastrous for both the party and the nation. With his focus on the world economy, Stassen advised: "It is my view that our Republican party can best honor Lincoln today, and best serve the people by facing in a very frank and forthright manner the great issues of our time. Chief among them is our world economic policy. The Republican party must recognize that a high tariff party no longer suit[s] America. This world cannot remain at peace unless there is a slow but steady improvement in the standards of living of other peoples everywhere." He emphasized that this could come about only under American leadership. "The result of abdication would be chaotic conditions in [the] world economy and a withering of [the] domestic economy with unemployment, bankruptcy, and less chance of lasting peace for all."[27]

Given these circumstances, Stassen would approve the Truman Doctrine to check Communist advances and the Marshall Plan to revive Europe's economy. This was not a tepid endorsement but a full-throated defense of the administration's initiatives. Speaking at the national convention of the American Legion in August 1947, he aroused the opponents of the Marshall Plan, who accused him of "rubber stamping the State Department." Striking back, Stassen asserted that anyone who opposed the plan would be giving aid and comfort to the Communists. His advocacy for the Marshall Plan helped defeat isolationist senator George Malone's (R-NV) minority report against it.[28]

Stassen's strong stance in favor of the European aid program was intended to be only a qualified endorsement of the Truman administration's policies. It was accompanied by a drumbeat of criticism for its mistakes. *New York Times* columnist Arthur Krock noted that at Topeka, Kansas, in his first formal speech since announcing his candidacy for the Republican nomination, Stassen had made economic policy the centerpiece of his address. He offered a clear picture of his social-economic philosophy, which devolved on the viability of small business. Krock observed that Stassen's understanding of the importance of big business in the American system included a caveat that the business component must not be permitted "to dominate the Republican party."[29]

Yet it was a precarious balance he had to maintain. There was no doubt about Stassen's sincerity in trying to extract the party from its isolationist past. But he had to do this without alienating the core of the party establishment. His means of achieving this result was to attack perceived weaknesses in the Truman administration's economic program. A month before his Lincoln Day address, he had called Truman's budget "wasteful and extravagant" and asserted that a cut of $5 billion would not impair government services. In criticizing the Truman budget, he joined Republican congressional opponents in estimating that the more effective management of federal agencies could reduce the total from $38.5 billion to $32.5 billion. Being an outsider to government, Stassen put his views on the budget in a memorandum for the Republican members of Congress. These included an income tax cut of 12.5 percent on individual incomes up to $30,000 and a 10 percent cut on those above $30,000.[30]

As Stassen and his devoted supporters looked ahead to 1948, the Dewey forces, veterans of the 1940 and 1944 campaigns, remained formidable. However, in light of some common ground on foreign affairs, they appeared less daunting than Taft. A leader of the former isolationists who controlled the party machine, the Ohio senator had been credited for returning the Republicans to power in the congressional elections of 1946. He had advantages that Stassen lacked. Even in the matter of an income tax cut, Stassen's 12.5 percent was topped by Taft's goal of 20 percent.[31]

Stassen had a legitimate claim as an innovator in labor relations. As governor, he had shown that labor and management could coexist amicably. But how could he deal with the Taft-Hartley Act of 1947, which limited the power of unions to control the workplace? Stassen endorsed the act, qualifying it with tepid criticisms. When he testified at a hearing of the Senate Committee on Labor and Public Welfare in February 1947, he challenged Taft on the issue of the closed shop with a ten-point program for "the peaceful settlement of industrial disputes." Though recognizing that organized labor had abused its power in recent years and that legislation was required to correct this situation, he feared the proposed legislation might weaken labor excessively. Taft dismissed such remedies as outlawing jurisdictional strikes and banning unionization of foremen as "trivial." Without a public platform similar to the one Dewey had as governor of New York and Taft had as arbiter of domestic policies in the Senate, Stassen had limited influence within his party. As Walter Davenport observed in *Collier's* in May 1946, the Minnesotan had considerable appeal as a presidential candidate but far less as a candidate for the Republican nomination.[32]

Taft's refusal to commit himself to seeking the presidency in 1948 did not prevent him from attacking the man who did. He felt that Stassen's political positions did not conform with Republican policy. In fact, as he wrote in 1945, if Stassen were to be nominated in 1948, it would once again reflect a lack of "a real party philosophy." His opinion of Stassen was more fully expressed a year later: "I have a pretty strong feeling about Stassen myself, because I think he is doing the Republican Party a tremendous amount of damage and will continue to do so if he is not nominated. If he is nominated he will be more of a New Dealer than Truman."[33]

Subsequently, Taft's objections to Stassen's candidacy disclosed his disdain for his rival as the primary campaigns of 1948 drew closer. In a speech at Steubenville (Ohio) Grant High School in April, after Stassen had violated protocol by entering the Ohio primary, Taft noted that, according to Stassen, he deserved the nomination because he was more liberal: "I can't get him to say exactly what it is that he is more liberal in. The fact is that my policies on domestic issues and foreign issues have been the same as the Republican majority of Congress. . . . If Mr. Stassen is in disagreement with Republican policy, what does he think is wrong with it?"[34]

Taft's personal animus then emerged. Rather than countering Stassen's specific objections to Republican policy, the Ohio senator launched an attack on his character: "Of course he could have participated in making that policy. After he was through from the Navy in 1946, he had the opportunity and considered running for the Senate and coming down to Washington and engaging in this battle, because the New Deal has still all the power which [is] necessary to overcome. But he chose instead of that to let Ed Thye run in the Senate, and then go out himself and spend two years campaigning for the Presidency, not getting down to brass tacks, but proclaiming general principles." He concluded by suggesting that if Stassen had been willing to join his party to fight the New Deal in the Senate, "he could have done so. It is ill-advised for him to criticize what the Republicans have done who have been fighting in the front ranks."[35]

The Moscow Ploy

To cope with the criticism of his political competitors, Stassen had to justify his decision to refrain from seeking a Senate seat and thus avoid its potential distractions from his goals. Stassen had held no office since resigning the governorship of Minnesota in 1943. But through a steady stream of lectures and travels after leaving the navy in 1945, he had managed to advance his name recognition and compensate for the lack of a political perch. After announcing his presidential ambitions in December 1946, his next step was to expand his travels to Europe, where he would polish his leadership qualifications by consulting with the heads of government in Britain, France, and, most importantly, the Soviet Union.

He set out on February 22, 1947, on a nine-week tour that would take him to eighteen countries. The ostensible objective was to examine the economic state of a world that was desperately in need of American aid and fearful of the intimidating power of Soviet-led communism. Stassen's youth and stamina were equal to the challenges of an extensive European tour. In Berlin he avoided specific comments about the Soviet-Western conflict over the sovereignty of Berlin, but in an informal press conference, he asked for unity among the four occupying powers and implicitly sustained the US position.[36]

It was his visit to the Kremlin and an interview with Joseph Stalin that attracted the most attention in the United States and Western Europe. Disclaiming any pretense of being an expert on foreign affairs, Stassen nonetheless took every opportunity to insert his judgments about the necessity of US support for the economic rehabilitation of Western Europe in the face of Communist pressures. He also used every opportunity to dispute the inevitability of war with the Soviet Union and went out of his way to say that although he would be in Moscow during the meeting of the Council of Foreign Ministers, he would not be discussing any of the matters addressed at the conference. He claimed that this was only a fact-finding tour to educate himself about Europe's economic problems. Under these circumstances, an invitation for a personal conversation with Stalin was unusual. Stassen held no official office and was on no official mission. But as one Soviet scholar noted, Stassen's April 9 interview with Stalin "may have been the most significant among Stalin's public pronouncements during this period."[37]

No matter how frequently he disclaimed any political motives in his meeting with Stalin, his devotion of a full chapter to the meeting in his campaign biography implies recognition of its value in terms of his presidential aspirations. It gave him an opportunity to contrast the US economic system, which sought to achieve a workable balance between unionized labor and dynamic capitalism, with the collective system dominated by a one-party dictatorship under the Communist Party.[38] It also gave him an opportunity to link socialism with communism as a threat to the American way of life. Referring to his meeting with Stalin at the Kremlin, Stassen observed, "This was an unusual place to be discussing our great system and its individual freedom and high production with a man who believes that the individual must be subjugated and all production controlled by Kremlin edict."[39]

The conversations were cordial, allowing Stalin an opening to defend censorship as a means of protecting his people from slanderous reporting. Stassen, however, managed to reverse the Kremlin's refusal to admit the *New York Herald Tribune*'s correspondent to Moscow on a permanent basis. Stalin called the denial "an accident and not our policy." Stalin saw no differences between the Republican and Democratic Parties, but he told Stassen that despite the differences between the US and Soviet political and economic systems, the two powers could coexist without conflict.[40]

It is unclear why the Soviet dictator considered the meeting with Stassen important enough to allow a partial transcript of the interview to be published. It is unlikely that he had any special interest in elevating Stassen's candidacy. Stalin may have wanted to use Stassen's visit to calm tensions aroused in the Council of Foreign Ministers' meeting in Moscow. The transcript was published just as the Soviets announced an end of their delay in settling differences over the Lend-Lease program from World War II. This is all speculation. What is clear is that Stassen's stature was enhanced by this unusually long exchange with Soviet officials. It gave credence to his claim that his European visit was an integral part of his effort to "construct a long-term economic policy that he advocated for the American people."[41]

As a grace note, after his return home a month later, Stassen linked his American and European economic concerns with what he called the Production for Peace Program. Its main feature involved setting aside 10 percent of the US gross national production of goods and foods for the next ten years to promote worldwide freedom from want. This proposal was not a "vague or hazily idealistic" notion but a sound approach to global poverty, and its "long-term cost will be less than the alternative cost of the current patchwork and partially misdirected loans" that yield economic instability. His program would rest "on a careful world-wide evaluation of the best long-term basis on which we can rebuild after the war. We should not expect repayments in dollars or manufactured goods, because the rest of the world cannot repay in either one of them, and we do not need either one of them." Instead, repayments would take the form of "long-term agreements for the fair access to raw materials in other parts of the world," so that "we do not further dissipate our own natural resources in this tremendous productive effort."[42]

Stassen's detailed program outlined in May reflected ideas he had presented to Stalin in April, particularly the ability of free enterprise to spread prosperity throughout the world. It condemned any steps that would undermine the freedoms the West enjoyed and the Soviet bloc lacked: "We should expect agreements that the governments with which we work will not move farther away from individual economic freedom and will not go down the sad trail of increasing nationalization or socialization or government ownership which would . . . negative the constructive efforts we are making and would make more difficult our own economic future." Stassen's proposals were delivered in Jefferson, Iowa, a small farming community, but they received nationwide attention through the National Broadcasting Company. It was a significant by-product of his visit to the Soviet Union.[43]

Stassen's meeting with Stalin drew its share of criticism in the United States. More immediately, the US delegates attending the Council of Foreign Ministers in Moscow felt that his interview with Stalin created an awkward situation, as it took place before Secretary of State George C. Marshall's request to see the Soviet leader. Other delegates found Stassen's behavior to be in bad taste.[44] But when the meeting was splashed across the front pages of US newspapers, it worked in Stassen's favor. Despite his lack of official credentials, Stassen had gained access to the Kremlin, allowing him to raise important questions with the Soviet leader.

How important, then, was this overseas tour in buttressing Stassen's presidential campaign? First, it underscored the impact of his speeches made around the country since leaving the navy in 1945. It is unlikely that Stalin would have extended the invitation had he not considered Stassen a major political figure in the United States. Second, the transcript of the conversations revealed Stassen to be a formidable antagonist to the Communist economic system. Assessing the economies of Europe was the primary purpose of his visit, and he proved himself to be an eloquent defender of American capitalism. Third, his European trip confirmed his position as a midwesterner who had abandoned the isolationism of many of his Republican colleagues. As Milburn Akers of the *Chicago Sun* had observed in 1946, Stassen was not an opportunist in his embrace of internationalism: "It is hard to make a case against his sincerity when one considers his early and vigorous espousal of internationalism in the days when the Middle West, Minnesota included, was rampant in its isolationism. Prior to World War II, Senators Vandenberg, Brooks, Nye, Shipstead, and others, none of whom can be considered unversed in the stratagems of politics, all stuck to the safest course for a Midwestern politician to pursue in those days."[45]

Stassen's Vulnerabilities

Stassen's ability to galvanize youthful audiences, particularly in the college circuit, should have enhanced his advantages of youth, eloquence, and internationalism. His defense of capitalism and condemnation of communism fit the mood of the nation as it faced an expanding Soviet power and the debilitating weakness of Western Europe. He firmly supported the Marshall Plan as an earnest expression of his concern for the economic recovery of the West. And he could do so without forfeiting his ability as a Republican to criticize the mistakes of the Truman Democrats.

Stassen's campaign activities made him a serious challenger to the veterans Dewey and Taft, but they also invited commentary on the shortcomings of his candidacy. He had to cope with the hostility of the Republican establishment. This was not a new experience. He had encountered that opposition in Minnesota in 1938 and neutralized it through an energetic campaign and the mistakes of his opponents. He would not be as fortunate in 1948. His opponents were skilled politicians who had access to delegates not only in their own states but also through alliances with other states whose favorite-son candidates could yield to a potential winner. Dewey in New York and Taft in Ohio had connections that Stassen lacked. The Willkie phenomenon of 1940 was unlikely to be replicated in 1948. Stassen's brashness in announcing his intentions a year and a half before the convention exposed him to the judgment that he had entered the race too early and would lose momentum long before June 1948. Likewise, a shrewder politician might have been less specific about his program, whereas Stassen eagerly presented his multinumbered plans.

These were genuine problems for the Minnesotan. He unwittingly compounded them with the early publication of his campaign autobiography, *Where I Stand,* in November 1947 under the rubric of a major New York publishing house. As Orville Prescott, book review editor of the *New York Times*, noted, "He has done it again. Just as in his announcement as presidential candidate, he has set himself up as a sitting duck for all his rivals and political enemies to shoot at."[46]

This reality left him unfazed. He promised to set forth his ideas clearly and frankly, "regardless of my political fortune or misfortune." He did so with anecdotes and in great detail, though very selectively. He was disingenuous in claiming that politics was not the centerpiece of *Where I Stand.* Some 60 of the slim book's 203 pages were devoted to the USSR and the problems of communism. It was an opportunity to remind readers of his contest with Stalin the year before and to alert them to the dangers of communism in America. In his customary fashion, he even listed twelve specific steps to combat communism and socialism in America.[47]

The other major theme of his book was the relationship between labor and capital. Again drawing on experience and long-held sentiments, he displayed sympathy with organized labor's goals, citing the Minnesota Labor Peace Act, passed in 1939 with his blessing as governor. Paying tepid respects to the Taft-Hartley Act of 1947, he implied in his testimony regarding that bill—accounting for more than fifty pages of his book—that his own views on labor relations provided a fairer balance between labor and management than did Taft's.[48]

The book suffered the fate of most campaign biographies. It contained little that was new. The notion that it might start a groundswell of enthusiasm for Stassen that would intimidate the Old Guard and replicate Willkie's success in 1944 was highly unlikely. The Republicans in 1940 had been ready for a savior after repeated defeats at the hands of Roosevelt. Eight years later, they faced a Democratic Party that was ambivalent about Truman's suitability as president, and at last they scented victory at the polls. In this context, the excitement of the Stassenites and the calculations of his loyal political cadre in Minnesota could not compete with the wiles of party leaders, who, according to journalist Fred Smith, "customarily decide upon the acceptability of nominees . . . and wield irresistible power over the delegates to the convention through party favors. Stassen's partisans could believe that his charisma would counteract this disadvantage."[49]

James Reston, Washington correspondent for the influential *New York Times,* took Stassen's book seriously but judged, "It isn't much of a book. It is a compilation of past speeches, Congressional testimony, and magazine articles tied together with a few new personal observations at the beginning of each chapter." Reston conceded that Stassen was a young man who looked at the big issues of the day without offering "the normal pat extremes of national politics" and presented them "as part of an open campaign for the Presidency. There is a wonderful young upstart quality about this man and his ideas. He wants the Presidency and says so." What disturbed Reston was Stassen's seeming departure from a sensible middle-of-the-road policy by equating socialism with communism. Even when recommending a special session of Congress to adopt the Marshall Plan as Europe's only alternative to communism, Stassen could not refrain from saying that those countries receiving American aid should not take steps toward increased nationalization or socialization. This warning appeared in a speech to the New York Chamber of Commerce two months before the book's publication. Reston found confusion in Stassen's sincere approval of economic aid to countries such as Britain while deploring a Socialist government that was anything but Communist in its democratic ideals and practices. Despite this flaw, Reston found that Stassen had a clearer vision of the country's direction than any of his rivals, a vision that should attract independents.[50]

Reston's mixed blessing was not a problem for the Stassenites. Nor was Smith's pessimistic forecast sufficient to dampen their spirits. Stassen knew the odds were against him, but he believed his path to the presidency was paved not by traditional political machines but by the newly energized supporters he would arouse through his barnstorming. In the end, the Old Guard would have no alternative but to choose him. This had been the case in Minnesota in 1938. Such was his expectation when he published his campaign biography.

Over the next six months, his journeys would take him to New Hampshire, Wisconsin, Nebraska, Ohio, and Oregon.[51] In New Hampshire, his two more experienced rivals did not loom large in his path during the early stages of the race. Taft chose not to campaign in the state, where he had little influence. Dewey, with a large contingent of potential delegates, saw no need to make a special effort there. Their decisions appeared to open the way for an aggressive outsider to make a move that might not end in victory but would attract positive attention. This was just what Stassen counted on. Displaying his usual energy, he crisscrossed the state, bypassing local leaders but picking up youthful admirers like those he had won over in his home state. He earned plaudits for his boldness.

The excitement Stassen's campaign generated may have led Governor Dewey to declare his own candidacy earlier than anticipated on January 8, 1948; the assumption had been that Dewey was confident enough to wait for others to press him to run. More likely it was the threat of General Eisenhower's popularity that animated Dewey. The possibility of an Eisenhower candidacy was a threat to Stassen as well. Seven New Hampshire delegates had filed for Eisenhower, two for Dewey, and one for Stassen when filing for candidates opened on January 9, 1948. Dewey and Stassen were relieved when, two weeks later, the general clearly rebuffed efforts to nominate him.[52]

There was a sharp contrast between Stassen's and Dewey's campaign styles. Dewey spoke in generalities, as if he were already the candidate, while Stassen displayed his customary energy in dealing with local issues and shaking every hand he could find after his speeches. It made little difference that Dewey barely stirred himself; he had the Republican establishment almost wholly in his corner. Stassen won only two delegates in the New Hampshire primary, yet the vigor of his campaign and the attention it generated compensated for the loss.

The next two primaries were in the Midwest—Wisconsin and Nebraska—and the Minnesotan won by wide margins. Dewey, who had bested both Stassen and Willkie in 1944, tried the same tactic in 1948: he barely made himself visible. Not until five days before the Wisconsin primary did Dewey visit the state, and then he stayed for only forty-eight hours. By contrast, enthusiastic young Paul Revere Riders—caravans of young drivers—blanketed the state with leaflets as they moved from town to town. On primary day, 150 University of Wisconsin students, calling themselves "Stassen Minutemen," canvassed the citizens of Madison for votes. For the student volunteers, Stassen's message of internationalism had resonance; for conservatives, his anticommunism resonated as well.

Although the Eisenhower cloud had passed, another World War II hero, General Douglas MacArthur, was once again a contender. Dewey deemed him a more formidable opponent than Stassen. The Minnesotan apparently recognized that MacArthur could be a problem, so he had his surrogate, Wisconsin's junior senator Joseph R. McCarthy, attack the general's divorce and remarriage.[53]

The Stassenites need not have been so concerned about the MacArthur boomlet. Despite his support from the Hearst newspaper chain and such prominent progressives as Philip LaFollette, MacArthur, who was in Tokyo, was even less visible in Wisconsin than Dewey was. The New York governor stayed in Albany, while Stassen scoured the Wisconsin countryside speaking before excited audiences throughout the state.[54] The result at the polls on April 3 was a decisive victory for Stassen, with nineteen delegates to MacArthur's eight; Dewey won no delegates. Stassen was further cheered a weekend before the convention by news from Iowa and Maine. Iowa Republicans had provided twelve delegates to Stassen, as opposed to six to Dewey and one to Taft. More surprising, considering the geography, he won seven of Maine's thirteen delegates.[55]

Less than two weeks later, on April 14, Stassen replicated his triumph in Nebraska. There really was no contest. Stassen won 43 percent of the votes; Dewey trailed with 35 percent and Taft with 11 percent.[56] The mistake the Minnesotan had made two years earlier, trying to oust conservative senator Hugh Butler in favor of the more liberal governor Dwight Griswold, was no longer a burning issue. Butler would have been in Taft's corner under any circumstance. It did not matter in 1948. Neither Taft nor Dewey were serious obstacles to the Stassen candidacy. Senator Vandenberg would have been, given his national image, but his firm rejection of another presidential bid gave the Minnesotan an opportunity to claim any potential Vandenberg votes for himself. His internationalist posture was close enough to Vandenberg's for him to assume that mantle. April was the high point of Stassen's bid for the presidency.

The next month did not match the expectations of April. Stassen's sense of destiny may have moved him to campaign in Ohio, where its favorite son was a chief rival for the party's nomination. Like his intrusion into Nebraska's Senate race in 1946, it was a gamble, and like the Nebraska venture, it failed. In addition to being Taft's home state, Ohio had a conservative heritage that was reflected in the dominance of the Republican Party. But Stassen saw an opening in the controversies over the Taft-Hartley Act, Taft's crowning achievement in the Eightieth Congress. Even though the Minnesotan had given his blessing to the act, he had reservations about it. He was on record as being in favor of those provisions of the act that would prevent strikes in essential industries and against secondary boycotts. Based on his own record of achieving harmony between labor and management, he saw himself as a mediator who could not only calm passions but also win votes from labor strongholds in industrial cities such as Akron and Youngstown. He courted favor with the unions by opposing those provisions of the law requiring union officers to sign affidavits attesting that they were not Communists. But he opened himself to charges of inconsistency when he also urged the outlawing of the Communist Party, a subject that would bedevil him in the Oregon primary.[57]

Stassen's main advantage was the contrast between his internationalist perspective—bringing the Republican Party into the postwar world—and Taft's remnants of isolationist thinking—rejecting the administration's proposals for reconstructing Europe. Following a familiar pattern, he identified himself as a moderate in foreign affairs, opposing both excessive concessions to the Soviet adversary and excessive rearmament based on the premise of inevitable war. He recognized the threat of Soviet aggression in an address in Dayton, not far from Taft's Cincinnati base, and at the same time, he urged negotiations to ease tensions. What he failed to address was how the banning of the Communist Party conformed with the moderate tone that characterized his campaign.[58]

Stassen's imposing figure, vigorous style, and rousing oratory drew passionate crowds that Taft's more prosaic manner could never match. His self-confidence was further buoyed by polls in April that showed him with a lead over Dewey and Taft. And when Dewey turned down a request for a meeting with the Minnesotan, charges of a Dewey-Taft cabal to stop the prospect of a Willkie-style bandwagon impact on convention delegates only bolstered Stassen's stock. The Paul Revere Riders campaigned once again, as Ohio volunteers covered the districts where Stassen was competing.[59]

The outcome of the contest in Ohio did not serve Stassen's image. Addressing the Cleveland City Club on May 1, 1948, Taft made a strong case for Ohioans to support "someone who has fought against the continued efforts to extend power of the Federal Government over the lives of its citizens. . . . Mr. Stassen has come late into Ohio and appealed to the voters to repudiate my course and select him for President. His criticisms of my course are trivial and inconsistent. . . . He has not participated in the development of the Republican program."[60]

The problem of an outsider invading the territory of a favorite son never faded. Stassen was hurt as well by the defection of a former protégé, Senator Joseph Ball of Minnesota. Taft won forty-four of Ohio's fifty-three delegates, and Stassen took only nine of the twenty-three districts where he competed with the Ohio senator. It was hardly a disaster, but it was a disappointment to both candidates. If there was a victor, it was Dewey, who profited from the relative damage done to his rivals.[61]

The Oregon Crisis

Only the Oregon and California primaries remained to be decided in May before the convention met in June. Stassen's last major contest would be in Oregon, where he should have been able to recapture the momentum lost in Ohio. Stassen entered the Oregon race as the more popular figure, so his defeat came as a shock to the Paul Revere Riders as well as to his Minnesota team. The May Gallup poll had Stassen ahead of Dewey by 37 percent to 24 percent. Joseph Alsop captured the mood of the Dewey camp when he likened "the delegates fleeing from a weakening candidate to rats leaving a sinking ship."[62]

So what went so wrong? Stassen's poor performance in the debate with Dewey on May 17 was decisive. A reinvigorated Dewey engaged in a more active campaign and adopted a more informal style in the Stassen mode. Stassen was often absent from the state, and the New Yorker poured money into the Oregon primary. However, it is unlikely that any maneuver on Dewey's part actually altered the course of the Minnesotan's decline.

The publicity given to the debate itself may have been a contributing factor. Thanks to Dewey's advisers, it was held in a small studio without the audiences that had followed Stassen so enthusiastically in the past. Stassen was so anxious to meet Dewey face-to-face that he agreed to a debate on Dewey's terms. This meant there would be no danger of the troubling image of a burly Stassen towering a foot taller than his New York opponent. But the setting alone cannot explain the reversal of fortunes. A better case can be made for the oratorical talents of Dewey, a former prosecutor who had put many racketeers behind bars. The debate, which was carried live from Portland over 900 stations across the United States, showed that Dewey was at least Stassen's equal as a debater.[63]

Both candidates gave reasonably smooth speeches, replicating lines they had honed on the hustings. The major issue was how to deal with the Communist menace. The Minnesotan accused the Communist Party of being a creature of the Kremlin of Moscow and of serving as a "fifth column": "I do not think it is generally realized in America that we do not now have any law to effectively oppose the actions of these Communist organizations." Although Stassen insisted on the maintenance of full constitutional rights and liberties in America, "there is no constitutional right to carry open organizations above ground or below ground directed by the rulers of the foreign power with the purpose of overthrowing the government of the United States."[64]

By contrast, Dewey responded that "this glib proposal to outlaw the Communist party would be quickly recognized everywhere as an abject surrender by the great United States to the methods of totalitarianism." He made a point of noting that a bill authored by Senator Karl Mundt (R-SD) and Representative Richard M. Nixon (R-CA) did not outlaw the party and stated, "I fear such action on the part of Congress would only tend to drive further underground the forces which are already largely concealed from public view." Dewey advocated "keeping the Communist party everlastingly out in the open so we can defeat it and all it stands for." And as an experienced prosecutor, he judged that outlawing the party would not work in this country any better than it had in czarist Russia.[65]

The press seized on Stassen's error in urging the outlawing of the Communist Party and his mistaken judgment that the Mundt-Nixon bill moving through congressional committees did just that. Oregon voters turned in their verdict three days later, giving 53 percent of the vote to Dewey. The Stassen bandwagon was halted.[66]

But why was Oregon such a disaster for Stassen? He had tossed no bombshell into the debate. The idea of outlawing the Communist Party had long been a major weapon in his armory. Granted, it did not appear in his campaign biography, but it was a staple of his speeches. Arguably, Stassen's position reflected the anti-Communist mood of the country more accurately than Dewey's less draconian approach. But Stassen's misstep in labeling the Mundt-Nixon bill as an attempt to outlaw the Communist Party provided an excuse to put Stassen into the extremist corner. This was hardly the appropriate characterization of the Minnesotan's record of internationalism, his defense of the United Nations, and his backing of the Truman administration's foreign aid bills. If there is a credible explanation for Stassen's defeat at the ballot box in the Oregon primary—which he lost by only 1,100 votes—it is Dewey's more active campaign in the state.

Stassen's bandwagon fell off its tracks and was never able to right itself and regain momentum. Despite an abortive effort on Taft's part to work with Stassen to derail the Dewey movement at the Philadelphia convention in June, the New Yorker's superior financial resources, political connections, and efficient political machine at the convention enabled Dewey to overcome the opposition. Warren Burger, one of Stassen's closest Minnesota friends and a future chief justice of the Supreme Court, wrote forty-five years after the election that had Stassen "prevailed in the Oregon primary . . . he might have got the nomination. If he had, I have not the slightest doubt that he would have defeated Truman. Dewey lost to Truman because he thought he had the election in the bag."[67] The former Minnesota governor surely would agree with this statement. His belief in his destiny would sustain him through the election cycles of the next forty-four years.

3

The Eisenhower Solution, 1948–1952

Stassen's failure to win the Republican nomination for president in June 1948 did not quench his thirst for high office. It merely necessitated another approach to the quest.

Presidency of the University of Pennsylvania

When Robert T. McCracken, chairman of the University of Pennsylvania's Board of Trustees, sounded out the Minnesotan's availability for the university's presidency, Stassen responded positively. He accepted an informal offer on July 12 and a formal invitation on July 28. The board officially elected him on September 17, 1948. The enthusiasm he had aroused among college students as a Republican candidate convinced Stassen that higher education had always been in the forefront of his ambitions. He knew that accepting this new office need not remove him from the public eye. The president of a prestigious university could be prominent in national affairs. He was well aware of Dwight Eisenhower's potential as a presidential candidate—either Republican or Democrat—and that the general had declined that honor to assume the presidency of Columbia University in the spring of 1948—not long before Stassen was offered the presidency of the University of Pennsylvania.[1]

Although Eisenhower's acceptance of a university presidency had not come on the heels of a failed Republican candidacy, Stassen saw himself in the same light—both were presidents of influential Ivy League universities. It is worth noting that almost immediately after assuming the presidency of Columbia in New York City, Eisenhower returned to Washington as chief military adviser to Secretary of Defense James V. Forrestal.

Stassen followed Eisenhower's example, maintaining and even expanding his Washington connections. Also of note, Stassen turned down the presidency of Johns Hopkins University, a distinguished institution but lacking the Ivy League credentials of Pennsylvania.[2]

When the Board of Trustees voted unanimously to appoint the former governor of Minnesota to the presidency of the University of Pennsylvania, Stassen responded that he would try "to the best of my ability to extend its service to and inspiration to young men and women of its student body." He was signaling to the board his long-standing interest in higher education and, by implication, the attraction his political campaigns had for a new generation of Republicans. At the same time, he made it clear that he had other interests and obligations: "As you understand I will continue a vigorous interest in public affairs. . . . Subject to the fulfillment of my speaking schedule on behalf of Governor Dewey I will be prepared to begin my duties at the opening of the university year in September."[3]

He had no difficulty winning the trustees' approval of his intention to campaign for Dewey, the Republican candidate, in the fall presidential race. This was a foregone conclusion. Stassen could not have been more candid about his determination to remain involved in national affairs. He made no secret of an invitation from Dewey to visit his farm and consult about a variety of critical issues.[4] The new president of the University of Pennsylvania saw no conflict between his duties to the university and his participation in the 1948 presidential campaign. He indicated, though, that his immediate future was with the university, and he was not contemplating a possible cabinet position in the Dewey administration. Beyond the matter of the presidential race, he claimed that his current immersion in higher education harmonized with his long-standing quest for peace and freedom in the postwar world: "In my opinion, peace and freedom are the overshadowing questions of our time, and I think education is the foundation on which to face them."[5]

Chairman McCracken expanded on this point. He emphasized the importance of education in the former governor's life, as evidenced by his relations with college youth. Stassen never passed up an opportunity to address students on college campuses. They became part of the youthful brigade that would accompany his future campaign rallies. In fact, they were the backbone of his campaigns as he regularly contrasted his appeal as a young liberal with the inflexible Old Guard of the Republican Party.

The *New York Times* gave its blessing to the appointment, noting that Stassen "comes with executive experiences gained as a three-time elected governor of Minnesota and as an active naval officer in the Second World War. . . . As he steps at least temporarily out of the political arena he will have the good wishes of Americans of both political parties. An idealistic college president can throw the shadow of his influence a long way in these days of change . . . we believe Mr. Stassen will do that."[6]

The Critics

For four years, until the election of President Eisenhower, Stassen walked a delicate line between his university obligations and his ambitions for political office. Inevitably, he had to confront criticism over his extracurricular activities. Although such criticism was mostly muted, one student newspaper initially worried about an absentee administration. Stassen's assurances of his primary loyalty satisfied the editors.[7] Moreover, the possibility of a cabinet appointment in a Dewey administration became irrelevant when President Truman won the election in November.

More troublesome were rumblings about Stassen's extensive leaves in 1949 and 1950, ostensibly to raise the visibility of the university as he examined the economies of European and Asian countries. That he was sensitive to the charge was reflected in his insistence on taking leave without pay when he went abroad for weeks at a time. This was prudent, given that by 1951 his Minnesota friends had already put his name forward as a Republican candidate for president in 1952. He had no need to worry about expenses; these would be covered by his backers. As usual, he won unanimous endorsement from the university's trustees.[8]

Given his many and varied public political activities, it is noteworthy that Stassen was able to turn aside most critics. The supportive Board of Trustees was a major factor. A few opponents surfaced with scathing comments but caused little damage to Stassen's stature. Francis Henry Taylor, director of New York's Metropolitan Museum of Art, wrote to Stassen in October 1951 to explain that his resignation from the Board of Trustees was a protest against the "exploitation of the presidency of the University for your own political ends." He blamed the board for allowing Stassen to "continue to prostitute the University in this fashion and there was nothing further for me to do but to resign."[9] Taylor's was a lone voice on the board with little resonance in the university community.

Potentially more damaging to Stassen's reputation was the threat of state representative Hiram G. Andrews to oppose further financial aid to the University of Pennsylvania if its president did not stop "political globetrotting." He warned the university trustees that they "very distinctly are not cultivating good will, legislative or otherwise, by continuing to employ and apparently encourage a perambulating migratory president." The legislator was referring to Stassen's frequent travels abroad. He was also referring to the university's receipt of $130 million in state aid, despite its status as a private institution. Although other equally annoyed politicians—not to mention members of the faculty—might have agreed with Andrews, his rant carried no more weight in Harrisburg than it did with the university trustees. Andrews, the Democratic minority leader in a Republican-dominated legislature, was unable to reduce state support for the university.[10] Stassen emerged untouched by this challenge. As the 1952 election year approached, however, sniping from Republicans as well as Democrats was inevitable.

Stassen managed to cope with sensitive problems that were afflicting all universities. The fear of Communist influence in the country was exacerbated by the wild accusations of Senator Joseph R. McCarthy (R-WI). Given Stassen's record of advocating the outlawing of the Communist Party, highlighted in the Oregon debate with Dewey in May 1948, he might have joined the McCarthy parade. The senator, after all, had been an important Wisconsin ally in Stassen's failed effort to win the Republican nomination in 1948. But in fact, Stassen's own anti-Communist credentials helped insulate him from McCarthyism as he defended academic freedom at his university. When a reporter for the student newspaper asked whether his support of the Nixon-Mundt bill barring Communist Party activities applied to campus groups, he diplomatically stated that any group openly declaring its affiliation would be protected on the campus. Only those with false fronts would be unwelcome. His response may have been equivocal, but it was not confrontational or an invitation to red-baiting. His defense of academic freedom was more pronounced when it came to faculty. When a prominent minister faulted a political science professor for blaming the United States rather than the Soviet Union for the Cold War, the professor was not fired. An investigation disclosed that the charges had been exaggerated, and Stassen closed the matter by writing a brief note to the complainant, assuring him that "a careful inquiry" would be conducted.[11]

Stassen's low-key handling of explosive issues that could become major crises typified his style. He dismissed similar accusations with an affirmation of the principle of academic freedom at a time when some universities were succumbing to witch hunts. When faculty loyalty oaths became a lively issue on American university campuses, Stassen resisted the Pennsylvania legislature's efforts to impose such oaths on his faculty. He testified at the state senate hearings on the issue, where he agreed with the bill's objective of ridding the state of Communist subversive activities but went on to denounce its methods. It was un-American, he pronounced, "to require all law-abiding and patriotic citizens to file reports that they are law-abiding and patriotic. This law would drop a smothering blanket over the freedom of thinking and the freedom of speaking that exists at present and should exist on our campuses." The bill never materialized, and Stassen was content with the substitute, requiring presidents of state-aided colleges to certify that their institutions employed no Communists on their campuses.[12]

Stassen's record of anticommunism served him well. He retained his reputation as a leading foe of communism while defending the freedoms of the academy. He also kept his standing as a liberal educator who sought students without discriminating along family, racial, or religious lines. In light of the red-baiting hysteria of the day, the University of Pennsylvania's president deserves credit for his leadership. No faculty member was dismissed for his or her views or associations during Stassen's tenure.

He was not as sure-footed on other matters relating to higher education. He took on the unlikely alliance of President Truman and Senator Taft over federal aid to education. It was not that Stassen was opposed in principle to government assistance to deprived areas, such as those in the South. He recognized a federal responsibility to raise the standards of education where needed. But he was wary of the precedent of federal interference with the independence of America's colleges. He warned a University of Pennsylvania alumni group in October 1949 that federal grants for general purposes were an inherent threat to academic freedom. Federal funds were currently earmarked for research, and additional aid from Washington would not be welcomed if there were any strings attached.[13]

In the National Arena

Stassen was even less sure-footed when he inserted himself into national issues unconnected to higher education. His relationship with Senator McCarthy, a prominent supporter of his candidacy in 1948, proved to be an embarrassment in later years. It opened him to ridicule from Harold Ickes as he was planning to enter the presidential fray once again in 1951. "McStassen," Ickes observed, "had hardly toddled his first ten steps from the cradle when it occurred to him that, since it was possible for any native-born male American to become President, it might as well be he." After Stassen made his formal announcement, Ickes specifically tied him to the Wisconsin demagogue, noting at a press conference in Philadelphia on December 27, 1951, that Stassen wanted "to impress people with all the precision of a Joe McCarthy." Should he be elected president, he would "lose no time in ridding the payroll of 200,000 loafers now included among the federal employees." There was an echo of McCarthyism in Ickes's use of the figure 200,000—the number of Communists McCarthy had allegedly removed from government. Stassen was pilloried in the *Nation* for employing McCarthy-like techniques in testifying against Philip Jessup's nomination as a delegate to the United Nations. Stassen cited a plot to "sell out India" in the way Nationalist China had been sold out four years earlier.[14]

Obviously, his perch as university president did not immunize him from sarcastic rebukes, playing on his hunger for newspaper headlines. Condemnation of Communist China's defeat of the Nationalists was a logical object of Stassen's complaints against the Truman administration. But Truman laughed off his assertion that, after the election, the administration would approve the admission of the People's Republic of China to the United Nations and turn Taiwan over to Mao. Stassen warned that granting the Communists another veto seat in the United Nations would be of greater value to them than their loss of South Korea. Truman claimed this information had not come from him; Stassen must have received it from the chairman of the Republican National Committee.

Stassen's statement just before General McArthur and President Truman met at Wake Island—he advised the president to place US foreign policy on Asia in the hands of the general—was no less embarrassing, in light of events later that year.[15]

No matter how opportunistic Stassen was being in exploiting current crises in foreign policy as a means of striking out at the Truman administration, his reference to the veto power of a Communist member of the UN Security Council evoked sentiments dating from the San Francisco Conference in 1945. There, he had voiced his concerns about the potential abuse of the veto by the major powers. And during one of his trips to Asia, he asserted at a press conference in Karachi, Pakistan, that the time had come to revise the veto provisions of the UN Charter. The veto power, he claimed, was the greatest weakness of the United Nations.[16] There is no reason to doubt the sincerity of this conviction, and it drew no negative reactions from Democrats or Republicans.

Stassen's many trips to Europe to mingle with British and NATO leaders did generate negative comments about the Truman administration's management of its military commitments. He attributed belated knowledge of the Soviet acquisition of an atomic device to lax behavior on the part of the Democrats. Upon returning to the United States in October 1949 after an inspection of the British health system, he gratuitously commented on the Soviets' successful detonation of an atomic bomb: "One reason the Russians are ahead of schedule on atomic development may be traced to the shipment from this country to Russia in 1947 of electronic Geiger counters and similar equipment in atomic research and development. It was a definite mistake to ship the material and I feel a thorough investigation should be made and the full responsibility fixed."[17] The administration ignored Stassen's comments. It had other problems to deal with—notably, the contribution of Soviet spies in the United States to the Soviets' atomic program. Stassen's criticism was a minor cloud in the political storm that followed.

A few months later, however, he seemed ready to work with the Truman administration in organizing a "major mid-century conference" with Soviet leaders in an effort, as he put it, to avert "the grim tragedy that would come to all mankind from a third world war." In typical fashion, he even suggested neutral sites for a conference, as well as individuals—Russian and American—who should attend. The US participants would headed by Truman, in deference to his office, and intraparty differences could be resolved by including Taft and Eisenhower among the delegates. Stassen believed such a conference should emphasize Republican leadership, and as a Republican figure of importance, he was prepared to propose an agenda that included a Marshall Plan for Asia (a continent he had recently visited) and a program of moderate economic aid to other less developed parts of the world.[18]

It should not have surprised anyone that the Truman administration ignored his suggestion. Stassen told the press he had come up with his proposal after reviewing Truman's foreign policies over the past five years and concluding that they had failed except for those that incorporated Republican contributions. A conference was necessary, he believed, given indications that the Soviet Union was continuing to build up its war potential in every way. Whatever value such a conference might yield, however, was undercut by the presumptions of the person who advocated it. How could he expect the Democrats to believe that he was speaking "without assessing blame or credit on a partisan basis."[19] More likely, this was another example of Stassen thrusting himself into the spotlight, as both Republicans and Democrats assumed.

Similarly, the Truman administration was unlikely to take seriously Stassen's call in March 1951 for a limited war in Korea, after Chinese intervention had thrown back the American march to the Yalu the previous November. He made this recommendation only a month before the president relieved MacArthur for insubordination.[20]

Stassen's positive assessment of MacArthur's actions was not altered by the general's clash with Truman and the subsequent ending of his military career. As Stassen pursued the presidency in January 1952, he won applause from audiences when he declared, "One of the first things I would do as Republican President would be to wipe out [the] tragic record of his terrible summary dismissal, call him to the White House and properly decorate him for his great service to America." He believed that the dismissal of MacArthur was one of the "worst blunders" the Truman administration ever made and that the general should be reinstated as the UN commander in the Pacific.[21]

MacArthur remained an icon of the Republican Party and was a presence at the 1952 Republican convention, even though he found less support for his candidacy than he had in the two preceding presidential elections. For Stassen, the general's heroic status remained in place, and he urged Congress to give him the honors he deserved.

Stassen used his own bully pulpit at the university to continue his commentary on US foreign policy. It grew more strident as the presidential election loomed. Occasionally it backfired. In November 1951, not long before he announced his availability as a presidential candidate, Stassen pronounced at the annual dinner of the Historical Society of New York that "a Russian type veto by United States government departments was handicapping the rearmament of Western Europe under the leadership of NATO's Supreme Allied Commander, Dwight D. Eisenhower." He was referring to the Mutual Assistance Advisory Committee, headed by the distinguished Democratic statesman W. Averell Harriman. He decried the delay that would weaken Western Europe's resistance to communism and demanded an explanation from the administration "as to what their motivations are and what their reasons may be for this apparently indefensible delay and unworkable machinery of administration." But according to the State Department press officer, monthly figures of economic and military aid did not back up Stassen's claims. There was no unauthorized committee thwarting the rearmament program with a Soviet-style veto. Harriman, the administrator for mutual security, chaired a committee that decided on the diversion of military funds for economic purposes, and there was no unanimity rule on the committee. Once again, the administration dismissed Stassen's charges with a touch of sarcasm: "It is somewhat characteristic that Mr. Stassen is long on assumptions and short on facts."[22]

Notwithstanding occasional stumbles, there was a consistent refrain in his periodic forays into the national arena between 1948 and 1952. Although some of the gloss of youth had worn off, he never wavered in advising his party to follow a progressive path in the future. The Republican defeat in the 1948 election should have been a lesson for the party in advance of the 1952 election. A clear liberal policy in domestic and foreign affairs was vital for its success. His views mirrored those of the New York Young Republican Club, which, in the wake of Truman's victory in 1948, called for new leadership of the party. Republican leaders in the Eightieth Congress had "failed to formulate and/or enunciate any long range integrated domestic policy for the advancement of the common welfare." The club asked for a national convention in 1949 to reexamine the policies of the party. Philip Willkie, son of the late Wendell Willkie and a member of the Indiana legislature, suggested that the meeting be held in Washington or Baltimore to accommodate congressional supporters.[23]

The proposal received a mixed response from party leaders. Both Hugh D. Scott Jr. of Pennsylvania, chairman of the Republican National Committee, and Representative Joseph Martin of Massachusetts, Speaker of the House of Representatives, were cool to the idea, merely responding that the plan was worthy of consideration by the National Committee at its next meeting. Stassen, however, enthusiastically endorsed it: "The Republican Party," he insisted, "must be rebuilt. . . . I think Mr. Willkie's idea is an excellent one and shows the type of imagination and purpose that the party needs. We should develop a dynamic program as a party and give it our backing."[24] Six months after his own defeat in the Republican presidential primary, and three months after assuming the presidency of the University of Pennsylvania, Stassen left little doubt about where the party should be looking for new leadership. He may have failed to win over many recruits, but not for lack of trying.

Pennsylvania state politics spawned just as much criticism of Stassen as did his engagement in national affairs. This was unusual, since the president of the University of Pennsylvania was operating in a favorable political environment; Pennsylvania was a Republican state that was prepared to welcome a Republican educator. But Stassen got caught up in a nasty feud between the conservative machine of Joseph R. Grundy, boss of the Pennsylvania party for thirty years and a personification of the Old Guard, and the more liberal governor James H. Duff. The break between the two men became evident in the 1948 election when the Grundy faction, over Duff's strong objections, threw most of Pennsylvania's votes to Dewey. It continued in 1950 when Governor Duff became a candidate for the US Senate and supported Judge John S. Fine as his successor against Jay Cooke, a Philadelphia banker. Given Stassen's liberal positions on Republican policy, he should have been in the Duff camp, supporting Fine in the primary. But Stassen was linked politically with Cooke, who made this connection clear when he told a statewide radio audience that he was backing Eisenhower for president in 1952 but preferred Stassen if Eisenhower failed to run. Duff won the senatorial primary by a landslide, and he carried Fine along with him in the race for governor. Stassen thus lost an opportunity to win Pennsylvania delegates over to his side in the contest for the presidential nomination two years later.[25]

Support from the Board of Trustees

Given the frequent criticism of Stassen nationally, in his adopted state, and, to a lesser extent, in the university community, it is noteworthy that he retained the confidence of the Board of Trustees throughout his stewardship as president. Partly it was the product of his successful wooing of alumni groups, to whom he often spoke. He was a stellar attraction who used the right language to appeal to university patrons. During a dinner he hosted at New York's Waldorf-Astoria Hotel honoring alumnus Bernard Gimbel, president of the Gimbel Brothers department store, Stassen asserted that the future freedom and peace of the world depended "to a very large degree" on the "business leadership" of the United States. In doing so, he affirmed his vision as a statesman concerned with America's role in the world, as well as a university administrator seeking new donors. Not incidentally, he used the occasion to mention the $100 million gift the Gimbel family had given to the Wharton School.[26]

Fund-raising is an important function for any president of a major university, and Stassen played his part successfully. The support of the Board of Trustees would not have been so secure without his financial efforts. During the four fiscal years of his presidency, the university's budget was always balanced. Its total assets in those years increased from $80 million to $98.4 million, and the president received credit for this improvement.[27]

Yet speeches to alumni groups that attracted revenue to the university were not the most important factors in the trustees' plaudits. As did Eisenhower at Columbia, Stassen elevated the brand of the University of Pennsylvania. He was appropriately sensitive about the many leaves he took as president, but he always pointed out that they were without cost to the university, and the trustees granted him time off without hesitation, risking complaints from others about an absentee president. The editors of the student newspaper, the *Daily Pennsylvanian,* observed that his political ambitions may have affected his conduct as president, but they praised him for his leadership when he resigned in 1952. The editors appreciated "his intellectual superiority and dynamic character" in serving the university community.[28]

The trustees had no reservations in judging his leadership: "President Stassen brought to the office of administrative head of the University a rich and varied experience in executive work; a broad vision; a deep insight into the fundamentals of American life; a lively interest in the problems of education and an unusual capacity for executive action."[29] Effusive as this statement sounds, it touched on many of the qualities that made Stassen a successful governor of Minnesota and an equally successful executive aide to Admiral Halsey in World War II.

Chairman McCracken in particular looked on Stassen's extracurricular activities as an important asset to the university. The president's missteps in national and state politics, as well as his misjudgments of the geopolitical situation in Asia—the fall of Nationalist China in 1949 and MacArthur's role in the Korean War—paled in contrast to his more carefully considered judgments of US policy in Europe and in the United Nations. Here, there was a convergence of interests that linked Stassen's political agenda with his faith in both the UN Charter and the Atlantic alliance, and both bolstered McCracken's assumption that Stassen's involvement in European affairs would enhance the stature of the university.

Stassen's program accorded with the liberal direction he hoped his party would follow. It included a recognition of the nation's anti-Communist mood and its suspicions about Soviet global aspirations. In August 1950, after the outbreak of the Korean War, he won newspaper headlines when he advised Congress to warn the Soviets of war if their aggression spread. Congressional action was necessary, he felt, because of "a series of tragic major mistakes in policy" by the Truman administration.[30]

Six months later, after returning from a round-the-world trip in December 1950, he reported unrest in the Soviet empire and advocated rearming to protect against the extreme evils of Communist imperialism. He called for solid support of General Eisenhower, the newly appointed Supreme Allied Commander of NATO in Europe. But he took the opportunity to criticize fellow Republicans, including former president Hoover and Senator Taft, who urged a return to isolationism. True to form, he identified a series of changes that should be sought from the Soviet Union.[31] Stassen's fears of Soviet ambitions were not simply political ploys;

they reflected his experience with Soviet leaders at the San Francisco Conference in 1945.

His experiences that year also accounted for the middle course he advocated in dealing with the Russians. Once again, he drew on his record in San Francisco and in his meetings with Stalin and the Politburo as he sought the Republican presidential nomination in 1952. In February 1950 he had proposed a conference with the Soviets in an attempt to avert war. When this recommendation went unanswered, he offered other solutions. Indeed, he thought one of his proposals—a private session with Stalin—was preferable to holding a summit meeting. It would also place Stassen at center stage. When he wrote to Stalin on October 1, 1950, suggesting a personal visit to the Kremlin to stop the drift toward war, he was seeking to replicate the meetings held in 1947 and so prominently recorded in his campaign biography. Although his letter, printed in full in the *New York Times,* was delivered on October 4, 1950, he had been planning it for weeks. He built suspense by sending a cryptic telegram from La Guardia Airport in New York on September 16, canceling a speaking engagement in Chicago because of "unforeseen developments connected with an important national move." He then promised to make a major announcement within ten days. Stassen delivered as promised. His letter was sent in advance of a planned leave of absence from the university to consult with Asian national leaders. Should a Moscow conference materialize, it would be possible to combine both visits. He stood ready to go to the Kremlin at any time.[32]

His letter to Stalin was blunt. In urging him to change the Soviet Union's present course, Stassen reminded the Soviet premier of his 1947 claim that he wanted world peace. "It was impossible," he wrote, "to reconcile that statement with the North Korean aggression, with the Soviet Union's refusal to cooperate in stopping this aggression, with the armament of eastern Germany and with other recent actions." He pointed out that he had written the letter without consulting with President Truman or the State Department. He did consult with John Foster Dulles, the presumptive secretary of state in a future Republican administration, and with Eisenhower, but he did not discuss the details of the letter with them. It primary purpose, he declared, was to ensure that the Soviet Union does not "miscalculate and underestimate the strength or intentions of the United States." Stassen then assured Stalin that the United

States would never consider attacking the Soviet Union without provocation: Americans "still remember the great sacrifices and heroic fighting of the Russian armies in our joint victories over Hitler's Nazi forces." Then, with his penchant for details, he laid out specific recommendations for Soviet behavior: stop attacking churches in the Balkans; open borders to tourists, merchants, and students; and join the United States in rewriting and strengthening the United Nations.[33]

It is hardly surprising that the Kremlin did not respond to his patronizing advice—there was only a negative comment from *Pravda*. Nor is it surprising that President Truman reportedly reacted, as he had to past Stassen outbursts, with amusement. Neither government took his letter seriously.[34] Conceivably, Stassen could have been charged with violating the Logan Act of 1798, which made it illegal for a private citizen to negotiate with a foreign government. But Stassen suffered no more grief for his interventions in 1947 and 1950 than did Pennsylvania Quaker George Logan for his efforts to end the conflict with France. When asked whether he had broken the law, Stassen replied, "Surely it's not against the law to work for world peace."[35]

There was a degree of political calculation in Stassen's efforts to engage with the Soviet Union, resolve the conflicts between the two countries, and achieve peace in the world. In pointing out the Truman administration's many errors and chastising Republican isolationists for their blinkered look at America's position in the world, he was seeking space for the presidential candidacy that had been denied him in the past. However, the controversies generated by his efforts did not distract him from his obligations to his current employer, the University of Pennsylvania. The Board of Trustees appreciated the attention its peripatetic president brought to the university. And Stassen himself was conscious of his usefulness in this respect.

Arguably, the most dramatic illustration of the symbiotic relationship between Stassen's ambitions and the university's prestige was an abortive attempt to bring Winston Churchill to Philadelphia in the spring of 1951. The university president, accompanied by the chairman of the University of Pennsylvania Library Bicentennial Committee, visited London to invite the former prime minister to deliver an address commemorating the 200th anniversary of the library's founding by Benjamin Franklin. The event would be held in the cavernous Convention Hall, and

Churchill's speech on the world situation and on British-American unity was expected to rival his Iron Curtain address at Westminster College in Fulton, Missouri, in 1946.[36]

The visit never took place. The possibility of a general election as a consequence of divisions within the Labour Party made Churchill hesitant to leave Britain. But it was the Senate hearing on the removal of MacArthur from his command in Korea that convinced Churchill to defer his Philadelphia talk. It was apparent that he wanted to avoid any involvement in the MacArthur controversy. At the very least, the hearings would overshadow his address at the university.[37]

Stassen and the Board of Trustees were disappointed. Churchill's presence at the convocation would have boosted the renown of the university as well as shined the spotlight on Stassen. Without ever acknowledging a rivalry with the former president of Columbia University, now the Supreme Allied Commander of NATO, Stassen was well aware of the impact Churchill's address could have had on his political future.

As the next presidential election drew closer, neither the Board of Trustees nor Stassen suffered from Churchill's absence. External circumstances, not internal missteps, were the reason for the declined invitation. Stassen's actions in this instance, as in so many others, justified the board's decision to name him president. He never hid his intention to combine his leadership of the university with activities to promote his candidacy for the Republican nomination in 1952. When he sought another leave of absence in December 1951—this time to enter the presidential race—both parties could take satisfaction in Stassen's stewardship as president. He need not have sounded apologetic when he explained to the chairman of the board, "A special situation has arisen due to circumstances which were not anticipated when the Trustees elected me and I accepted in September 1948." The trustees did not even bother to question the veracity of the statement that these special circumstances had not been anticipated. They unanimously agreed the next day to grant Stassen leave without pay.[38]

The Election of 1952: The Stealth Candidate

In 1990, the centennial of Eisenhower's birth, eighty-three-year-old Stassen was persuaded to write an account of his important role in Eisenhower's presidency. He emphasized his contributions to Eisenhower's successful nomination. Meeting the general at his NATO headquarters outside Paris in December 1951, Stassen recalled the exact words he used to tell the Supreme Allied Commander, "You should be the next president of the United States. It would be best for future world peace, and best for the national security and economic prosperity of the United States." He went on to assure him that "your election as President will provide the world with the best chance for continuing peace. You have the best prospects to become President of all the people since George Washington." However, he concluded with a warning: "You will not be elected without a detailed program to bring about your nomination as a Republican."[39]

To win the Republican nomination, Eisenhower would have to overcome Taft's formidable lead. In light of the difficulties the general would face if he openly sought the nomination from his position within both NATO and the US military establishment, Stassen offered to enter the contest to reduce Taft's advantage, to "dent his support and slow him down and develop a preconvention stalemate."[40]

To make this tactic credible, Stassen would have to launch a serious campaign and avoid charges of being a "stalking horse" for the general. He was prepared to have his friends introduce his candidacy and "make it clear that in [the] beginning . . . it will be an all out campaign" because he "did not believe it could be effective on any other basis." He assumed this would "result in a head-on clash with Taft in Wisconsin" and in other states and thus prevent him from sewing up the nomination. He admitted that the possibility of slowing Taft down enough to deprive him of a first-ballot nomination was remote. His efforts, he insisted, were intended to get the general to at least hint that he would be willing to accept the Republican nomination if it were offered. In initiating this course, he would work with Eisenhower's key allies—Governor Thomas Dewey of New York and Senator Henry Cabot Lodge of Massachusetts.[41]

For the most part, Stassen biographers Alec Kirby, David G. Dalin, and John F. Rothmann accepted Stassen's rationale at face value. They recognized the doubts and suspicions of Dewey and Lodge, who distrusted the ambitious Minnesotan but were willing to work with him as long as they could maintain some control over his behavior. As Dewey wrote to General Lucius Clay, another Eisenhower confidant, Stassen could be useful in preventing Taft from taking the nomination "by default." Stassen's biographers, however, appreciated the possibility that the general, on duty in Europe, might refuse to enter the race, just as he had in 1948. They were also aware of a "slow descent [in] his popularity from the stratospheric heights of 1948 when both parties envisioned him as the ideal candidate." Cabell Phillips of the *New York Times* asked, "Would an available Citizen Dwight D. Eisenhower in 1952 stir up the same frenzied excitement that the glamorous but unattainable general did in 1948?" While this question may have occurred to Stassen as well, his biographers agreed that he did not enter the race to win the nomination for himself.[42]

Still, given Stassen's personality, the possibility of taking the nomination was always in his mind. The trajectory of Stassen's life, reflected in his successive presidential campaigns, suggests that the boy governor of Minnesota was never able to look at himself candidly. His ambitions remained constant. He believed there was no one more qualified than himself to lead the nation. Although there is no reason to doubt his sincerity in fearing the isolationist background of Taft and valuing the superb qualifications of Eisenhower, there is also no reason to question his expectations if an Eisenhower candidacy failed to materialize. His campaign was positioned to take on the Taft forces and raise the banner of a rejuvenated Republican Party fully committed to a new role in the world.

There was nothing subtle or secretive about Stassen's political activities while serving as president of the University of Pennsylvania. His presence on the lecture circuit carried a clear message, always buttressed by specific recommendations. Whether speaking to Pennsylvania alumni, to Republican gatherings, or at national forums, he continued to see himself as the youngblood with international concerns who could rescue the Republican Party from the grip of the Old Guard.

Yet he periodically attempted to minimize his aspirations, no matter how unconvincingly. He spoke of supporting worthy candidates, and as early as October 1950, he identified three leading figures as possible Republican candidates in 1952—Dewey, Eisenhower, and himself—although he added, "It is more likely I will be supporting someone else." He noted, however, that Dewey was unlikely to be tapped a third time and that Eisenhower's possible appointment as NATO commander in Europe might rule him out in 1952. This left Stassen himself as the most viable prospect. Although he omitted Taft's name from the list of those he would support for the nomination, he offered to help Taft campaign for reelection to the Senate if asked.[43]

An Eisenhower candidacy in 1952 was always a possibility, even as Stassen gave reasons why the general would not compete. He was well aware of Dewey's decision to place his well-oiled political machine in the service of an Eisenhower candidacy. In August 1950 party leaders from seven southern states indicated that the general was their first choice for president in 1952. When asked to rate potential candidates, they ranked Eisenhower first, Taft second, and Stassen third. The party consensus in 1950 seemed to suggest that Stassen had lost ground since 1948, not least in Pennsylvania, where he had antagonized the popular Governor Duff. This judgment did not discourage the former Minnesota governor. When he was asked point-blank by a dignified white-haired man in a Washington audience in April 1951, "Are your political ambitions dead?" Stassen was silent for a minute and then admitted, with a wry smile on his face, "No—I'm not dead in any respect, I hope."[44]

If lightning should strike at the Republican convention next year, Stassen would be ready for it. He had formed an organization that was even more prepared to serve his cause than his youthful followers had been in 1948. He called a meeting on June 17, 1951, at the home of Amos J. Peaslee in Clarksboro, New Jersey. The association between Peaslee, an internationally minded lawyer, and Stassen had begun in San Francisco, where they had shared their concern for the future of US relations with the United Nations. Forty-one veterans of the 1948 campaign attended. They agreed to assist Eisenhower and dispatched Stassen to Paris to assure the general of their support, should he decide to seek the nomination. If Eisenhower declined or delayed his response too long, Stassen would be their alternative. The week before the Clarksboro meeting, Stassen had consulted with the Dewey team, which was firmly committed to an Eisenhower candidacy. Dewey came away from that meeting pleased that Stassen had "pledged himself 'one thousand percent' and with no reservations to the movement as long as our friend was available and said all he wanted was cooperation and orders."[45]

Dewey's associates, especially Lodge, the manager of Eisenhower's preconvention campaign, did not share the New York governor's initial enthusiasm. They mistrusted Stassen's motives for conducting his own campaign and disputed his rationale for entering the race. When Stassen left for Europe to meet Eisenhower at NATO headquarters, General Clay warned his friend, "Please be careful with him. No one, I repeat, no one of your group trusts him fully."[46] Given his personality and his ambitions, Stassen's offer to place himself unconditionally under the orders of the Eisenhower camp understandably inspired skepticism among the general's supporters.

The Campaign

The elaborate campaign that Stassen set in motion surely increased suspicion among the Eisenhower campaign organizers. The president of the University of Pennsylvania, now on leave from his post, announced formally on December 27, 1951, that he would seek the Republican presidential nomination in 1952. He made this announcement at the Warwick Hotel in Philadelphia, at a dinner given by the Friends of Stassen Committee. It appeared to be a well-organized event timed to follow his return from his meeting with Eisenhower. As usual with Stassen, he accompanied his announcement with a list of "clear-cut, outspoken objectives." But unlike in the past, these were generalities rather than specifics.[47]

What attracted the attention of the Eisenhower team was a press conference Stassen held prior to his announcement, where he linked his recent visit to Paris with his decision to seek the nomination once again. He stated that his talk with Eisenhower had a "direct bearing" on his decision to run. When asked if this meant that Eisenhower would not be a candidate, he refused to "authorize any assumptions." Although this hedged statement could fit into the grand scheme Stassen had proposed to the Eisenhower team, it could also be interpreted as a swipe against Eisenhower's potential nomination. In any event, it drew an angry response from Lodge, asserting that "nothing happened at the conference between Eisenhower and Stassen to justify any inference whatsoever that Eisenhower would not be a candidate." Responding to rumors from Stassen's supporters that he really was running for president, Dewey asked Stassen if his commitment to serve Eisenhower was still good. Bernard Shanley, Eisenhower's campaign manager and his future appointments secretary, recorded Stassen's response in his diary: "Tom, I want this clearly understood—I have no commitment." Stassen would throw his support to Eisenhower at the most effective time. So much for Dewey's belief that Stassen's campaign would take orders from the Eisenhower team. Stassen denied firmly and frequently any pledge to aid Eisenhower. In entering the fray, he wanted foreign policy to be aired as an issue to counter the neo-isolationist positions he attributed to Taft. With Eisenhower out of the country and unable to speak freely, Stassen's would be the only voice to combat the Old Guard.[48]

For distinguished journalist James Reston, Stassen's behavior was a disappointment. He remembered the exciting pilgrimage of "Childe Harold" in 1944 and 1948, as the young Minnesotan tried to reenergize a tired party. At the 1940 convention, he had been the late Wendell Willkie's keynote speaker, a powerful, balding youth with voice that boomed out against the Old Guard of the party. In 1944 he had been the lonely symbol of men fighting in the Pacific for a better world, and in 1948, after a personal triumph at the San Francisco Conference on the United Nations, he had campaigned alone for more than a year before anyone else entered the field. "Where was that exciting reformer in 1952?" Reston saw only a cautious contender at the press conference following his announcement, careful not to ruffle anyone's sensibilities. He seemed to be entering the race from the right, invoking the names of Herbert Hoover, Douglas MacArthur, and Bernard Baruch. He refused to commit himself on anything substantive, not even whether his program was nearer to Taft's or Eisenhower's or whether he would support either of those men if the convention did not nominate him. And his program, such as it was, consisted of banalities rather than the fresh ideas associated with him in the past. Could it be, Reston speculated, that Stassen recognized a decline in his political fortunes and was willing to settle for a cabinet post or the vice presidency? Whatever the reason for his new persona, it was a puzzle as well as a disappointment to the *New York Times*' foreign policy expert. If Stassen "ducked more questions this afternoon than any politician since Calvin Coolidge," as Reston asserted, it may have been part of his devious plan to lure Eisenhower into the race. Given the strategy he had outlined to Eisenhower's sponsors, however, he was unable to clearly identify the tactics he proposed to use.[49]

Blocking Taft

Stassen left no doubt from the onset of his campaign that he hoped his candidacy would not only prevent a runaway Taft victory at the convention but also stop him in his tracks. At a Republican dinner in Decatur,

Illinois, he equated Taft with Truman: "I do not agree that America must be either internationalized into failures and probably war by President Truman or isolationized into failure and probable war by Senator Taft. Both irresponsible internationalism and regressive isolationism were equal dangers to America . . . and both have been and would be very bad for America." He urged a new approach to foreign policy that could win "a victory for peace and freedom over communism and war."[50]

He expanded on this theme a month later at a meeting of the Republican Club of the District of Columbia. He repeated his judgment about Truman's and Taft's foreign policies and then responded to a skeptical questioner who asked: "Is there any third course that American could follow?" Stassen was prepared to offer solutions that involved "neither of the extreme alternatives presented with heat and excitement by the press." These included vigorous advocacy of freedom for captive peoples in the Soviet empires; a reorganization of the State Department, removing those personnel, including the Voice of America, responsible for soft policies toward communism; and a reorganization of the United Nations and a revision of its charter, "which has failed to maintain the peace and provide for the advance of freedom for which it was with high purpose formed." He worried that false reliance on the current UN machinery would prevent America "from following a strong and consistent foreign policy." He did not seek American domination of other peoples but "would insist upon respect for the American Flag and American citizens wherever they were rightfully found around the globe." He asserted that his policies would be more closely related to Teddy Roosevelt's than to Truman's or Taft's.[51] Whether these generalities really opened a third way for America's foreign relations is questionable and was immaterial to Stassen's purposes. He had a stick to beat both Truman and Taft—particularly Taft.

There was nothing subtle about Stassen's opposition to Taft's candidacy. In a speech during a one-day visit to Harvard University, he combined his recommendation for a School of Diplomacy equal in standing to the US Military and Naval Academies with a denigration of Taft. Asked about Taft's candidacy, Stassen replied: "Senator Taft, for a man of his views, has the poorest chances of winning in November." He did not confine his criticism to foreign policy. Although he had been generally supportive of the Taft-Hartley Act in the past, he proposed an amendment to the party's platform committee that would be acceptable to labor without reverting to what he considered the Wagner Act's bias against management.[52]

Taft's response to Stassen's challenge was understandably ill-tempered. He wrote to a friend and supporter, Nebraska senator Hugh Butler: "Stassen's announcement yesterday seems to have produced a very poor impression in Washington. The reporters seem to think he is slightly off the beam. Nevertheless, I suppose his very stupidity will lead him to file in various states."[53] Yet his disparagement may have masked Taft's uneasiness about Stassen's strength as a candidate. In 1949, just a few months after Stassen accepted the University of Pennsylvania presidency, Taft confided to a friend that he believed the Republican failure in 1948 had been Dewey's fault. And he thought that Dewey's surrogates, "the Eastern and international crowd," were "going to use Stassen or Lodge in 1952," handing one of them the Republican nomination.[54]

The Stassen threat helped account for the Ohioan's tactic of announcing his intentions well in advance of the Chicago convention, just as Stassen had done in 1948. Taft campaigned strenuously in the states critical to his success, focusing on Illinois, Wisconsin, and Nebraska. He was pleased with the results in those states, as he won all three primaries by substantial margins in April. He savored victory in Illinois even as he fully recognized that his major opponent was not Stassen but Eisenhower: "It is not an easy task to defeat a popular war-time general in successive elections. In the fourth largest state in the Union, I have carried the state by a smashing margin of 6 to 1 against him. . . . My vote was 6 times more than Harold Stassen and at least 6 times more than General Eisenhower. Incidentally, it was the second time even Stassen has defeated Eisenhower—Minnesota and Illinois."[55]

Taft's jubilation should have been more muted, despite his successes in the Midwest. Granted that, up to that point, the write-in votes for Eisenhower had been "pitifully small," as Taft put it, but the write-in votes for Eisenhower in Minnesota numbered 108,000, compared with Taft's 24,000. The general's success in Minnesota was a factor in his decision to commit himself to the campaign. Although Eisenhower was only virtually present, Stassen's large physical presence in the spring of 1952 played a role in blocking a runaway by the Taft bandwagon.[56]

The Stassen team had its plans in place within a few weeks of his December 1951 announcement, identifying him as the Ohio senator's major opponent. When he filed for candidacy in Illinois, he knew that Taft would be the only other contestant for that state's delegates at the Republican convention in July. Similarly, he moved into Wisconsin with a slate of thirty delegates, many of them veterans of the 1948 campaign. Senator McCarthy's name was absent from the 1952 slate.[57]

The reason for this rapid action, according to the Minnesotan, was the current political atmosphere. He warned that "the nomination of one candidate is now certain given commitments already made to the Ohio senator. . . . In other words the Presidency is already zippered up in a plush-lined bag waiting only for the opening of the zipper by expert hands six months hence." But, he claimed, "it will soon be found that the plush-lined bag has not been zippered shut and that the help of a majority of voters in primaries is necessary before it can be closed."[58]

Stassen's imagery suggested a confidence that Eisenhower's advisers did not share in December 1951. General Clay pointed out that the price of Eisenhower's failure to commit himself to the campaign was complicated by the mutual dislike between Senator Lodge and Governor Duff. The intrusion of Stassen into the picture added another layer of mistrust within the Eisenhower ranks. The upcoming state conventions posed the problem of trying to attract delegates who could not be sure that Ike was even a candidate. The general signaled to his supporters his interest in the campaign without giving them a flat commitment. In this vacuum, Stassen's involvement could serve as a surrogate for the absent general.[59]

It was obvious in January 1952 that Stassen wanted to give the impression of a two-man contest between himself and Taft. When the senator announced his intention to enter primaries in Stassen's home state of Minnesota and his adopted state of Pennsylvania, Stassen took up the challenge by entering the Ohio primary. Four years earlier, in the bitter campaign of 1948, he had opposed Taft in twenty-five of the fifty-three convention seats and won nine. This time, he put together a full slate composed of liberal-minded leaders who had supported Taft's reelection to the Senate in 1950. He asserted pro forma that this was not a "stop-Taft move"; he would never make personal attacks and would speak only on issues affecting the future of the country, foreign policy in particular.[60] Opening his Ohio campaign in Akron, Stassen asked why Taft had voted against the Atlantic pact. US commitment to the Western alliance was key to his charge that the senator was bound by the isolationist issues of the past that had damaged the reputation of the Republican Party.[61]

By so clearly making the campaign a two-man contest, Stassen risked disturbing the Eisenhower faction and reviving distrust of his motives. When asked whether he was running against Taft or Eisenhower, his reply in January was, "I am running affirmatively to get the nomination." What else could he say? Yet in the course of publicly positioning himself as Taft's opponent, in January he indirectly let it be known that "all the pre-convention speeches and conferences of candidates are of no account, that nothing important will happen until Chicago six months from now when the khaki curtain will roll back and the next President will take his bow."[62] Was this a signal to Eisenhower and his supporters that Stassen was still honoring the pledges he had made the month before?

If that was his purpose, his subsequent entry into the New Hampshire primary race raised questions once again from the Eisenhower devotees about his intentions. His action was potentially damaging to the Eisenhower cause. New England, with its strong internationalist base, was expected to be Eisenhower territory. But since Taft had chosen to compete in New Hampshire, Stassen had little choice but to do so if his campaign was to remain credible. He could not decline the competition, having sought New Hampshire delegates in 1948. There may have been a special incentive for Stassen to compete in New Hampshire: his expectation that Governor Sherman Adams would throw the state's support to him if Eisenhower chose not to run. The Minnesotan's campaign centered on attacking Taft's isolationist principles and, at the same time, hinting that Eisenhower's involvement with the Truman administration, even though peripheral, would preclude his entry into the race. The results were startling and an affirmation of Eisenhower's appeal—he received 46,661 votes, to Taft's 35,838 and Stassen's 6,754.[63]

As indicated earlier, Stassen could not afford to be seen as a stalking horse for the general, which might have been the case had he avoided New Hampshire. His behavior in January 1952 was intended to demonstrate his independent course. It is doubtful that he genuinely believed he was in a two-man contest and had a chance to win the nomination by challenging the Ohio senator. A deadlock between Taft and Eisenhower, or an ultimate refusal by Eisenhower to pursue the presidency, were more likely scenarios that might leave the field open for Stassen.

Long before June, the former Minnesota governor understood that his chances of winning the nomination were remote. He was no longer the youthful avatar rejuvenating his party. He could barely be considered a serious rival to Taft after his defeat in Pennsylvania, where Taft had received 50,000 more write-in votes than Stassen. "He has lost more ground in four years," according to James Reston, "than probably any other Presidential candidate of his generation, and he knows it."[64] He also knew that if Taft's momentum were stopped, it would be because of the Eisenhower name rather than his own activities as a candidate. But he could take comfort and pride in knowing that in late 1951 and early 1952, when Taft seemed unstoppable and Eisenhower was still hesitating, his participation in the presidential race made a difference. It bought time for the Eisenhower forces to mobilize. As for his own fortunes in the presidential race, Stassen would stay the course, as he had promised, until the general had defined his policies and outlined a program he could accept. Then he would openly campaign for the general and use whatever political power he still retained to secure Eisenhower's nomination.

On balance, Stassen was indeed a stalking horse for Eisenhower, despite his denials. If he could deliver the nomination by continuing his campaign all the way into the convention, he would not reject a reward—a cabinet position or the vice presidency. But he also recognized that a deadlock could open the path for a dark-horse candidate. That he was not unaware of this possibility was evident in the statement he made upon his arrival in Chicago on July 1, expressing some doubt that either General Eisenhower or Senator Taft could win the nomination. He went on to say that the contest between them "is very tight. I feel certain that both sides have been making overclaims of support. I expect that the nominee for President will be other than one of the front runners." When asked if he was still in the picture, he replied, "Definitely. And that goes for Governor Warren [of California] and Gen. MacArthur."[65]

This was bravado. Stassen gave the illusion of exuding confidence about his prospects when he talked with the press that day. He urged the platform drafters to avoid taking "positions so conservative that they would be wrong in principle [and] disastrous at the polls next November." It was vital for the party to introduce foreign policy plans, as well as those relating to labor, that were more liberal than some factions in the party would be willing to accept. His prescription for a more dynamic American foreign policy included recommendations for a more imaginative Voice of America and a complete reorganization of the State Department. He also proposed an academy of diplomacy—something he had advocated in the past. Though not quite credible, at least the manner and advice were vintage Stassen.[66]

Not unexpectedly, statements of this kind disturbed Eisenhower's supporters, who wondered where Stassen was taking his campaign. Even Shanley, Eisenhower's campaign manager, was worried that his candidate had lost his bearings. He wrote in his diary that he was depressed as the convention opened "because I can't help believe Harold is going to play for a deadlock and may very well attempt to force one, which if he does, whether it misses or doesn't miss, would be fatal to the country, the party, certainly to Harold Stassen."[67]

Stassen's actions on the convention floor, however, did not corroborate the fears of the Eisenhower team. His promise to serve the Eisenhower candidacy was redeemed at a crucial moment that made all the difference in the nomination process.

Stassen's Role at the Convention

In the first ballot, Eisenhower received 596 votes and Taft 500, with 604 required to win the nomination. Stassen may have stopped the Taft bandwagon, but he had not stopped Taft's expectations of victory. It was at this point that Stassen intended to have his Minnesota delegation cast a unanimous vote for the general. Actually, Stassen had been disappointed by the initial split in the Minnesota delegation—with nineteen votes for him and nine for Eisenhower. "Several delegates became impatient to climb aboard the Eisenhower bandwagon early, too eager to wait for us to execute our plan for the dramatic ending by giving Minnesota recognition for putting Eisenhower over the top."[68] The delegates' impatience did not spoil the psychological impact of Minnesota's vote. Stassen deserved the thanks he received from the successful Republican candidate.

New York Times pundit Arthur Krock posed a different, more cynical scenario. He had envisioned two obstacles facing Eisenhower on the first ballot, neither of which was Taft. One was the favorite-son campaign of Governor Earl Warren of California, with his state's seventy delegates, and the other was Minnesota's favorite son Harold Stassen, with his state's twenty-eight-member delegation. "Their idea," as Krock saw it, "was to stop Eisenhower from a first-ballot nomination, on the judgment—shared by the Eisenhower managers—that this could open the way for a nominee other than Taft, whose name Warren or Stassen could readily have supplied if called upon." As for the nine Minnesotans who defected prematurely to Eisenhower, Krock claimed that Stassen had pleaded unsuccessfully with Minnesota's national committeewoman, Mrs. Peavey Heffelfinger, to stay with him until the delegation was released.[69] This was speculation on Krock's part. If Stassen had any last-minute doubts about the Eisenhower candidacy, he did not act on them. The outcome of the nomination followed what he claimed to be his script.

Eisenhower's reaction when the head of the Minnesota delegation, Senator Edward Thye, switched his state's nineteen votes from Stassen was certainly not effusive. Eisenhower's memoirs give no indication that he thanked Stassen for his help. But the Minnesotan had achieved his goal: his state was credited with Eisenhower's victory at the convention, sweeping aside whatever lack of enthusiasm he might have perceived.

Stassen did not play a major role in the subsequent campaign, but he always made his presence known and took appropriate credit for Eisenhower's success in November. As he asserted, he "jump[ed] into the campaign with both feet."[70] He linked himself to Herbert Brownell, a former Dewey adviser, and to C. D. Jackson, a *Time-Life* executive whom Eisenhower had known during World War II, to form a team that he believed was more useful and more influential than the Republican National Committee.[71]

He relished his assignment as liaison to General MacArthur, cloistered in New York's Waldorf Towers, and the general assured him that he did not want a candidate supported by President Truman to be elected. This was not a difficult role for Stassen. More difficult was rationalizing Eisenhower's seeming capitulation to McCarthy over the patriotism of General George C. Marshall, the architect of victory in World War II. Stassen distanced himself from the decision to omit the pro-Marshall speech Eisenhower wanted to deliver in Wisconsin, although in his later book about Eisenhower, he included a letter from the general acknowledging his criticism of that decision.[72]

All things considered, Stassen's recollection of events forty years earlier inevitably cast him in a positive light. The recognition he subsequently received from the president in the wake of his victory in November justified the plaudits he gave himself during the 1952 campaign.

4

The Mutual Security Agency and Foreign Operations Administration, 1953–1955

After Eisenhower's nomination as the Republican candidate, Stassen predicted that he would be a great president. He even had praise for his former rivals, calling Taft a "great man and a great American" and expressing admiration for California governor Earl Warren.[1] That exuberance continued after the election.

Joining the Team

Stassen's immediate reaction when President-elect Eisenhower offered him the post of director of mutual security was to exclaim that he was "thrilled" to undertake a task that was "so vitally related to [Eisenhower's] top objective of peace and prosperity and involves the program for mutual security in which I have always believed in so deeply."[2] His wholehearted acceptance of the assignment cast some doubt on his claim of regret at having to sever his connection with the University of Pennsylvania, although, as he recalled two generations later, moving to Washington meant disrupting his children's lives in Philadelphia.[3]

Stassen insisted that only Ike's special invitation changed his mind. He was intrigued by the promise of something more than a regular cabinet post. Stassen's practical experience in the political world would compensate for Eisenhower's lack of direct experience working with "the professional politicians who actually run the political parties and the government as a whole." If this were not incentive enough, Stassen's assignment as director of mutual security was expected to surpass Averell Harriman's responsibility in the Truman administration. He would be in charge of all foreign operations—foreign aid and military and defense assistance programs, including economic and technical assistance. He would have cabinet rank and, as underscored by the president-elect, he would serve as a special consultant that the president could "bounce things off of." As Eisenhower told him, "From time to time, I'll want you to sit quietly and listen in on conferences and later give me your reactions."[4] How could he resist such an invitation? He envisioned the post as equal in importance to secretary of state.

Stassen did not pass up this opportunity. Nor is there any evidence that he joined the administration reluctantly. The university's Board of Trustees expressed regret at losing its president, but as the chairman quickly noted, "neither this nor any other group of men should attempt to stand in the way when a distinguished American is called to service to his country as this appointment presages."[5]

When the *New York Times* checked the list of Eisenhower's cabinet appointments, it found Stassen a worthy addition. It recited his credentials as governor, university president, and energetic contributor to the United Nations, particularly his efforts to keep the veto clause out of the UN Charter as a member of the US delegation in 1945. "Whatever else may be said of him he can never be charged with affiliating with the isolationist wing of his party."[6] Less enthusiastic but nonetheless supportive were Arthur Krock's observations. He noted that Stassen's many years of studying collective security in the face of "world bolshevism," as well as his meetings and correspondence with Stalin, would make him sensitive to the challenges the Soviet Union presented to the United States. Even though Stassen had tried to prevent Eisenhower's nomination, his subsequent activity in the Eisenhower campaign, along with his popularity as a liberal Republican, accounted for his selection as director of mutual security.[7] There was an element of skepticism in Krock's endorsement, as there had been in his evaluation of Stassen's campaign for the Republican nomination six months before.

Less than two weeks after the president-elect announced Stassen's appointment, Stassen was consulting Averell Harriman about the problems and personnel of what Harriman called his "nonpolitical organization." Stassen diplomatically avoided repeating his earlier criticism about the need for a more businesslike administration of the program, as well as his wish to withhold assistance to those countries engaged in "socialist experimentation." After meeting with Harriman, he emphasized that Eisenhower "has made Mutual Security the cornerstone of his foreign policy."[8]

Stassen developed this theme in an extensive interview with Ernest K. Lindley, chief of *Newsweek*'s Washington bureau, a few days later. While he could not provide specific information about future changes in the program, he hedged on the reduction of foreign aid, which embraced both military and economic components. "Security," he asserted, "never turns out to be cheap, even though in the long run it is never so expensive as insecurity."[9]

Lindley raised the sensitive issue of his relationship with John Foster Dulles, the secretary of state–designate. Stassen assured Lindley that he recognized that the head of the State Department was the president's chief adviser on foreign policy: "I want to emphasize my recognition of the leadership of the Secretary of State in foreign policy matters. I have spoken often in the past and want to restate it now."[10] Whether this acceptance of a subordinate position under Dulles could survive the range of Stassen's perceived assignments was not a subject that either man wished to consider at the outset of the new administration. But his membership in the cabinet and the National Security Council, along with his special assignments from the president, would inevitably invite conflict with the secretary of state. As director of the Mutual Security Agency (MSA), Stassen was only nominally part of the State Department.

None of these potential problems emerged in the Senate Foreign Relations Committee hearings on January 21, just one day after Eisenhower's inauguration. Not surprisingly, the senators were concerned about the MSA's bloated number of employees, particularly overseas, as well as the question of loyalty. Stassen conceded that he had "the impression at this time that it will be possible to make some reduction in the number of personnel who are in the Mutual Security Program." But this was as far as he would go in criticizing Harriman, and the senators did not press him further. He was appropriately deferential to congressional authority and responded satisfactorily to the statement that the MSA was "an implementing office" that "primarily is not concerned with the overall policy that is worked out by the State Department in connection with the Congress." On the strength of his performance, the committee approved his nomination unanimously.[11]

Senator Wayne Morse of Oregon (a former Republican but now an Independent) was the only one to sound a sour note. He accused Stassen of taking distinctly contradictory positions on whether US foreign aid would be used to exert political pressure on the beneficiaries. At one time, he noted, Stassen had charged that aid should be withheld from "socialistic" countries. Morse was referring to the British Labour Party's nationalization of the country's steel industry. Stassen responded by asserting that he would be faithful to Eisenhower's statement in his inaugural address about never using "our strength to impress upon another people our own cherished political and social institutions" Morse was not impressed: "I have formed the opinion that clarity of expression is not one of Mr. Stassen's fortes." But, he added, "We have appointed here a very able politician, and if the President wants a very able politician in this position he is certainly welcome to him." On this sarcastic note, Morse joined his colleagues in approving Stassen's appointment.[12]

Stassen was aware of congressional hostility to foreign aid in general and to the MSA in particular. He responded cautiously when asked whether he thought the MSA should be incorporated into the State Department or remain separate. He said the question should be decided by Congress and the president. From his perspective, the agency could be administered in a number of different ways. The issue gave him an opportunity to show his respect for the leadership of the Dulles State Department in foreign policy formulation: "I feel one of the important aspects of the director of Mutual Security is to operate a program that is in the maximum degree implementing the foreign and defense policies of the country in accordance with the actions of Congress, the decisions of the President, and the more direct policy decisions in Defense and State."[13]

Relations with Dulles

Inevitably, there would be tension and ultimately conflict between Stassen and Dulles over the management of foreign policy. The ambitious and relatively youthful Stassen faced off against a secretary of state who was twenty years his senior and had acquired an incomparable record of involvement in diplomacy extending back to the Hague Peace Conference of 1911 and the Paris Peace Conference of 1919. After World War I, Dulles had been a spokesman on foreign relations for the Federal Council of Churches and special assistant in the Truman administration negotiating the peace treaty with Japan. There was no way Stassen's credentials could compete with Dulles's record.

This disparity in experience never daunted him, however. The sense of entitlement that motivated his perennial candidacy for the presidency over a forty-year period gave him the confidence to stand up to the secretary of state. It was buttressed by his successful service as governor, university president, and wartime aide to Admiral Halsey. Always full of ideas for every occasion, he planned to make the mutual security program a vehicle for a more effective American role in foreign relations. Stassen could claim that his concern for foreign policy had always been in the forefront of his vision for a liberal Republican Party. Though he lacked Dulles's long years of preparation, he could cite his major role in the San Francisco Conference on the UN Charter, his extensive travels in Europe and Asia during his presidency of the University of Pennsylvania, and his conversations with Stalin and other Soviet leaders to burnish his reputation not only as a foreign policy expert but also as someone who understood the paramount threat of his generation—Soviet expansion. Armed with a belief in his competence, he was ready to become much more than an implementer of directives from the State Department or the Defense Department. And he clearly believed he had the president's imprimatur as his sounding board in developing US foreign policy.

The ambiguities in the relationship between the MSA and the State Department presented an opportunity for Stassen to minimize State's oversight. While Dulles lacked the temperament for and interest in administrative detail—one of Stassen's strengths—he was sensitive to challenges to his authority as the primary formulator of foreign policy under the president.

Conflict between Stassen and Dulles was obscured in the early days of the Eisenhower administration by the Minnesotan's efforts to present himself as a cooperative member of the Eisenhower team. Less than a week after his appointment, Stassen was effusive in his appreciation for Dulles's "gracious hospitality at lunch" and said he looked forward to working "under your leadership in President Eisenhower's administration." He concluded by stating his confidence "that you will be one of the

John Foster Dulles, Dwight D. Eisenhower, and Harold E. Stassen, circa 1953. (Minnesota Historical Society)

greatest Secretaries of State in American history." Dulles responded with thanks for Stassen's generous comments and expressed his expectation "that we can cooperate to the advantage of the nation and that there will be coordination rather than competition in the making and implementing of foreign policies." He contrasted this potential future "with the old set-up of uncoordinated and jealous departments and agencies."[14]

Stassen's advantage with the president was their shared belief that strengthening the NATO alliance was a priority in their foreign policy objectives. The more skeptical Dulles had harsher views of the allies and was more impatient with their objections to the integrated defense system that Dulles and the Joint Chiefs of Staff wanted. Stassen felt he understood the paradox: "Dulles, the man of diplomacy, preaching force, and threats of force, and Eisenhower, the military man, searching desperately for diplomatic breakthroughs; the diplomat ready to 'go to the brink' to reach his goals, while the general of the armies sought peaceful solutions to prevent the need for brinkmanship."[15]

In this context, the new president repeatedly expressed his support for the MSA mission, especially its economic benefits: "The most expensive way to insure security is to pile up our money for defense. . . . We are talking about the security of the country—nothing more."[16] His immediate target was Congress, which refused to fund the foreign aid the administration requested. Dulles agreed with the president, but without the distress that Stassen exhibited. The director of the MSA left no doubt that he was on Eisenhower's side. Still, the special harmony between the president and his like-minded aide was undercut by the suspicion of most of the Eisenhower team, and occasionally Eisenhower himself, that Stassen was serving himself more than the administration or the nation.

A joint mission to visit the capitals of seven European allies was the first assignment of the two statesmen. They departed on January 30, 1953, for a nine-day inspection tour. Dulles's task was to reassure the allies about America's commitment to Western Europe, while Stassen would deal with the many economic issues that accompanied the military buildup. They agreed that the European allies needed to exert a more energetic effort to coordinate their defense buildups. The faltering European Defense Community, undercut by France, was a case in point. Stassen's strong anti-Communist sentiments were in accord with Dulles's. But whereas Dulles's account of their trip implied a unified stance, Stassen was unusually quiet, suggesting some unease with the secretary's optimistic report.[17]

Stassen's friend and fellow Minnesotan Robert E. Matteson was serving as assistant director for research at the MSA. His explanation for Stassen's silence was that he disagreed with Dulles's aggressive behavior toward the allies. Rather than simply assessing the European scene in support of their efforts, the secretary of state had antagonized the British by asserting that containment of the Soviet menace, the objective of the Truman administration, was insufficient. Liberation, even at the risk of war, was his message. The French, in Stassen's judgment, resented the implied threat that if they did not ratify the treaty establishing the European Defense Community, American aid might be withheld. Dulles showed too little understanding of France's fears about a revived Germany. Stassen, by contrast, claimed to advocate the positive approach the president seemed to prefer and found Dulles too rigid and too dismissive of Europe's concerns.[18]

According to historian Stephen Ambrose, the purpose of this brief visit to Europe was to pressure the Europeans to fulfill their promises to build up their defenses in an integrated European Defense Community, undergirded by a US-led NATO. This was certainly Dulles's primary objective. But Stassen's biographers have pointed out that in his autobiography, Eisenhower emphasized reassuring the Europeans, along the lines Stassen followed. Stassen's function as head of the MSA appropriately played up the importance of the economic dimension in American foreign policy.[19]

A generation later, Stassen recalled his uneasiness during his travels with Dulles. The secretary's visceral hatred of communism and the Soviet leaders compelled him to think primarily of containment by force: any other attitude, he thought, would be a show of weakness that might invite aggressive moves. Stassen observed, "I studied hard but could find no basic differences between Dulles' fundamental approaches and the Truman policies that we considered bankrupt. Dulles' mindset left no room for Eisenhower's policy of reaching out in an effort to change directions."[20] Stassen made it clear that there were two ways of dealing with the Soviets—Eisenhower's and Dulles's—and that he followed the president's way.

Stassen's assessment of Dulles's limitations as the nation's primary foreign policy adviser to the president did not surface in communications between the two men in 1953. Their correspondence was filled with expressions of mutual respect and gratitude for the other's efforts to work together. When Stassen reported on indoctrination meetings for new MSA evaluation teams in February 1953, Dulles acknowledged that Stassen had "taken the trouble to write me regarding the success" of those meetings: "You may be sure that I shall do everything possible to see that you continue to receive any necessary assistance or support from the State Department or its personnel." Eisenhower speechwriter Emmett Hughes noted Stassen's "easy mastery of the vocabulary of self-effacement: 'Whatever you think, Foster,' and (as suffix to all suggestions) ' . . . under your leadership, of course, Foster.'" Dulles appeared to be appreciative of Stassen's deference.[21]

This display of apparent friendship continued into 1954, when Dulles praised Stassen at a forum in Philadelphia about the forthcoming Geneva Conference: "May I add that if I have been able to accomplish some results in the last year, it has been to a considerable extent due to your energetic support in many places and in many ways, for which I am truly grateful."[22]

Beneath the veneer of amity was another message that separated the two diplomatists. Dulles asked Stassen to read and comment on a draft of his upcoming address at the next session of the North Atlantic Council in Paris.[23] Stassen responded to this "gracious invitation" in a memorandum that underscored the point that "the United States considers the combined strength of NATO as of crucial significance." Throughout much of the memorandum, Stassen's words reflected Dulles's ideas and language: "The United States is confident that if free nations as a whole each do their reasonable share and continue in voluntary cooperation with each other, they can indefinitely maintain such world-wide military strength that will at all times have the capability of defeating the Soviet Union if aggression begins."[24]

The thrust of his memorandum, however, was the balance between economic and military power. He urged Dulles to say that "the United States considers that a sound economic base is essential in the free nations; it recognizes the interrelationship of economic health between the free nations; and it is determined to do its full share for that economic health." Parenthetically, he inserted a paragraph observing that, "from the long range standpoint, the United States considers it to be very important that underdeveloped areas should make progress." In another section, he asked Dulles to consider that the most effective allocation of the financial resources available for defense purposes from the NATO nations required careful study. "The United States for its part is re-studying its use of both its financial resources and its forces in being in an endeavor to place them in the most effective position to contribute to the total military capability and thereby to increase their deterring power as well as their fighting power in any eventuality."[25]

None of the foregoing contradicted the message Dulles wished to send. But by demonstrating the linkage of the allies' economic health, Stassen intruded his own convictions, which equated the economic aspect of mutual security with the military aspect—an equation Dulles chose not to make in his speech, even though Stassen's views accorded with Eisenhower's. Moreover, it would be understandable if Dulles resented the patronizing tone in Stassen's addendum a few days later: "I believe you could revise the approach to European integration to emphasize approval and support for the leadership of European statesmen in this and the essential success of such European leadership and avoid a possible reaction to 'over-lecturing' the Europeans."[26] Stassen could comment, but he could not convince his colleague.

The McCarthy Challenge

Stassen's approach to foreign relations differed critically from Dulles's, but not visibly in the first year of the Eisenhower administration. Where they differed markedly at this time was in their treatment of Senator McCarthy. The Wisconsin senator's challenge to the State Department and to the Republican administration in general provided a case in point. His wild and unsubstantiated charges in 1950 that there were Communists in the Truman State Department aroused the public and played a role in the Republican victory in the presidential and congressional elections of 1952. The Truman administration tried to demonize the senator as a demagogic threat to the nation, but given the anti-Communist hysteria of the time, press attention only increased McCarthy's influence. Truman's campaign backfired. Singling McCarthy out as a prime issue in the 1952 presidential campaign only seemed to make him more powerful.

McCarthy's behavior intimidated Republicans as well as Democrats. Influential Republicans such as Taft may have deplored McCarthy's tactics, but they were convinced he could be a "useful idiot" (to use the Lenin image) in the contest with the Democrats. Dulles, too, had little use for McCarthy's methods, but he was willing to appease the senator by hiring one of McCarthy's acolytes, Scott McLeod, to authenticate the anti-Communist credentials of State Department employees. Others—including President Eisenhower—were appalled by McCarthy's antics but felt that responding too stridently would give the Wisconsin senator even more prominence. They could cite the failure of the Truman administration to defeat McCarthy as reason for restraint. As Stassen recalled, Eisenhower felt that "Harry Truman really created Joe McCarthy. If Truman had ignored those charges McCarthy made down here in West Virginia about all those Communists in the State Department, the matter would have died out soon enough, even though McCarthy yelped a time or two more."[27]

McCarthy initially regarded Stassen as an ally, or at least a sympathizer. Their connections went back to the Minnesotan's 1952 presidential campaign, when McCarthy had been one of his backers. In fact, McCarthy had announced his support for Stassen within twenty-four hours of the declaration of his candidacy. As head of the State Department, Dulles, not Stassen, was the focus of the senator's charges of communism in that department. The notion of Stassen as a McCarthyite had led Harold Ickes to label him "McStassen." This was unfair. Stassen may have enjoyed a camaraderie with McCarthy early in his career, but he was not willing to participate in or condone the character assassinations the Wisconsin senator indulged in.[28]

By contrast to Dulles and Eisenhower, the director of the Mutual Security Agency openly and provocatively took up the McCarthy challenge early in his tenure. He asserted that the senator interfered in the operations of the administration by having his Senate Permanent Investigations Subcommittee conduct secret negotiations with Greek ship owners over the delivery of strategic supplies to Communist countries. The headline on the front page of the *New York Times* laid down the gauntlet more openly than the Democrats had done in the Truman administration. It read: "Stassen Charges McCarthy Impedes Red Cargo Curbs."[29]

Instead of immediately vilifying the director of mutual security as some kind of Communist, McCarthy seemed taken aback by Stassen's attack. The two men knew each other well. Ideologically, they should have been allies. Stassen's condemnation of Soviet communism and his equally strong animus against domestic Communists should have made them a match. In fact, McCarthy thought he would be applauded for his initiative in getting the Greek owners of 242 cargo vessels, often flying British flags, to stop shipments of strategic supplies behind the Iron Curtain. In a televised hearing he boasted that he had done what Dulles and the State Department had failed to do. He estimated that 10 to 45 percent of the flow of strategic materials to China and to Soviet bloc ports had been cut off. If he had kept the negotiations secret, it was because of the "extreme delicacy" of the negotiations. Disappointed with Stassen's reaction, he blurted: "I frankly feel, Mr. Stassen that we are helping you."[30]

Stassen did not agree, despite the unusually mild language the senator used. He responded that the subcommittee was hampering the efforts of the State and Defense Departments to stop shipments that served the enemy in Korea: "You are in effect undermining and are harmful to our objective." Stassen went on to raise another objection: "May I ask whether this agreement was accompanied by a promise that those Greek ship owners who joined it would not be investigated." At this point, McCarthy lost his temper and replied, "That is no concern of yours, Mr. Stassen," although he subsequently said that no immunities had been promised.[31]

Conceivably, if McCarthy had his way, Dulles would be his prime target as the leader of the State Department. Without winning any credit from the secretary, Stassen was defending the administration against inappropriate interference from another branch of government. That Stassen's stance was an act of courage was undeniable in the toxic atmosphere of the day. Whatever he may have thought of Dulles's bending to McCarthy, he never blamed the president. He was fully convinced that McCarthy "won't last. He'll thrash himself out, if we don't give him some more publicity that gives him a new spurt of life."[32]

McCarthy's more immediate target was the deputy director of the MSA, Kenneth Hanson. When the senator subpoenaed Hanson and asked his first question, Stassen recalled that he intervened and said, "I am answering you because I am in charge." Stassen appreciated the president's support in his confrontation with McCarthy. As Eisenhower recalled, he told Stassen: "I don't want any misunderstanding about what's happened. You are in charge of the Mutual Security Administration. . . . You apparently protected your man from the kind of attacks McCarthy's been giving other witnesses." But there was a caveat in the president's response. Stassen had used the word "undermine" in accusing the Wisconsin demagogue of interfering with the executive branch. Dulles thought that term was too strong and preferred the milder "infringe." Eisenhower explained, "He's afraid that your fight with McCarthy might have a bad effect on foreign appropriations later on." Stassen accepted the change, "as long as McCarthy and others on the Hill know that at any time they try to 'infringe' or 'undermine' one of my employees, I'll confront them."[33]

Harnessing the MSA

Eisenhower's tactics with McCarthy were successful, and the Senate ultimately acted to stop him. But the crisis gave Stassen an opportunity to show his colors. He was no McCarthy manqué. His record of defending civil rights and academic freedom and supporting a democratic West was long-standing and prevailed over occasional lapses and political accommodations. His embrace of the United Nations was enduring, as reflected in his enthusiasm for the Point 4 program of technical assistance to undeveloped countries. He played a leading role in negotiating trusteeship arrangements for many of the countries in the Middle East and Asia that participated in Point 4 arrangements. It was expected that in the forthcoming reorganization of the State Department, he would be responsible for managing a program that Secretary Dulles had identified as one of the shortcomings of the Truman administration.

Stassen had staked out a position that he would repeat in different forums throughout his years as director of mutual security and, later, foreign operations. It involved de-emphasizing the military component of aid, promoting technical aid to Asia and Africa, and, not least, supporting East-West trade as long as it served Western interests. As he observed in June 1953, we should not put up a "trade curtain" on our side to "fit the Iron Curtain on the other side. We should be understanding and far-seeing in the fact that non-strategic trade may be one of the factors that ultimately leads to a better position in the prospect for peace."[34] He pursued his objective with considerable success, minimizing differences with Congress and his cabinet colleagues whenever he could. James Reston quickly recognized the advantages Stassen brought to the new administration, beyond his progressive outlook. Most notably, his administrative experience in Minnesota and the navy was unmatched by the other political appointees in the cabinet. Reston judged that the former governor's reputation was on the rise after his political eclipse in 1948.[35]

Stassen's assets as an administrator were visible from the moment he accepted Eisenhower's assignment. Despite his reputation for aggressive self-aggrandizement, he displayed in Washington the tact and initiative that had made his tenure as governor of Minnesota so successful. He listened to all sides and sought accommodation whenever possible, which explains his success with organized labor in his state. He did not follow the guidelines of the Republican establishment by slashing the budget of the MSA or immediately firing incompetents and potential security risks. He recognized that, being new to the office, he needed to absorb as much information as he could as quickly as possible. Not until he had gathered a task force and visited MSA personnel in Europe did he recommend reductions in manpower. Traveling with Dulles to Europe, he saw flabbiness in the agency and the reluctance of the European beneficiaries to accept responsibility for implementing the program. He also recognized the dangers in Dulles's rigid outlook on foreign policy and in excessive cost-cutting.

Dulles would concur with the latter concern, but the differences between the two men centered on their respective world outlooks. Dulles believed that foreign aid had to be directed primarily toward the military preparedness of the beneficiary countries. Stassen placed aid in a broader context, embracing economic and technical assistance. Writing to the president-elect in November 1952, Stassen granted that, "in the cold war struggle versus Kremlin-directed communism, the Atlantic Pact countries are our main center force," but he urged Eisenhower to take into account the political and economic aspirations of millions of Asians and Africans who could fall victim to the blandishments of the Communists.[36] It was not that he disagreed with Dulles about pressing the Europeans to shoulder their appropriate share of the burden of Western defense. Rather, it was the secretary's tone of intimidation that bothered him. It could alienate allies that were vital to the success of NATO's mission.

As Stassen prepared to assume his new duties, he had no illusions about congressional hostility to the principle and the cost of foreign aid. He was aware of efforts by the European allies to take advantage of the North Atlantic Treaty's article 3 to emphasize "mutual aid" at the expense of "self-help." The difficulties the Truman administration had encountered in pushing the Mutual Assistance Defense Program through Congress testified to congressional feelings. Members resented both the competition among the allies to be first in line for American military aid and their reluctance to make maximal use of their own resources to serve the common cause. Congress wanted an integration of Western forces in return for US assistance. This was the atmosphere Stassen encountered when he visited Washington in advance of his appointment in 1952.

In recognition of congressional attitudes, Stassen enlisted a task force of prominent businessmen and bankers to evaluate how the beneficiaries utilized aid and to recommend ways to make the agency more efficient.[37] This initiative could help protect the MSA from those members of Congress who were anxious to cut costs at the agency's expense. Stassen did his best to forestall the predictions of Senator Homer Capehart (R-IN), chairman of the Senate Banking Committee, who said that his committee planned to target foreign aid to balance the budget. The new director for mutual security dismissed as "premature" any speculation that foreign aid would be cut. Speaking on NBC's *Meet the Press,* he said he did not think the Republicans had been given a mandate to cut costs in this area. What the public wanted, he asserted, was "an efficient and effective job," and this is what he set out to provide. He went on to emphasize his disagreement with congressional leaders who suggested that $10 billion in unspent foreign aid funds indicated that no additional appropriations were needed.[38]

In the spring of 1953 Dulles and Stassen worked in tandem to give the congressional committees an optimistic evaluation of Europe's growing military strength. Dulles estimated a 30 percent gain for NATO in his briefing of the House Foreign Affairs Committee in April, while Stassen presented an equally optimistic report to the Senate Foreign Relations Committee. In his habitual detailed fashion, Stassen provided a list of six accomplishments at the NATO meeting, including the adoption of firm force goals based on the allies' capabilities. But unlike Dulles, who envisioned the creation of ten divisions over the existing twenty-five active and twenty-five reserve divisions, Stassen stressed the realistic character of the goals for 1953, which he distinguished from the "nebulous" objective of nearly a hundred divisions set at the Lisbon meeting of the North Atlantic Council in 1952. He doubted that the revised foreign aid estimate submitted to Congress would allow cuts of $2 billion below President Truman's preliminary budget allocation of $7.8 billion, which might have followed from Dulles's optimistic forecast. Moreover, a close inspection of Stassen's six major results of the Paris meeting reveals an easily overlooked reservation: the NATO allies had to develop "an understanding . . . of the limitations on future United States programs" and "shape their plans accordingly."[39]

This phrasing suggests Stassen's limited expectations from the NATO allies. Dulles's radio address the next day, in which he warned against future delays in the creation of a European army, cast doubts about his rosy estimates of NATO's gains. What was obvious in the judgments of the two officials with responsibility in the realm of foreign affairs was that Stassen, presumably subordinate to Dulles, was intruding on the secretary's territory.

Inevitably, the foreign aid budget proposed by Eisenhower for fiscal year 1954 was considerably lower than the Truman estimates. He asked for $5.8 billion, of which $2 billion would be earmarked for defense support (essentially economic aid) to Western Europe and basic materials under the Point 4 program. Stassen, backed by the State Department, still hoped that mutual security funds would be increased to a minimum of $4.7 billion to $5.2 billion. But given France's plight in Indochina, Dulles was more concerned about funds for Southeast Asia than for the NATO allies. There was little Stassen could do to prevent the House Appropriations Committee from recommending that $1.1 billion be cut from the mutual security budget.[40]

Stassen responded by asserting that these cuts "were a serious matter" directly involving the nation's security. When he was interviewed by CBS's *Man of the Week* program, he noted that the NATO allies were training divisions to use the equipment that would have been provided by these funds. Congress had mistakenly concentrated on the $400 million in previous appropriations that had not been spent. This money was earmarked for equipment that would be sent to Korea instead. Not all was lost, however. The Senate subsequently restored almost half of the $1.1 billion aid bill.[41]

In his many travels during his service as director of the MSA and, later, the Foreign Operations Administration (FOA), Stassen displayed more support for economic aid and technical assistance to Asian and African countries than he did for the NATO allies. His worries over the rise of anti-American sentiment among former colonial states mounted as he recognized that many of the NATO allies were themselves colonial powers. By concentrating on the problems of Europe, the United States was complicating its relations with Asia. In response, Stassen recommended a Marshall Plan for Asia.[42] He envisioned a counterpart to the successful Organization for European Economic Cooperation that would make it easier for Asian recipients of American aid to trade with one another.

A Marshall Plan for Asia was not possible in 1954. But in light of France's difficulties in coping with the Vietminh in Indochina, Stassen went on record to support in April 1954—just a month before the French debacle at Dien Bien Phu—emergency aid to the beleaguered country. He could appease congressional critics by asking for $1 billion less than funds appropriated in 1954 and $2.5 billion less than funds appropriated in 1953. The remaining unobligated monies would be shifted to Asia, at the expense of economic aid to Europe. Asia and the Pacific regions would receive $1.7 billion, while Europe's portion would be less than $1 billion. The plight of French forces in Indochina made the new priorities palatable to critics of foreign aid. Under the rubric of crisis in Southeast Asia, the director of the MSA was able to focus national attention on the importance of technical assistance to the struggle against Soviet-led communism.[43] It also allowed him to pursue his own objectives in US foreign policy.

Stassen's support for anti-Communist South Vietnam after the division of Indochina at the Geneva Conference in 1954 was not a cynical ploy to win congressional votes for his vision of Point 4. He believed that the survival of South Vietnam was vital to success in the Cold War. He therefore launched a crash program that could add $1 billion to the defense of South Vietnam in the current fiscal year.

Stassen's most outspoken adversary as he pivoted toward Asia was not Dulles but Secretary of the Treasury George Humphrey, a conservative Ohio industrialist. Humphrey believed that Stassen was moving too fast in embracing the underdeveloped world, and he wanted to delay implementing the transition from military aid to economic aid. When the press played up the conflict with Humphrey over the proposed aid program for Asia, Stassen was quick to condemn the reports as "extremely unfortunate." He claimed there was no rift between the two cabinet officials. Praising Humphrey as "one of the ablest men in the country," he hoped that an "executive agreement would be ready by March 1955, and would go a long way in thwarting communist aims in Asia." It was understandable that Stassen would play down Humphrey's opposition. He had already won his case with the president, who confirmed that large-scale grants to Asia were in the works, even if the exact scope had not yet been determined.[44]

Whatever Humphrey's objections to Stassen's massive aid projections, they were essentially less important than Stassen's differences with Dulles over what was then being called the "Third World."[45] Technical assistance—Point 4 of the Truman's administration's International Development Act of 1950—was Stassen's focus. He succeeded in removing shared responsibility with the State Department and took over, as he put it, "the monitoring of the supply end of those who entered into contracts with the Mutual Security Administration to supply goods and services, and to watch those who dispensed them in the country of destination." He noted that "our productions ran the gamut of human activity from fertilizer plants to improve[d] food supplies . . . to economic advisers to help ruined economies regain their viability."[46]

Stassen would agree with the secretary of state and other colleagues in the administration that economic aid should be minimally applied to Western Europe. He was convinced that the European allies, having profited from the largess of the Marshall Plan, would be able to use their common resources to participate in keeping Asia and Africa in the Western camp. As he recorded at the end of his tenure as director of the Foreign Operations Administration, "the original Marshall Plan countries of the area no longer require economic aid. The average European today enjoys a higher standard of living than ever." He hoped that an expanded economic aid program for Asia would be carried out with a minimum of US funds. He made this clear in a news conference in December 1954, when he cited encouraging responses to the US proposal that the Western European allies participate in the enlarged economic aid project.[47]

For the most part, Stassen's manner was conciliatory rather than confrontational. It reflected a sense of accomplishment in his posts. He claimed in 1953 that his agency's new budget would show reductions in military and economic aid, as well as in administrative costs. The next year, he assured, would be one of "more trade and less aid," as he expected Congress to adopt a more liberal trade policy. Since military and economic aid were never the priority that technical assistance was, the new budget reflected a modest increase in this area. Although funding for mutual security fell from more than $6 billion in 1953 to less than $3 billion in 1955, Stassen made the most of his considerable talents as an administrator to use his funds efficiently. At the end of his first year in office, he reported that industrial and agricultural production in Western Europe had reached an all-time high. In his familiar style, he cited a series of factors that accounted for this progress.[48]

Director of the Foreign Operations Administration

Almost from the beginning of his tenure as director of the MSA, Stassen was aware and supportive of Eisenhower's intention to restore the State Department's traditional policy-making role, which had been distorted by the addition of new responsibilities since World War II. These included military aid as well as information programs such as Voice of America. Military and economic aid embodied in the MSA would become the nucleus for a new Foreign Operations Administration that would take over the various programs for technical, economic, and military assistance. The unification of these programs would take place under Stassen's aegis as director of the FOA. Dulles would offer policy guidance, but the new agency would have wide latitude in developing its own programs.[49]

In his message to Congress on June 1, 1953, the president recognized that "our organization for the conduct of foreign affairs has been built upon a patchwork of statutes which needs careful restudy as a basis for new legislation." He found that the organization of foreign affairs was deficient in two major aspects: (1) "there has been no clear assignment of central responsibility for foreign policy below the President," and (2) "a number of programs which implement our foreign policy have been scattered within the Executive Branch rather than being grouped together for the most efficient and economical administration." Until Congress passed new legislation, the president cited his authority to make these corrections through executive order. This consolidation was intended to centralize the operations, control, and direction of all foreign and technical assistance programs and to coordinate mutual security activities.[50]

Although Stassen would lose authority over information programs to the new US Information Agency, he would be vested with responsibility for "continuous supervision, general direction and coordination of all foreign assistance programs." Along with military assistance, the FOA would oversee the Technical Cooperation Administration, which had previously functioned under both the State Department and the MSA. Now these programs would be wholly under Stassen's supervision—an assignment he welcomed, in light of his long-standing conviction that economic and technical aid abroad had more impact than military assistance. As director of the FOA, he could distance himself from the supervision of the secretary of state, extend the range of his operations, and enlarge his presence in the Eisenhower administration.[51]

Stassen's awkward relationship with Dulles was eased by two aspects of this change—one explicit in the president's message, and the other implicit in Dulles's relative lack of interest in administrative affairs. Eisenhower reassured Dulles that "the over-all foreign affairs reorganization which I desire to achieve is designed to emphasize the primary position of the secretary of state within the executive branch in matters of foreign policy. I personally wish to emphasize that I shall regard the secretary of state as the Cabinet officer responsible for advising and assisting me in the formulation and control of foreign policy."[52]

Eisenhower's underscoring of Dulles's primacy in foreign affairs validated a State Department memorandum of March 21, 1953, recommending that "the Secretary of State have sole responsibility (subject to the President) in the formulation and control of foreign policy" and that his primacy should be maintained "through the President's consistent practice of employing the Secretary of State as the Executive's channel of authority on foreign affairs questions."[53] That this draft emanated from Dulles's office suggests the secretary's insecurity inspired by Stassen's presence in the cabinet. A particular point of friction centered on the competing roles of the ambassadors and the MSA mission heads in European capitals. This issue was clarified in the president's memorandum to Stassen, where he stated, "The Chief of the United States diplomatic missions in each foreign country must provide effective coordination with respect to all United States Government activities in the country. . . . Appointments of the chiefs of military assistance advisory groups abroad should be cleared with the Secretary of State."[54] The subordination of military aid to the ambassadors secured Dulles's authority abroad as well as at home. If Dulles did not frame these recommendations personally, the authors clearly knew his position.

The second element of the reorganization was never clearly defined. By transferring to the new Foreign Operations Administration a host of responsibilities acquired by the State Department during the Truman administration, such as US participation in the United Nations International Children's Emergency Fund and the Intergovernmental Committee for European Migration, these duties would be lifted from the secretary. The State Department's report strongly recommended the creation of a new agency to undertake these duties, although it did not include the director's membership in the cabinet.[55] The president's decision made it possible for the secretary of state to unload many administrative tasks onto the head of the FOA, who relished them.

In a sense, the creation of the new agency cleared the air between the two statesmen. Dulles could concentrate on the primary functions of his office—namely, the conduct of foreign relations—without having to attend to the time-consuming details involved in foreign aid and public information. Stassen, in turn, was happy to enlarge the scope of foreign aid and was not worried about the administrative burden imposed on his agency.

Despite its promise, the FOA was not destined for a long life. Established in August 1953, it expired in June 1955 after the president decided to phase it out and transfer its functions to the State and Defense Departments.[56] In terminating the FOA, the president claimed that, having realized its goal of centralizing all government operations connected with foreign relations, its function could be returned to the State Department. Whether this judgment was accurate is questionable, and Stassen certainly had his doubts. In part, the FOA's demise was a product of the conflict that pitted Stassen against his many adversaries in the State and Defense Departments.

This was not a decision Stassen welcomed. He would have continued to develop a Marshall Plan for Asia if he had had his way. In fact, his Asian reset elicited some positive reactions from those who were worried about the vacuum left by France's departure from Southeast Asia. In early 1955 the FOA director explained that such a program would not only stimulate the economic development of free nations in the area but also create conditions to counter political and economic aggression and subversion on the part of the Communists. The alternative, he wrote to the president after attending a Southeast Asia Treaty Organization conference in February 1955, was "an Asian wildfire with Communists included and white men excluded."[57] Still, the image of billions of dollars in American aid to Asia made Stassen and his agency vulnerable to attack, not only from enemies in the State Department but also from budget cutters in Congress.

When Congress voted to put an end to the FOA as an independent agency, it intended to phase out economic assistance over the next two years. Eisenhower then set up a new entity, the International Cooperation Agency, as part of the State Department. Its head was a former law partner of Senator Taft, an appointment that reflected congressional discomfort with Stassen's ambitious plans. The military component of foreign aid would formally belong to the Defense Department. There would be no overall coordinator of foreign aid with a seat in the cabinet. John

Hollister, Stassen's successor in this new arrangement, would administer economic aid and occupy a lesser role in the administration's hierarchy.[58] It was not a situation Stassen intended to contest.

The president's decision had other origins. He valued Stassen's approach to easing tensions in the Cold War, which matched his own and contrasted with Dulles's rigidity in dealing with the Soviet Union. Eisenhower had a new assignment for the former director of the MSA and the FOA—special assistant for disarmament—and Stassen welcomed the opportunity. The new assignment more than compensated for the loss of his agency.

Stassen's record as director of the two agencies won plaudits from most of his constituency. Of particular note was the contrast to the chaotic conditions Averell Harriman had left him. In an appreciative editorial in 1956, the *New York Times* observed, "Those who feared that a Republican administration would mean . . . the beginning of the end in foreign aid were wrong." Stassen deserved credit for successfully integrating foreign aid into the long-term foreign policy of the United States.[59] When Congress voted the FOA out of existence in July 1955, Stassen's outline of an ambitious program for Asia was his valedictory.

5

Special Assistant for Disarmament, 1955–1958

It was apparent from the beginning that the Foreign Operations Administration would have a short life. Although it did not formally expire until June 1955, its fate was determined as early as February of that year. The problems of arms control and disarmament occupied a larger place in Eisenhower's mind than the management of foreign aid. If UN control of atomic weapons was impossible in light of the Soviet veto power, the president sought other ways of achieving nuclear disarmament. On December 8, 1953, his "Atoms for Peace" proposal to the UN General Assembly offered an alternative to the abolition of nuclear weaponry by calling for the creation of an international atomic energy agency that would contain fissionable materials from the stockpiles of contributing nations.[1]

Undeterred by the failure to convince his own foreign policy establishment, let alone the Soviet adversary, the president continued his efforts to slow the nuclear arms race and take specific steps to avoid a future nuclear disaster.[2] But advances in nuclear technology, resulting in a series of new tests by all three nuclear powers by 1954, made it difficult to reach the level of trust with the Soviet leadership needed to achieve his goals. He also had to contend with the influence of a February 1955 report from the Atomic Energy Commission that underscored the importance of tests: "If we had not conducted full-scale thermonuclear tests . . . we would be in ignorance of the extent of the effects of radioactive fallout."[3]

While the president remained steadfast in his determination to reduce the threat of war with the Soviet empire, he recognized that nuclear testing would have to continue until he could come up with a workable disarmament agreement.[4] It was in this context that Robert W. Bowie, director of the State Department's Policy Planning Staff, proposed the creation of a cabinet-level position: special assistant to the president for disarmament. This official would draw from the many agencies involved in national security issues to devise a unified US position on disarmament. Bowie presented his views on February 10, 1955. Harold Stassen, with Dulles's approval, was his choice.[5]

Was Stassen the right choice, or even the obvious choice, for this position? He was in the midst of an inspection of foreign aid projects in Karachi, checking on the progress of the aid program in Pakistan. The director of the FOA enjoyed his job, which required extensive travel. He felt it was important to win friends for America in a divided world where Soviet propaganda was often more influential than US efforts to solve Asian and African problems. Stassen was an effective administrator, but the opportunity to lead a team whose goal was to remove the threat of global destruction was far more exciting than promoting and managing foreign aid programs. When the telegram offering him the new post reached him in Karachi, he seemed to have few compunctions, beyond consulting his wife, about accepting it. He continued in his role as FOA director until the agency ended in June 1955. He gladly relinquished his old responsibilities to take on new and more interesting challenges and terminated his FOA obligations on a positive note.

His final report as FOA director was delivered while he was fully absorbed in his new and more ambitious assignments as special assistant to the president for disarmament. He was pleased to report that "the list of free-world accomplishments—to many of which our programs of mutual security have made a significant contribution—is long." He went on to identify the areas where the program had made a positive difference in foreign relations. NATO Europe, he noted, was particularly responsive to US aid. But Stassen's attention centered on the condition of the underdeveloped world: "The task of building peace must not be confined primarily to armaments and alliances. There will be little hope for enduring world tranquility unless the vast segments of humanity in the underdeveloped areas succeed in lifting themselves into a higher economic plane and develop political and social institutions responsive to their cultural and spiritual values. . . . It is in our own interest as well as theirs to help them to succeed."[6]

The language and spirit were vintage Stassen. His final report encompassed his enthusiasm and optimism as well as his idealism and ambition.

The task of providing economic aid on a global basis had been grandiose in scope, but he had never doubted that he could achieve the results he sought. His new challenge was even grander and more vital. Nothing less than the survival of civilization was at stake. The opportunity to make the world a better place made the mission of developing the Third World less pressing. If he succeeded in resolving the nuclear threat to humanity, he would be doing more than saving Asians and Africans from the lures of communism.

His appointment became official on March 19, 1955. According to the White House, the failure of the UN Disarmament Commission's meeting in London to generate any progress or even "clear thinking on the subject" had prompted the president to create the new post.[7]

An additional incentive for Eisenhower's action was his dismay over the Soviet Union's unilateral proposal in February 1955 to freeze the two nations' armed forces at January 1, 1955, levels and to rid both sides of nuclear weapons. The United States saw this as a means of preventing the rearming of West Germany and removing the US ability to depend on nuclear weapons to counter the USSR's superiority in conventional weapons. Given the Soviet rejection of US proposals in 1945 to surrender its atomic monopoly to the United Nations, the new initiative was seen a cynical maneuver to put the United States on the defensive before the court of world opinion. The Soviet action evoked memories, the president noted, of the "tragic consequences of unilateral disarmament, the reckless moves of Hitler when the United States was weak, the Korean aggression when our armed strength had been rapidly diminished."[8] Eisenhower's appointment of Stassen was designed to demonstrate America's resolve to change these perceptions.

When Eisenhower was asked "what his 'thinking' was on the newly created position," he replied: "There was nobody in the government, up until I appointed Governor Stassen to this post that was responsible for getting together all of the different ideas affecting disarmament and putting them together so the administration can say, 'This is our program, and this is what we are trying to do in this field.' . . . Let us have somebody with a small staff who cannot only do something to bring together, draw together, these views, but to devise a short, easily expressed program, maybe that all of us here could adopt."[9]

Stassen believed his new position was unique in the nation's and the world's history. Neither the United States nor any other major power had ever appointed an official of such rank. With a seat in the cabinet, he would devote his time wholly to the possibilities of world disarmament and the means of achieving it.[10]

He expressed no sense of loss when his fiefdom in the FOA was split into pieces and parceled out to lesser officials in the State and Defense Departments. Given the grand vistas he saw beckoning as special assistant to the president, he was not bothered by the appointment of a Taft acolyte to head the successor agency. This easy acceptance might not have been his reaction had he not been given a more attractive assignment. Under other circumstances, he would have happily continued running the programs he had developed in the FOA, despite Congress's inherent hostility to foreign aid and his unsuccessful efforts to demonstrate its positive effects on America's national interests. But Stassen was off to a more promising arena with greater advantages. He expected to be better armed to deal with his old adversary Secretary Dulles.

Certainly, Stassen recognized that, as special assistant to the president, he would be a more formidable rival to Dulles in influencing American foreign policy, with closer personal ties to the president than the secretary of state possessed—or so he believed. He may have disavowed the sobriquet "Secretary of Peace," but it was a halfhearted disavowal.[11] He was convinced that Eisenhower saw him as a kindred spirit in his approach to the Cold War, as opposed to the secretary's rigid anti-Communist stance. He would be a better instrument than Dulles to carry out the president's initiatives on disarmament. In his retrospective appreciation of Eisenhower's presidency, Stassen quoted at length journalist Richard Rovere's judgment that his appointment had been a rebuke to Dulles.[12]

Stassen's assumption of Dulles's personal animus was not misplaced, but he may have missed the nuances behind Dulles's acceptance of Stassen's appointment. The secretary of state agreed with the president's decision to create the new position of disarmament adviser. He even gave lip service to the need for a single policy on disarmament. But Dulles may have backed Stassen's appointment because he knew there would be strong opposition from affected agencies—State, Defense, the Joint Chiefs of Staff, and the Atomic Energy Commission. In fact, Dulles downplayed Stassen's threat to his authority because he believed that progress on arms control and disarmament was unlikely. The president's appointee, Dulles said, would be in charge of a "highly technical dead-end job, just the place for Harold Stassen."[13]

Dulles's opinion was widely shared by Stassen's enemies in the State Department. Ambassador Robert Murphy assumed that Eisenhower's offer was a polite way of pushing Stassen out of the limelight. Murphy recalled, "When he was offered the job I don't believe anybody expected that he would accept it," including the president. Instead, "he grabbed the ball and ran very hard with it," in the expectation that a successful disarmament agreement would have his name attached to it.[14] Given Stassen's drive and ambition, as well as his organizing abilities, Murphy was mistaken in thinking Dulles had disposed of a rival.

The Geneva Summit

Stassen quickly immersed himself in his new job. He immediately appointed a White House disarmament staff to assist in policy recommendations. It consisted in part of specialists on loan from other government agencies and members of the teams he had created in the FOA. To advance the possibilities for disarmament, he established eight task forces to deal with the requirements for effective international inspection and control. Heading these task forces were such distinguished figures as Ernest Lawrence, director of the University of California's Radiation Laboratories, and Lieutenant General James H. Doolittle, vice president and director of the Shell Oil Company and leader of the American raid on Tokyo in 1942.

The task forces and their chairmen, as well as their respective functions, were in place by August 1955, and their report was completed by October of that year. Consisting of preliminary recommendations on inspections, it was presented on October 22, 1955, at a joint meeting with the disarmament staff at the Marine Corps base in Quantico, Virginia. It was an impressive beginning. For the first time, there was an operating manual on disarmament inspections. It offered comprehensive guidance on what would be inspected and how the inspections would take place. Essentially, the manual identified what could profitably be inspected in seeking safeguards against a surprise attack.[15]

While Stassen was pressing the task forces to come up with ideas to advance disarmament, outside events managed to accelerate the process. The Soviets, conceding that they had failed to keep West Germany out of NATO, set off on a new path to minimize Western defense programs. One step was to announce their readiness to make a peace treaty with Austria that would neutralize that country in the Cold War. A neutral Austria was acceptable to the United States, but the Soviets' second announcement in May was met by reservations from a skeptical West. At a meeting of the UN Disarmament Subcommittee in London in May 1955, the Soviets introduced a comprehensive plan to control the atom. Abandoning their earlier insistence on the abolition of nuclear weapons as the initial step toward disarmament, they now seemed to accept some kind of inspection.[16]

Specifically, they proposed a moratorium on the production of weapons beginning in 1956, followed by the "progressive 'dismantling' of all bases to be completed by 1957." Not incidentally, they intended to evacuate all foreign troops from Germany. Stassen's special staff study reported to the president: "The USSR has thus placed disarmament in a political package in which it hints at the possibility of the withdrawal of USSR troops from positions in Central Europe in exchange for a pull-back of United States bases abroad." There was no provision for the cessation of nuclear production "until the second stage."[17] Although inspection machinery was conspicuously absent from the Soviets' proposals, they seemed willing to at least discuss the process of international controls.

Energized by this possible change of heart, Eisenhower took the opportunity to spur Stassen, along with Nelson Rockefeller, to come up with a new American initiative. Rockefeller also held the rank of presidential assistant, but without the prestige of Stassen's job description. Actually, Rockefeller's credentials as an internationalist and liberal Republican were even more impressive than Stassen's. Scion of one of America's most prominent families, Rockefeller was the same age as Stassen and had made a name for himself in his thirties when Roosevelt appointed him assistant secretary of state for American republic affairs during World War II. He actively promoted the Act of Chapultepec and the Monroe Doctrine, ensuring, as a US delegate to the San Francisco Conference on the UN Charter, that regional organizations were recognized. Eisenhower entrusted Rockefeller with directing Cold War strategy, and his mission overlapped Stassen's.[18]

Given their complementary interests and ambitions, it is not surprising that Rockefeller claimed credit for the major proposal to emerge from the Geneva summit in the summer of 1955. This was modeled on "Open Skies," the principle of mutual air inspections identified by Rockefeller's team of experts at Quantico. In an interview a decade later, Rockefeller told Stassen's former chief of staff, Robert Matteson, that the idea for Open Skies was contained in a memorandum written by Rockefeller. Stassen then drafted the document that "without too much change became the text of the President's statement."[19]

Stassen did not claim responsibility for the idea, but he recalled a generation later how impressed he had been with General Doolittle, who accompanied him on his flight from Tokyo to Washington as he prepared to take over his duties as the president's special assistant for disarmament. Doolittle, who subsequently chaired the task force for aerial inspection, was the fabled World War II hero who had lifted the nation's morale in 1942 with a daring bombing of Tokyo. In conversations with Stassen during that flight, Doolittle made the simple statement that, "in today's world of the most destructive weapons of all time, the most important consideration is the mutual, reciprocal fear of all nations of a *surprise attack.* In this context our prime goal should be some formula to ensure against such a disaster. And if all nations could be similarly insulated there would be less need for a continuing armament race."[20]

Stassen was excited by Doolittle's particular solution: "a formula to permit each side to *fly over* the other at any time to be sure that no military build-ups developed, no armies massed for movement."[21] He promised to present this idea to the president at the forthcoming Geneva summit. In this circuitous way, Stassen could identify himself with the inspiration for Eisenhower's Open Skies initiative in July 1955.

There was one significant obstacle both to holding the summit and to having the president offer a dramatic shift in policy in the presence of Soviet leaders: the secretary of state. Dulles had numerous reservations about the president's presence in Geneva, not least of which stemmed from his memories of Woodrow Wilson's experience in Paris in 1919. The president, who was the head of state as well as the head of the US government, would be seen as equal to the other heads of government at the meeting, thereby diminishing the stature of his office. Unstated was Dulles's fear that Eisenhower, like Wilson, would be taken advantage of by shrewder politicians unless an experienced diplomat such as himself was conducting the negotiations. The secretary, to Eisenhower's annoyance, did not take into account the president's many years of experience in diplomacy as Supreme Allied Commander in Europe during World War II and in NATO in 1951 and 1952.[22]

Dulles's concerns transcended the issue of protocol. They reflected the difference in temperament between the president and the secretary. The president certainly respected Dulles's expertise and, for the most part, followed his lead. But Eisenhower the optimist clashed with Dulles the pessimist. Neither man had any illusions about the Soviet challenge and the dangers it posed. But the president was always looking for ways to bring the two sides together, while Dulles had no expectation that any bridge could be found to link Western democracy and Soviet communism. If the Soviets could be deterred from aggression, from Dulles's perspective, it would require methods such as massive retaliation.

The idea that a summit meeting could open a path to accommodation was a dangerous illusion, in Dulles's judgment. The president's optimism would play into the hands of the Russian adversary, and the possibility of mutual disarmament was the most dangerous illusion of all. The secretary of state elaborated on his fears in a memorandum written just before the Geneva summit. He noted that there was really no substitute for massive retaliation against Soviet provocations. Any dilution of America's retaliatory powers would provoke further aggression. Moreover, reducing nuclear weaponry in any exchange would deprive the United States of the keystone to its security. There was no possibility of matching Soviet ground forces in the event of a Soviet invasion of the east. The Eisenhower administration, Dulles was convinced, must remain vigilant not only in maintaining its military defense structure but also in resisting Soviet propaganda appeals for a reduction of nuclear weaponry.[23]

The president's appointment of Stassen as his special assistant for disarmament was needless, from Dulles's perspective, and it would have been acceptable to him only if it were meaningless. The toxic personal relationship between the two men was always a factor, exacerbated by a recognition that Eisenhower had brought Stassen into his administration as a counterweight to the secretary of state. Dulles had locked horns with Stassen in his capacity as director of the MSA and FOA. Now it appeared that Stassen's new post would not neutralize but rather empower his intrusion into matters that were appropriately the realm of the State Department.

Stassen was a self-aggrandizing amateur in the sensitive field of nuclear issues, and he could do considerable damage to American diplomacy. The media's insistence on calling Stassen the "Secretary of Peace" was particularly offensive to Dulles. "Not that I had any personal feelings," he professed, but "it was not good for the State Department and Foreign Service to feel that some outside agency had primary responsibility for peace." Stassen's efforts to distance himself from the title were not convincing, particularly when the president himself casually employed it.[24]

No matter how clearly Dulles expressed his opposition to Stassen's personality and policies, Eisenhower's need to respond to the Communist propaganda campaign outweighed the secretary's objections. The most Dulles would concede under pressure was to consider the possibility of limited mutual inspections, but he would not condone a comprehensive arms limitation agreement without stringent political conditions.[25] This concession was swept away by Stassen's enthusiasm for his own proposal. By May 26, he submitted to the president and the National Security Council (NSC) a progress report on disarmament. His aim was to facilitate the process "by bringing into focus areas of agreement and of disagreement and by suggesting solutions." This was the first product of the group he had assembled in Quantico.[26]

Since the abolition of nuclear weapons was not possible, the report advocated that "United States policy on the question of disarmament in the present state of world tensions should be directed primarily toward preventing the USSR from attaining a capability of destroying the United States through a surprise attack." Consequently, it "should be concentrated on the method of a multilateral arms limitation agreement to reach this aim." Admitting that "it is not possible by any known scientific or other, means to be absolutely certain of the control of all future production of nuclear weapons materials," the report proposed the creation of an International Armaments Commission "to inspect by land, sea, or air, with the aid of scientific instruments, all existing armaments and to communicate the observations to an international center outside the country being inspected without interference." The operation would include stationing US nationals in the Communist bloc and Soviet observers in the United States. This would be the first step in preventing a surprise attack. The report recommended that after this plan had been presented to the Senate, the president and secretary of state should find an appropriate occasion to explain its merits to the nation and, through the United Nations, to the world.[27]

To Dulles's dismay, this report was just what the president was seeking. And a summit meeting with the Soviets was precisely the venue where further progress might be made. Even before the report was delivered, Eisenhower had made it clear to a reluctant Dulles that he should "let other countries know that if they want a summit, I am ready to go to one. I want to take the affirmative approach to bring about a summit at an early date." There was little the opponents of a summit could do to deter the president at this point. Military leaders joined Dulles in expressing their disapproval of a summit conference.[28]

At least Dulles could take comfort in his success at keeping members of Congress from attending the summit meeting. He was worried about the effect of a congressional delegation on the British and French, who had been assured that attendance would be restricted to a small number. He warned Eisenhower: "If, for example, four Congressmen were to be there it would not only quite change the character of the conference, it would create difficult problems for Eden and Pinay. Therefore, I am confirmed in the view which you expressed to Senator George that the time for Congressional representation may be when we get to the second phase, namely, the substantive negotiations rather than at this initial phase." This was a minor victory for the secretary of state. He never expected the conference to reach a "second stage."[29]

Lewis Strauss, chairman of the Atomic Energy Commission, shared Dulles's and the Pentagon's pessimism about any kind of nuclear test moratorium. As he told the secretary of state, "A moratorium on the testing of large weapons would be to our advantage if it could be arranged by a *dependable* agreement. A dependable agreement with the present Soviet Government is *illusory*." Strauss underscored his concerns about Stassen's disarmament proposals in a letter to Undersecretary of State Herbert Hoover Jr.: "In the absence of complete reliance upon Soviet good faith, I do not believe that any arrangements can be devised concerning disclosure and verification of information about atomic weapons that might not be prejudicial, to some extent, to the security of the United States."[30]

Their voices on the main issue went unheeded. Eisenhower and Stassen disagreed with Dulles, Hoover, and Strauss. The president and his disarmament adviser believed that an arrangement could be reached between

East and West, but complete disarmament—desirable as that goal might be—was an impossible ideal. In the context of the Cold War, arms control would be an incremental step toward eventual disarmament after a warming of the Cold War.

The president took up the theme in a nationwide television address on July 15, 1955, in which he expressed his hopes: "I say to you, if we can change the spirit in which these conferences are conducted, we will have taken the greatest step toward peace that can be conducted in the history of mankind."[31] In light of this rhetoric it was obvious there was no stopping Eisenhower's journey to Geneva, but Dulles still hoped to keep Stassen and Rockefeller from joining him there. Both Stassen and the president were aware that Dulles did not want Stassen in Geneva. But as the Minnesotan later recalled, Eisenhower was fully supportive of his ideas about breaking the Cold War stalemate. Furthermore, he believed that Dulles's inflexibility would have exactly the opposite effect. So the president's solution was to have Stassen and Rockefeller, along with Admiral Radford, quietly fly to Paris. They would wait there, ready to leave for Geneva as soon as Eisenhower sent for them.[32]

This was an artful compromise, but it also reflected the president's caution. He did not want to bruise Dulles's feelings any more than necessary. He had not ruled out a future confrontation with the Soviets, and Dulles's experience at that juncture would be invaluable. His continued reliance on the secretary of state was evident in a letter to Vice President Richard Nixon after Eisenhower's heart attack in September, in which he emphasized Dulles's importance in securing whatever gains were possible at the foreign ministers' meeting in Geneva following the summit meeting in July: "I hope that each one in Government will do whatever he can to make Foster's task easier. The Secretary of State must have the discretionary authority which is needed if there is to be effective negotiation. . . . He must be the one who both at the Conference table and before the world speaks with authority for our country."[33]

The call to Paris came on July 19. Colonel Andrew J. Goodpaster, the president's staff secretary, informed Stassen and Rockefeller that the subject of disarmament would be the sole topic of the July 21 session at Geneva.[34] This was the occasion for the presentation of Open Skies, a version of General Doolittle's principles that Stassen had adopted. Dulles did his best to frustrate Stassen's contribution. At the end of the internal debates, he dissented from the basic principles of Stassen's draft on mutual inspections and the exchange of information on military installations: "It has not been my thinking of what should be included in this summit meeting." Stassen recalled that these were Dulles's exact words.[35]

The president overruled Dulles, who reluctantly conceded that "the result of Soviet disarmament propaganda plus our allies' weakness . . . combine to create a popular and diplomatic pressure for limitation of armament that cannot be resisted by the United States without our forfeiting the good will of our allies." Consequently, Dulles recognized that the United States must support some plan for limiting armaments but warned, "We should not proceed quickly or radically to alter the present situation. We should proceed cautiously so long as the present situation gives us important bargaining power and so long as Soviet leadership continues basically hostile, autocratic and controlled by those who are not inhibited by any moral scruples." At a meeting on the same day with Stassen and the principals from the Department of Defense, the Atomic Energy Commission, and the CIA, Dulles was dispirited. Gratuitously, he observed that Stassen "did not add anything new to the positions outlined in his various earlier memoranda."[36]

But Stassen had won his case with the president. The NSC recommended that he develop methods of inspection and incorporate the international pool of atomic energy materials for peaceful use, as outlined by the president in his speech on December 8, 1953. This was the substance of the disarmament statement Eisenhower offered at the eighth plenary session on July 23, 1955, in Geneva.[37]

In his Open Skies speech, Eisenhower proposed practical steps that began with the two sides exchanging complete blueprints of their military establishments and then establishing facilities in both countries for aerial photography: "We to provide you . . . ample facilities for aerial reconnaissance, where you can take all the pictures you choose and take them to your own country to study, you to provide exactly the same facilities for us." By taking these steps, Eisenhower believed that he could not only remove the danger of surprise attacks but also lessen the tensions between the opposing powers.[38]

But as Eisenhower admitted in his memoirs, disillusionment quickly followed the termination of the Geneva Conference: "At the October Foreign Ministers' conference, held in the same room as the Summit Conference, the Soviets had repudiated every measure to which they had agreed in July. . . . To those of us responsible for the conduct of foreign relations, the Soviet duplicity was a grievous disappointment."[39]

Open Skies, however, won applause even from adversaries. Premier Nikolai Bulganin, the nominal Soviet leader, hailed the proposal as sincere and worthy of study. This gracious response was typical of the language Bulganin used in his correspondence with Eisenhower. It prompted Dulles to be wary of the premier's politesse. He urged the president to be cautious in his response to Bulganin's flattery. He noted that whatever concessions the Soviets appeared to offer over disarmament had to be balanced against their repeated assertions that the incorporation of West Germany into NATO would preclude the possibility of German unification. Concerns about Germany joining NATO in 1955 were more compelling than any aspect of arms control.[40]

Not that aerial inspection was ignored. Nikita Khrushchev, secretary of the Communist Party and a more powerful voice in the Kremlin than Bulganin, pointedly disagreed with Bulganin's apparent acceptance of Open Skies. He saw the proposal as a ruse to spy on Russian facilities. According to Ambassador Charles E. Bohlen, who served as translator, Khrushchev asked Eisenhower "whom he was trying to fool? In our eyes, this is a very transparent espionage device. . . .You could hardly expect us to take this seriously."[41]

On this sour note, the summit meeting essentially ended. Even without a formal rejection of Open Skies, the idea would, Bohlen predicted, "die of malnutrition." Understandably, Eisenhower was disappointed by the outcome of the meetings. He had hoped that aerial inspections and an exchange of blueprints would be a first step in confidence building between East and West. But, "as always, the result was nothing but disappointment." All that was accomplished, he told his cabinet, was "a new atmosphere." But he admitted that, "in the final analysis, . . . I believe the Geneva Conference represented a limited success." There were "small beginnings, but they could not have transpired in the atmosphere prevailing before Geneva."[42]

If the Geneva Conference of the Big Four had been a total failure, there would not have been the jockeying for credit that accompanied the unveiling of Open Skies. Rockefeller advanced his own assessment of the results of the Quantico meeting, asserting that he had initiated the idea of mutual aerial inspections in the face of Stassen's opposition. In recalling the development of Open Skies, the president did not claim credit for originating the concept but seemed pleased to have his name associated with it. Stassen transmitted Doolittle's musings, which expressed sentiments the president had been ruminating on since assuming office. While Eisenhower made no mention of Stassen's specific contributions to Open Skies, the Minnesotan did so in considerable detail in his history of the Eisenhower administration. It was Stassen's draft, acknowledging Rockefeller's contribution, that Eisenhower presented to the Soviets.[43]

If the Geneva Conference had a permanent impact on American nuclear policy, it was less from the lively imagery associated with aerial photographs of military sites than from an understanding that abolition of nuclear weapons was an impossibility. The most that could be achieved was arms limitation and control. Open Skies was a step toward that goal. The term "disarmament," however, was too attractive to be discarded. Although the UN Disarmament Commission was eventually retitled the Arms Control Committee, Stassen's title as special assistant to the president for disarmament remained untouched.

After Geneva

On July 28, less than a week after the Geneva summit adjourned, Eisenhower appointed Stassen US deputy representative on the UN Disarmament Commission, where he could apply his passion for Open Skies to a new venue. The president's draft letter to Stassen outlining the terms of his appointment noted that he would serve as US representative at the forthcoming subcommittee meeting, where he would be under Ambassador Lodge's direction on matters relating to his work with the United Nations. But the letter also noted that on matters relating to negotiations with other governments, Stassen would be under the direction of the secretary of atate.[44] The latter directive was obviously intended to bolster Dulles's amour propre.

Stassen's proposals to the UN Disarmament Commission—ostensibly preliminary but, as usual, ambitious—provoked Dulles to respond with a series of reservations. He squelched Stassen's recommendations for immediate action. "There are as of now no known inspection procedures," he asserted, "which could provide adequate support for an agreement to eliminate atomic weapons." Moreover, no actions should be taken before coming to a consensus with Britain and France. Consequently, consideration of any decisions would be "premature."[45]

It was unlikely that Dulles expected Stassen to follow his advice. He had not done so in the past, and it was quickly obvious that Stassen would again go his own independent way. Stassen was heartened by the areas of agreement he perceived in the Soviets' behavior at Geneva. He was convinced that the United States enjoyed a sufficient lead in nuclear weapons to permit bold initiatives. The point was to get started and allow momentum for change to build. The odds against success never restrained him.[46]

He wasted little time in letting the Soviets know that the United States would be open to partial measures to implement the Open Skies proposals. He disregarded the concession for "reserved and inactive status," pending further studies of inspections, the secretary of state thought he had extracted. Instead, Stassen informed Secretary of Defense Charles Wilson that he was proceeding to implement the NSC decisions of June 30, which were essentially his own interpretations of the administration's plans for developing feasible methods of inspection. He would "actively seek an international system for the regulation and reduction of armed forces and armaments." He had his special task forces in place to implement his plans.[47]

Not surprisingly, Stassen moved swiftly prior to the August 29, 1955, meeting of the subcommittee to invite the chargé d'affaires and the first secretary of the Soviet embassy to meet informally with him. He suggested that the first meeting of the subcommittee dispense with ceremonial and procedural matters and begin substantive discussion. He reminded them that both President Eisenhower and Premier Bulganin "had found merit in the concept of reciprocal visits and technical exchanges between the USSR and the U.S." Acting on the basis of this apparent imprimatur, Stassen made specific reference to the "creation of a panel of technical panels of experts to test the various methods of inspection which might be employed in the control of arms and armed forces." To advance this idea, he invited members of the Soviet delegation to lunch on August 29, convinced that informal social conferences had proved productive at Geneva. The Soviet diplomats appeared somewhat flustered by Stassen's enthusiasm but diplomatically responded with expressions of appreciation.[48]

Stassen's impulsive moves disturbed his cabinet colleagues. Secretary

Wilson responded that the Defense Department was undertaking studies for the military portions of the comprehensive inspection plan, and he urged that comments from his department be taken into account before drafting any formal proposal. Secretary Dulles wanted a simple theme, comparable to the Soviets' "Ban the Bomb," and feared that introducing the complicated subject of inspections to the UN General Assembly would permit the Soviets "to bog the matter down in discussion of details while they went ahead with their own simple 'Ban the Bomb' program."[49]

Dulles was subsequently more blunt in his criticism when Stassen continued to press his proposals. On September 1 the secretary began a letter to Stassen with a clear rejection: "I remain convinced that it will militate against the President's program if we go all out for this panel proposal on the scale and to the degree your draft suggests." He claimed he had no objection to setting up a group to study methods of conducting inspections, but "to go on and give the study group authority themselves to become a pilot plan inspection group . . . seems to me to be so spectacular and far reaching that it will greatly dilute attention to and interest in the President's proposal."[50]

The deputy representative paid lip service to the concerns of his colleagues and then proceeded along his own path. He agreed that, in light of State and Defense positions, it would be better to make no proposal until the Soviets had clarified their reaction to the Eisenhower plan: "An anemic study group would weaken the United States position in world opinion" without winning a satisfactory response from the USSR. But unlike the perennially suspicious secretary of state, Stassen thought the Soviets might be open to a more conciliatory approach, as suggested by the US Information Agency's Andrew H. Berding. A first move would be to exchange blueprints at one port and one aerodrome and then exchange aerial photography at those sites. Stassen felt that a step-by-step, phased approach would achieve both world support and a more flexible response from the Soviet Union.[51]

Dulles ignored Stassen's approach and continued to advocate a minimal statement to the UN General Assembly; he was doubtful that a favorable response from the Soviets could be expected under any circumstances. Stassen disagreed. The Soviets "were showing unusual reserve and respect for the President's proposal," he observed, and he blamed US behavior, exemplified by a bellicose speech from Secretary of the Air Force Donald A. Quarles on September 3, for stoking Soviet fears that the United States was not moving toward a reduction in armaments. He cautioned his colleagues to be mindful of how America's adversaries might interpret speeches dealing with disarmament.[52]

After meeting with the president at his summer home in Denver on September 16, Stassen informed the press that the odds were favorable for an eventual Soviet acceptance of the Open Skies proposal, even though "the United States delegation realizes that it will take some time for the Soviet Union to reach a decision." He professed to be encouraged "by the kinds of question they are asking about the manner in which the plan would go into effect."[53]

Sensing flexibility in the Soviet position, he moved against the advice of Dulles to frame a resolution to the United Nations based on reports that his task forces would deliver in October. He was buoyed by the conviction that he was acting in accordance with Eisenhower's objectives. Dulles, on the contrary, continued to believe that the Soviets would try to finesse anything the administration proposed. His skepticism seemed justified when Bulganin's letter to Eisenhower on September 19 reverted to the familiar Soviet ploy of demanding the prohibition of nuclear weapons.[54]

Dulles's reservations, shared by most of the cabinet, did not delay Stassen's preparations for a major report by his staff. He summarized its contents before the National Security Council on October 13, emphasizing specific suggestions for winning passage of the resolution on disarmament in the UN General Assembly. He elaborated on the advantages of the United States seizing the initiative rather than leaving it to the Soviet Union. His aim was a preliminary agreement by the NSC for a modest aerial inspection in an area 100 to 200 miles in breadth. This initiative would mobilize world opinion in favor of the United States and give the secretary of state a negotiating edge vis-à-vis the Soviet Union. Dulles predictably deprecated Stassen's suggestions, saying they "were still in an embryonic stage as far as we in the State Department are concerned." Dulles wanted the report to dispense with technical details. He emphasized that the president's Geneva proposal on inspection "was not really offered so much as a technical proposal or a cure-all as it was a means designed primarily to change the atmosphere of the world." Stassen's recommendations, he felt, would diminish the vision Eisenhower had projected and let the Russians off the hook by concentrating on relatively minor issues.[55]

As these discussions proceeded in October, the president was still recovering from a heart attack suffered on September 24 while on vacation in Denver. Indirectly, Stassen won Eisenhower's approval of his approach, as Lodge reported to Dulles after visiting the president in Denver. Lodge agreed with the president that getting an endorsement from the UN General Assembly would put pressure on the Soviets to allow aerial inspections. Failure to do so would expose them to censure for violating a UN resolution and the possibility of being "branded by the United Nations as the troublemaker and war-monger of the world." Such wishful thinking by the convalescing president fitted Stassen's worldview.[56]

Obstacles at the UN Subcommittee Meetings

When Stassen finally unveiled his progress report to the administration on November 1, 1955, it fleshed out ideas he had been touting since his appointment to the subcommittee: namely, the importance of taking detailed initial steps toward nuclear arms control as the primary goal, with disarmament relegated to the background. The report assured that a "comprehensive, effective, feasible, reciprocally acceptable international inspection and control system for armaments and armed forces could be established to serve certain limited but very important objectives of the United States, if agreed to by the USSR and by the other states involved." He took as his point of departure the Soviets' offer to allow outside observers into the country and expanded it exponentially.[57]

The essence of the report's recommendations involved ground inspectors operating through five regions and approximately 280 posts in the USSR and Warsaw bloc nations. The aerial inspectors would originate in four external bases, and the inspection forces in the USSR and its satellite area would total between 20,000 and 30,000 personnel. A reciprocal arrangement would be made for inspectors in the United States.[58] This interpretation of Open Skies was in direct opposition to the expectations of Secretary Dulles and the State Department.

Dulles's response was negative. He harped on Stassen's denigration of disarmament in favor of inspection, a posture that would make the United States vulnerable to negative world opinion as well as Soviet criticism. The secretary felt that from a foreign policy standpoint, the report failed to give a clear indication of the US attitude toward the reduction of armed forces and conventional armaments. Moreover, in his judgment, the outline of the inspection and control system lacked the details necessary to evaluate Stassen's policy suggestions.[59]

At the meeting of the National Security Council ten days later, with the president present, Dulles was more caustic in his criticisms and arguably unfair to Stassen. After complaining that there was insufficient detail for State Department planning, he mocked the excessively elaborate inspection plan: "We can be absolutely sure that the Russians will never accept any arms inspection system which involved twenty to thirty thousand non-Russian inspectors on Russian soil. Such an all-or-nothing proposition—that is, no steps toward disarmament until this elaborate inspection system was in operation—would make the United States a laughing stock."[60] For one who was suspicious of any disarmament program, it seemed hypocritical to fault Stassen for taking inadequate steps toward disarmament.

Dulles went on to accuse him of inconsistency: "Governor Stassen himself had not consistently followed his professed position that no steps toward disarmament could be taken until this great inspection plan had been accepted by the Russians and put into operation." Actually, Stassen's report did call for modest reductions of conventional armed forces before the inspection process was completed. When Stassen admitted that this was his intention, the secretary asserted that "he was compelled to describe this position as completely unrealistic."[61]

It was obvious that whatever course Stassen pursued, he would meet resistance from the secretary of state. The "Secretary of Peace" was acting on assumptions that were unacceptable to Dulles: namely, that flexibility by the United States would soften Soviet resistance to an ultimate deal on arms limitation. Dulles, in contrast, remained convinced that the Soviet Communists were immune to change and could never be trusted to fulfill any agreement on disarmament.

What was surprising was the president's reaction to Stassen's progress report. His special assistant for disarmament had always counted on having common objectives that connected him with Eisenhower. They both believed in the need to de-escalate the Cold War and were ready to offer ways to do so. Open Skies in this context was more than a symbol; it would be integrated into a series of steps that would transform the relationship between the United States and the Soviet Union. Yet Eisenhower appeared to reject Stassen's report by agreeing with Dulles that there had to some Soviet political concessions to accompany arms control. Stassen's failure to consider the political role in negotiations with the Kremlin was Eisenhower's major criticism of the report. He stressed the necessity of developing programs that covered a political settlement as well as arms control. No progress could be made on one program without progress on the other. The president then observed that if the Soviets gave the United States a blueprint of all their military installations and allowed reconnaissance over Soviet territory, some kind of agreement on armament reduction would be reasonable. "Thus you would not be killing the whole plan from the very outset. We must not appear to the world . . . to be laying on the table so large and complicated [an] inspection system that other nations will accuse us of blatant insincerity. The United States could not get anywhere if it followed such a course." To Stassen, the insertion of the issue of political concessions came as an unwelcome and confusing surprise.[62]

The president appeared to be unnerved by the complicated program Stassen had put before him. He was particularly put off by the numbers—the 20,000 to 30,000 non-Russian inspectors on Russian soil that Dulles had derided as unrealistic. Stassen, on the contrary, claimed that the vast size of the Soviet Union required the number of inspectors he had recommended. The president was not convinced. In the judgment of historian H. W. Brands, Stassen failed to win Eisenhower over to his plan. Political scientist David Tal phrased Eisenhower's disapproval more starkly; he "excoriated the plan," pointing out that the only thing it achieved was to unite the Atomic Energy Commission, the CIA, the Defense Department, and the Joint Chiefs of Staff against Stassen's ambitious program.[63]

The special assistant for disarmament, it seemed, had overstepped the boundaries of his position and had been appropriately reprimanded for it. Dulles made the most of the apparent breach between Eisenhower and Stassen by asking what kind of installations and armaments could be inspected "without having recourse to the full and all-out inspection called for by Governor Stassen."[64]

Was this a change of heart by the president? Was he now moving away from Open Skies by linking arms control to diplomatic approaches that were unrelated to aerial inspection? Had he returned to the concept of disarmament in place of arms control? Or was this new attitude toward

Stassen an expression of long-held feelings of distrust dating back to suspicions in 1952 that Stassen's professed advocacy of an Eisenhower presidency had masked his own ambitions for the presidency?

Eisenhower may have had some questions about Stassen's ambitions, but none of the foregoing speculations was applicable. He had brought Stassen into his cabinet to serve as a check on the presumptions of the secretary of state, but he had never intended to displace Dulles. Rather, Stassen provided an alternative way of looking at foreign policy, one to which the president was more sympathetic than he was to Dulles's hardened position on the Soviet Union. Brands judged that Eisenhower drew closer to Dulles when the latter softened his approach to disarmament. Whatever his genuine feelings may have been, the secretary recognized both the global support for arms control in the United Nations and the need to respond to it. Besides, minor reductions in conventional weapons might divert world attention from Soviet pressure for the abolition of nuclear weapons—the United States' critical strategic advantage over the Kremlin. Brands also speculated that in light of the USSR's ambiguous response to Open Skies, Eisenhower had an open mind about the future of disarmament, and he seemed prepared to follow Dulles in attaching political preconditions to it.[65]

Other factors may have been in play to account for Eisenhower's shifting position. The foreign ministers of the four major powers had adjourned their meetings in Geneva on November 16, 1955, with no plans to resume them. The matter of disarmament would be returned to the UN Subcommittee on Disarmament.[66] The failure of these talks devolved on the US insistence that inspection and control of nuclear sites and weapons be the starting point for any disarmament plan. By contrast, the Soviets continued to press for agreement on the reduction of some armaments and the prohibition of others, regardless of whether adequate controls and safeguards could be established. Important as disarmament was, however, the unsettled ending of the Geneva talks most likely centered on the new membership of the Federal Republic of Germany in NATO. To the Soviets, inspections of nuclear facilities were basically opportunities for intolerable Western intrusion into the USSR's territory, as Khrushchev had charged at the end of the Geneva Conference. Whatever concessions the Soviets were willing to make to world opinion or to US pressure had to be weighed against their primary objective—disarmament of Germany.

Consequently, the president's reaction to Stassen's report on disarmament seemed to presage a movement away from Open Skies and the first incremental steps toward disarmament, of which arms control was a basic element. In this contest, Stassen would be out of favor, and Dulles's influence would correspondingly increase. Such was not the case. Stassen's behavior did not reflect a loss of the president's confidence in his judgment. Granted that Stassen was not always attuned to the nuances of interpersonal relations, but he certainly would have been aware of a change in their relationship.

One reason for Stassen's self-confidence may be that Dulles pressed his advantage too far. For example, Dulles claimed it would be possible to control the construction of submarines in the Soviet Union without the large numbers of inspectors Stassen's plan required. The president's special assistant immediately and forcefully challenged the secretary, warning that limited inspections could give the West a false sense of security. The president backed up Stassen and expressed his reluctance "to say or do anything which would discourage Governor Stassen, and [he] suggested that Governor Stassen's people get together with General Twining's experts on aerial photography and find out from them just exactly what we could and could not effectively inspect through the agency of aerial reconnaissance." These supportive comments were made at the same session of the NSC where Eisenhower appeared to join Dulles in dismissing Stassen's report.[67]

Given these circumstances, it is not surprising that Stassen felt that he had the president's encouragement, even as he accepted Eisenhower's agreement with Dulles to require political concessions from the Soviets. Although Eisenhower never fully subscribed to Stassen's positive attitude in negotiating with the Russians, his hopes for the future at the end of 1955 were closer to Stassen's optimism than to Dulles's pessimism.

When the UN General Assembly met in December, it endorsed the resolution submitted by the United States, Britain, and France by a vote of fifty-six to seven. It reflected the principle of Eisenhower's Open Skies and the priority of the initial steps proposed by Stassen, along with Bulganin's plan for establishing control posts at strategic centers.[68] Implementation of these confidence-building measures, however, was not on the General Assembly's agenda.

6

The Illusion of Progress, 1956

Whatever reservations Eisenhower may have had about Stassen's plan in December 1955, they did not keep his special assistant from unveiling a new package of proposals in January 1956 that included letters to Bulganin and to Congress. As always when he went to work, Stassen's progress was fast and thorough. He characterized the results as a compromise, although Dulles and the Joint Chiefs of Staff groused that they could find no evidence of it. His plan contained elements of both the incremental approach to disarmament that he and the president had advocated in the past and other more extravagant ideas that encompassed a wide range of steps toward disarmament. He believed that the UN General Assembly had substantially endorsed his views on December 16.[1]

Stassen justified his haste, noting that "delay in [a] US decision would cause a serious loss of US initiative in world public opinion, would result in a gain for the Soviet Union, and would prejudice many other important interests of the U.S." Not surprisingly, he had to face the continuing hostility of Dulles, who "believed that adoption by the US of the position which you recommend would not be sufficient to maintain for us our leadership in the free world coalition and to secure the essential support of world public opinion."[2]

The secretary of state's opposition reflected his persistent suspicion of any Soviet concessions on the issue of Open Skies. Nonetheless, Stassen did not retreat from his position. He explained why a large-scale system of some 30,000 or 40,000 inspectors was necessary, given the enormous size of the territory occupied by the Soviet Union. If the Russians reciprocated, he predicted that a 5 percent reduction in the defense budget would be possible by the end of the first year of the inspection program. He suggested that if the Soviet Union genuinely opened itself to aerial inspection, "as well as to *external* internal inspection, the United States would agree at this point of time . . . that all future nuclear production would be for peaceful purposes only."[3]

Dulles's many criticisms of Stassen's presentation devolved on the latter's unrealistic optimism that he could win over the Soviets on "the most difficult field of inspection and control, namely; the field of ground forces. In that field the Soviet totalitarian system provided Russia with the greatest advantages over the United States. . . . Historically, indeed, reduction of military manpower had always proved the hardest nut to crack in all past disarmament schemes, yet Governor Stassen has picked this very nut as the one to be cracked."[4]

Stassen countered that his proposals would be a test of the Soviets' seriousness about disarmament. And in this objective he had the president's full approval. Eisenhower left no doubt of his intention to support his disarmament adviser in testing the USSR's good faith. They both believed that the size of the inspection teams would not, by itself, be a sufficient reason for a Soviet rejection of Stassen's proposals. Eisenhower was looking at Soviet reactions to see whether he had a partner "in trying to lead the world back from the brink of disaster." In the mild-mannered, gracious Bulganin, Eisenhower thought he had such a partner. Their correspondence following the Geneva Conference, filled with comforting pieties about the spirit of the meetings, seemed to support the prospect of a mutual understanding on disarmament between East and West. Yet Eisenhower never carried his enthusiasm to excess. He recognized that "the heart of the problem was this: We are trying to bargain in good faith with a fellow whose good faith we have every reason to doubt."[5] That "fellow" was certainly not Bulganin. It was the Communist system. Stassen disagreed. While ready to criticize the Soviets when crossed, he always envisioned a positive outcome in future negotiations.

Dulles was not alone in his criticisms of Stassen's proposals. The Defense Department, particularly Admiral Arthur M. Radford, chairman of the Joint Chiefs of Staff, was concerned less with the particulars of his proposals than with the implications of his strategy. The United States was dealing not with ordinary diplomatic adversaries but with "a people who had no intention whatever of keeping any agreement if they can get out of it to their advantage." He cited historical examples between 1945 and 1950 to make his point. The only reason there appeared to be a new appetite for negotiation on disarmament, he declared, was because US military strength vis-à-vis the Russians had developed so greatly in recent years.[6]

Stassen would certainly agree that the newly favorable atmosphere was due, in large part, to America's substantial military buildup at home and abroad. But his conclusion was the opposite of Radford's. Because of America's defense efforts, successful negotiations were now possible. While the admiral agreed that negotiations were likely, he was also convinced they would be unsuccessful.[7]

The president concurred with Stassen's judgment. It was obvious that his views were closer to those of his disarmament adviser than to Stassen's challengers in the State and Defense Departments. He observed, "We had given Governor Stassen a pretty good 'going over' at this meeting, and it was now time to provide him with some useful guidance. How were we going to give Governor Stassen's proposals some real appeal, both to our own people and the people of the world?" He wanted "something of Governor Stassen's policy proposals worked up in the form of a speech or statement by the President which would provide a kind of test of the reaction of our allies and of world public opinion." As Eisenhower asserted repeatedly, the goal was to "secure some slight easing of the world situation without damaging our own national security." He felt that even the Joint Chiefs would agree with this goal. This NSC meeting on January 26, 1956, adjourned without acting on Stassen's recommendations. But the NSC accepted Eisenhower's advice that Stassen's arguments be used as the basis for a speech "by a responsible spokesman for the Administration" that assessed their probable impact on both allied and Soviet governments. That "responsible spokesman" would be Stassen. He was also charged with refining a letter the president would send to Premier Bulganin.[8]

Given the support of the president, it would be understandable if Stassen had assumed that his proposals would be formally accepted by the NSC at its meeting on February 7, 1956. They were not. In fact, the record of actions taken at that meeting noted that the draft statement of February 2 "will not be used." While this sounded like a curt rejection, it was cushioned by the authorization "to explore and develop as a basis for negotiation with the USSR, his proposal of small strips of territory in the US and USSR within which the feasibility of inspection systems would be tested."[9] This permission did not encompass all that Stassen advocated, but it was an endorsement that he could use as a platform for expansion. The venue for future development would be the forthcoming meeting of the UN Subcommittee on Disarmament, to which Stassen had been appointed the US deputy delegate in July 1955.

The UN Subcommittee on Disarmament

The meeting of the subcommittee would proceed in two stages, the first taking place in March and April 1956. Not until the Suez crisis had passed and the presidential election in the fall had been decided was the second stage possible. The meetings resumed in March 1957 and concluded in August of that year. Stassen was a prominent participant in both stages.

To prepare for the March 1956 meetings, the president made it clear that Stassen would be the key interpreter of US positions on disarmament. His letter of guidance to Stassen revealed his discomfort with the secretary of state's blunt rejection of technical inspections and the incremental measures of disarmament they signified. Eisenhower stated, "By flatly rejecting technical inspection as providing any practical basis for disarmament we thereby give to the Russians a great opportunity for hurting us politically."[10]

Stassen had won his case. In his letter of guidance, Eisenhower seemed to take direct aim at Dulles's dismissal of Stassen's proposal to reduce the size of US and USSR armed forces to 2.5 million and the military budget by 5 percent. The president believed that if aerial inspections and accompanying ground inspections were operating satisfactorily, he would authorize his representative to indicate the acceptability of mutually agreed force levels of 2.5 million men for the United States and the USSR.[11] Although he linked China to this figure as well, which softened Dulles's opposition, Eisenhower, intentionally or not, clearly rejected the position of his secretary of state.

Even as the president recognized the visceral hostility of the Soviet leadership to intrusive inspections, he was hoping to build mutual confidence based on Bulganin's putative willingness to establish control posts at transportation facilities, as the Soviet premier had suggested in his letter of May 10, 1955. Eisenhower, however, was well aware of how "the United Nations inspection teams in Korea, tied down to fixed locations, were freely bypassed by the Communist air and ground forces; . . . thus

[they] were able to dispose their units with impunity and strengthen their forces at will."[12]

The thrust of the president's letter to Stassen on the eve of his departure for London was his approval of the small steps Stassen had long championed, as opposed to the State Department's demand that a complete disarmament package, along with a political settlement, precede disarmament talks. The key was using small strips of territory in the United States and USSR to test the feasibility of the work of "a small number of inspection personnel," with the emphasis on "small" in taking steps toward the larger goal.[13]

Armed with Eisenhower's optimism, Stassen spent two months in London—March and April 1956—at meetings of the UN Disarmament Subcommittee. There he joined a distinguished company of veteran diplomats—the Soviet Union's Andrei Gromyko, Britain's Harold Nutting, France's Jules Moch, and Canada's Norman Robertson. He had known Gromyko since his days at the San Francisco Conference in 1945, and he was well aware of Moch's difficult personality. He anticipated some familiar problems in negotiating with his Soviet counterparts but was less prepared for serious conflicts with the chief NATO allies.

Dulles, whose diplomatic responsibilities were wider than Stassen's, had to bear the brunt of the world's criticism of the US refusal to accept Soviet demands for the immediate suspension of nuclear testing in December 1955. Cries for a test ban came from Nehru in India to the pope at the Vatican. These were echoed by the Soviets, who, as Dulles bitterly noted, advocated suspension only after they had completed their own test series. Stassen also occupied a lesser role when he testified in January 1956 before the newly created disarmament subcommittee of the Senate Foreign Relations Committee. He argued that testing was only a symptom of international tensions and that weapons tests were necessary for national security. But it was the secretary of state who made the major case for continuing nuclear tests; Stassen was more open to test-ban arguments.[14]

Arguably, Dulles was less surprised at the British and French dissent over Stassen's proposals. He was worried about the allies linking disarmament talks to German reunification: "It would be only playing into Soviet hands if we allowed ourselves to be drawn into discussing the substance of this matter even tentatively in the disarmament talks."[15]

Reunification was not the only problem. A new Anglo-French initiative following the Geneva Conference was distinctly different from Stassen's—or Dulles's—views on disarmament. The initiative was primarily the work of France's Jules Moch, a longtime Socialist leader and defense specialist. He saw the Soviet threat from a French perspective that was widely shared by the European NATO allies. Moch worried about a surprise attack coming from conventional rather than nuclear forces. This fear reflected the numerical superiority of Soviet ground forces in Europe. He did not disagree with Stassen's (and now Eisenhower's) idea of using small strips of territory to test the success of the inspection process. But Europeans were uncomfortable with the concurrent emphasis on deterrence in place of disarmament. While they were prepared to accept a link between arms inspection and arms control, they felt the Americans' primary interest was in the threat posed by a surprise attack.[16]

The contrast between the American and European positions on disarmament was sharper than Stassen had anticipated. He had always promoted interim steps centered on credible inspections before arms reduction could be concluded. The Anglo-French plan, in contrast, proposed to craft a comprehensive agreement with the Soviets even if the inspection procedures were faulty or incomplete. Moch's alternative would exclude the Open Skies initiative, which he believed the Soviet Union would never accept.

Disturbing as the French position was, the United States was more concerned with Britain's association with it than with the content of the proposal itself. The transatlantic differences never reached a breaking point that might have jeopardized the alliance. But until the divergences were bridged, neither side could come up with a joint position paper for the subcommittee. The best they could manage was to identify the French plan as a "working paper" rather than a formal proposal.[17]

The Anglo-French issue was resolved in May when Stassen was able to convince Premier Guy Mollet, over Moch's protests, to accept the US approach to disarmament. Soviet initiatives were more subtle and more difficult to address. The Soviets appeared to endorse Stassen's proposals, including substantial reductions in conventional forces, which the Soviets had already begun to implement unilaterally as early as August 1955. Given the enormous disparity in the number of Western versus Soviet ground forces, this gesture was hardly a genuine concession. On the issue that was highest on the US agenda—nuclear arms control—the Russians were prepared to consider intrusive aerial photography, the heart of Eisenhower's Open Skies, but only in the final stages of a comprehensive disarmament agreement. In the meantime, they were willing to allow the inspection of armaments in selected areas of Germany—East and West—but only if there were a ban on nuclear testing and all nuclear weapons were removed from West German territory.[18]

The Soviet proposal did not meet the US requirements for a settlement, but its tone was sufficiently conciliatory to raise Stassen's hopes for an agreement in the near future. These hopes were nourished in part by events in the Soviet Union, especially when Khrushchev, first secretary of the Communist Party, denounced Stalinism in 1956 before the Twentieth Soviet Party Congress. It was understandable that optimists in the West envisioned an improved environment, and Stassen was among them. Gromyko raised expectations for positive change when he expressly asked Stassen to maintain informal personal channels. It was likely that Gromyko regarded Stassen as a softer target than his State Department colleagues.[19]

There was, however, a troubling theme embedded in Soviet indications of their more flexible stance. This was the German question. The Soviet endgame in the negotiations with the West was the detachment of the Federal Republic of Germany from NATO. The removal of nuclear weapons from West German territory was just one step in that direction.

Chancellor Konrad Adenauer was well aware of the potential dangers to West Germany. In his letter to Dulles on the eve of the subcommittee meetings in March, he reminded the secretary that "the Federal Republic is not represented in the Disarmament Subcommittee of the United Nations and, therefore, has no possibility to express her views. I believe, however, that her cooperation is necessary in the interest and the spirit of Atlantic solidarity." Since the negotiations would involve the military security of his country, he wanted assurance that no decisions would be made without its approval.[20]

The German problem was very much on Dulles's mind when he urged the US delegation "to keep the discussion of this subject there centered on the questions within the competence of the Subcommittee." He was disturbed by indications that Stassen's team might lean toward accepting additional force reductions or weapons limitations in return for German reunification. He made it clear that the issues of German reunification and European security were too complex for the subcommittee to handle and should be managed through regular channels. His intention was not to downplay the importance of unification but to ensure that its pursuit did not come at the expense of dangerous force reductions.[21]

Despite Dulles's usual misgivings about Stassen's diplomatic skills and the ends he hoped to achieve, the State Department's reaction to his conversations with Gromyko over German reunification was positive. Stassen gave the impression of taking a harder stance on the relationship between disarmament and political settlement than he actually held. Responding to Gromyko's query if further progress on disarmament was dependent on the reunification of Germany, Stassen replied that although a prompt solution to the German problem was desirable, its absence was no obstacle to reducing the size of US and USSR forces to 2.5 million. While the tone of the conversation might have disturbed the German chancellor, given that disarmament trumped German reunification among Stassen's priorities, nothing in that conversation suggested that the United States was considering decoupling disarmament from German reunification.[22]

If Adenauer had any doubts about Stassen's dependability, he could always count on Dulles to maintain a hard line. But it was not so hard that it precluded a warning to Adenauer not to stand in the way of US tactics on disarmament. Still, the chancellor could take comfort when the secretary denounced the Soviet plan as a sham, on the grounds that a limited inspection zone was a pretext for legitimating the division of Germany. Dulles perceived additional Soviet designs on Germany when he accused the USSR of seeking to prevent the deployment of NATO forces in West Germany.[23]

After almost two months of intensive negotiations, an impasse developed that was not readily resolved. The Soviets had repeatedly turned down aerial photography and offered instead reductions in armaments and manpower without inspections. The Americans criticized the Russians for wanting disarmament without inspection, while the Russians denounced the Americans for wanting inspection without disarmament.

It is worth noting that at the elaborate Soviet reception at the Claridge Hotel on April 24, shortly after the talks formally concluded, Gromyko asked Stassen to meet informally with Bulganin and Khrushchev to discuss once again their differences over disarmament. Nothing concrete emerged from this impromptu meeting, but Gromyko's special effort to bring Stassen together with Bulganin and Khrushchev suggested an awareness of Stassen's flexibility on this subject and the potential to take advantage of his vulnerability.[24] Gromyko continued talks with Stassen the next day, implying an ongoing hope of exploiting Stassen's passion for collaborative action to serve Soviet interests. But when the Soviets floated the idea of a small step involving no more than 10,000 men, their apparent agreement with Stassen's approach failed over the issue of inspection. Stassen's putative flexibility did not encompass a retreat from this fundamental US requirement.[25]

The subcommittee adjourned on May 4 without resolving the substantive differences between East and West. For Stassen, the fundamental clash centered on his conviction that aerial surveillance was essential to any inspection system. Khrushchev had engaged in a tirade against aerial photography during their informal meeting at the Claridge. He claimed the Soviet Union could not understand why the United States insisted on it. Only his respect for President Eisenhower restrained Soviet diplomats from "openly rejecting it." In his customary hyperbolic way, Khrushchev asserted that "the US should not seek to know everything, that the US should not try to look in everybody's bedroom." Stassen responded that a disarmament agreement would be sound only if both sides felt confident that the agreement was being respected. In sum, they talked past each other.[26]

But it was not only the credibility of an inspection system that doomed Soviet overtures. Testing remained a formidable obstacle to an agreement. As Stassen told the Senate subcommittee in June, nuclear weapons were too important for America's security to be compromised by a test ban unaccompanied by a general disarmament agreement. "It is essential that the United States continue exploration and testing in the field of thermonuclear weapons." The subcommittee's work thus ended in a familiar impasse.[27]

Neither Dulles's skepticism over the sincerity of Soviet overtures nor the French-inspired disagreement over negotiating priorities nor the Soviets' persistent unwillingness to allow credible nuclear test inspections did much to damage Stassen's optimism about the prospects for a settlement in the near future. The transatlantic split, for example, had been resolved when he convinced French premier Mollet to accept the US approach to disarmament.[28] Moreover, the subcommittee had just completed round one. He perceived enough progress to hope for better results when the subcommittee reconvened in 1957. Above all, he felt he had the president's continuing confidence in his mission.

Aftermath of the London Meetings

A man of Stassen's temperament could envision a potential breakthrough: for the first time, the Soviets had demonstrated a willingness to discuss disarmament without explicitly tying it to a prohibition of all nuclear weapons. Moreover, his embrace of nuclear testing was not as firm as his testimony suggested. Had his scientific advisers, especially Ernest Lawrence and Edward Teller, not objected so vigorously, Stassen might have moved in the direction of a test ban, without all the restrictions placed on it. World opinion and his own sensibilities responded to the appeal of a nuclear test ban, even though he pointedly disagreed with Democratic presidential candidate Adlai Stevenson's April 21 speech urging an end to nuclear testing.[29]

But the subject of nuclear testing was now problematic. From May 5 to July 22, 1956, the United States conducted a series of nuclear tests in the Marshall Islands in the Pacific. The official account of the maneuvers emphasized the benefits of new information obtained on the long-range detonation of nuclear weapons.[30] In essence, the United States was catching up with Soviet nuclear activities over the past year. Nonetheless, this news did not affect Stassen's own long-range sense of the future, as reflected in his official report to the National Security Council.

Stassen began his report on May 10 by spelling out the results of the disarmament negotiations at the London meetings of the UN subcommittee. It contained a positive gloss, focusing less on Soviet relations than on his success in deterring the British and French from submitting their own plan. "As a result of negotiations with the British and French," he noted, "the latter not only modified their disarmament plan, but agreed to put it forward as a working paper rather than as a fixed position of their governments." He also succeeded in winning German as well as British and French approval for the reduction of US forces to 2.5 million men prior to any agreement with the Soviets on German reunification. The four Western powers, including Canada, were in harmony over presenting a united front vis-à-vis the Soviets.[31]

Relations with the USSR, he admitted, continued to be marked by its resistance to aerial inspection and to linking German reunification with the reduction of armaments. Yet he believed the Soviets had made significant moves toward the Western position on ground inspections. Their next step, he hoped, would be accepting the Western position on aerial inspections. He was particularly pleased that the Soviets had abandoned the prerequisite of banning the bomb. He speculated that the Soviets had finally realized there was no hope of ever inducing the United States to agree to an immediate and outright ban of nuclear weapons.[32]

Buoyed by his perceptions of American diplomatic superiority, he was convinced that success had been achieved largely through his own tactics. The special assistant posited five major areas where American policy on disarmament should be concentrated. They were all interrelated and centered on the need to convince the Soviets to reduce their hostility to Eisenhower's aerial inspection plans and to reach an agreement before other governments began developing their own nuclear weapons. He concluded with the observation that despite the Soviets' continuing use of propaganda based on the disarmament problem, "they are at long last aware of the suicidal character of a nuclear war. In short, they are beginning to see the problem of a general war with nuclear weapons much as we see it in the United States."[33]

The tenor of Stassen's report conformed with his vision of the future. In the spirit of his ten-year advocacy of the United Nations, his last point proposed the earmarking of some portion of the nuclear stockpiles of several nations for the support of UN resolutions against aggression. This would have the advantage of freeing nations from having to maintain large military establishments. Instead, resources spent on self-defense could be diverted to economic development. "Thus the atoms-for-police program," he contended, "would be an important factor in countering the economic offensive aimed at the underdeveloped nations of the world."[34]

From Stassen's perspective, the objectives he had sought as director of the FOA might be achieved under the rubric of a reorganized nuclear program. His upbeat judgment of the progress of the UN Disarmament Subcommittee was submitted on May 10, just six days after it adjourned on May 4. Actually, there seemed to be little reason for optimism. The four Western powers officially conceded that, after a seven-week effort to frame an acceptable world disarmament plan, "the differences between the position of the Soviet delegations and those of the other four delegations were not reconciled in the meetings of the subcommittee." The division was sharp. The United States, Britain, France, and Canada pointed to the need to proceed by cautious stages toward disarmament, to be carried out with parallel with the settlement of international disputes. The progress report reiterated the familiar demand that effective control measures had to be in place before disarmament could begin.[35]

Given the termination of the subcommittee's negotiations without a resolution of the differences between the United States and USSR, it was hardly surprising that there would be some negative reactions to Stassen's optimistic appraisal of conditions. Even the president, usually a cheerleader, suggested that the "atoms-for-police" proposal be carefully defined before any steps were taken to implement the concept. The NSC tabled Stassen's report and asked him for a new review, taking into account the US response to a possible unilateral Soviet reduction of conventional weapons. The NSC decided that Stassen should conduct more studies of US policy on the control of armaments before the United States committed to any new aspects of a disarmament policy. The NSC overlooked the details of Stassen's report, as well as the enthusiasm with which he presented them.[36]

What the administration faced in May 1956 was a full-blown peace offensive by the Soviets, highlighted by their May 14 announcement of a reduction in their armed forces as an earnest indication of their move toward disarmament. State and Defense Department officials denounced this as a ruse to weaken the West. General Alfred Gruenther, Supreme Allied Commander in Europe, feared that this apparently conciliatory act would undercut vital congressional aid to Europe and noted that, in light of their superiority in manpower, the Russians' capability for offensive action would not be "substantially affected at all." Influential military analyst Hanson Baldwin dismissed the Soviet announcement as a gesture to back up its "peaceful coexistence" theme and put the United States on the defensive. If carried out, its military power relative to the West would hardly be changed.[37]

No US reaction was more vigorous than that of Secretary of State Dulles. Rather than citing Soviet troop reductions as evidence of peaceful intentions, he saw the release of soldiers and sailors into industry and agriculture as a means of increasing the USSR's war-making power. The Soviet move was prompted not by "a love of peace" but by "solid and compelling economic reasons." He claimed that efforts to develop new weapons on a grand scale had overextended the USSR's resources. At a point "where it could cut with the greatest advantage to itself," it decided to take men out of uniform and move them into factories and farms. He subsequently brushed aside a Soviet invitation to General Nathan F. Twining, the US Air Force chief of staff, as just another propaganda ploy.[38]

Stassen was disturbed by what he considered to be an overly negative reaction by the cabinet, Secretary Dulles in particular, to the Soviet action. He made a point of balancing the judgments of his colleagues by telling the press that the Soviets' decision to reduce the number of troops "was an initiative we wanted them to take." He elaborated on the reasons why they had acted, which were more nuanced than those cited by Dulles. Stassen noted the low birthrate in the late 1930s and early 1940s, which accounted for an usually small pool of young manpower at this time; the rising demands among the Soviet people for more consumer goods; and, most important, a conviction in the Kremlin that the United States had no intention of starting a war, given the devastating effects on both sides of a thermonuclear conflict. He was convinced that the Soviet announcement made the prospects for peace "a few degrees brighter." He further denied that the force reduction was just a propaganda move.[39]

Stassen's attempts to counter the State Department's negativism received support from both President Eisenhower and General Secretary Khrushchev. He would not have spoken so freely had he not gained the president's quiet approval of his efforts to generate momentum on disarmament. Khrushchev was effusive in hailing Stassen as "a serious man," and he referred to their productive talks in London in April. He used the occasion of a diplomatic reception at the French embassy in Moscow to compare Dulles unfavorably with Stassen, mocking the secretary for "guessing" that the USSR would reduce its military forces by 1.2 million men, "as if he got that out of the stars." Dulles, he asserted to US Ambassador Bohlen, knew the exact figures, since he had given them to Stassen in London. In a further conversation with Bohlen, he intimated a camaraderie with Stassen and told him, "[I hope] you don't mind, but when I was in London I invited Mr. Stassen to come here and stay at your house." The Communist leader displayed more than his brand of humor in this exchange. Stassen obviously occupied a special—and arguably vulnerable—place in his perception of American policy.[40]

The Kremlin made the most of its efforts to sow confusion about its disarmament measures, and it succeeded up to a point. The troop reduction issue pushed aside the ongoing Soviet refusal to accept nuclear inspection plans that were acceptable to the US negotiators, including Stassen. In fact, it induced a powerful military critic of Stassen's policies, Admiral Radford, to consider reducing US troops in Europe, but only in the context of a strong, credible nuclear force. And the widespread concerns over nuclear testing had an effect as well: Stassen testified on June 7 before the Senate Foreign Relations Committee's subcommittee on disarmament that the United States was willing to discuss a test ban as part of a comprehensive disarmament agreement, but not as "an isolated advance agreement."[41] He was responding to pressure from both Democrats and the Soviets in considering a suspension of nuclear tests. But the idea was attractive to him as well, under the right conditions.

The summer of 1956 turned out to be unproductive with respect to disarmament issues. Policies were not fully established, despite Stassen's efforts to press the bureaucracy into decisions that he believed were vital for the future. Opponents feared that the United States would not suspend its agreements with the USSR if the adversary disregarded them. Stassen did not object, though, to the contention that the creation of a NATO or a UN force should not restrict the United States from using its nuclear capability. As he noted on July 20, "A sound policy now, leading either to a sound agreement or to no agreement, is preferable to the alternative of leaving a vacuum of undecided policy, with adverse effects at home and abroad."[42]

There was never a doubt about Stassen's willingness and ability to fill any vacuum. But the opportunities were limited by the State Department's questions about the timing and form of a UN "Atoms for Peace" police force. Deputy Undersecretary of State Robert Murphy asserted, "In general, I have always felt that the concept of a United Nations military force is a good one," but the obstacles in implementing it at this time were formidable. Dillon Anderson, the president's special assistant for national security affairs, identified a "stumbling block which at present prevents progress toward the policy decisions which Governor Stassen and you [deputy special assistant Amos J. Peaslee] have had in mind. This was the absence of any *interdepartmentally agreed* inspection system." Consequently, he felt that it would be "well nigh impossible" to complete any major policy decisions in this area.[43]

From another direction, Murphy raised the prospect of the United States taking the initiative in limiting the testing of nuclear weapons. Because of rising American worries about the health effects of nuclear testing and Soviet pressure for the discontinuation of tests independent of a general agreement on disarmament, the State Department floated the idea of a unilateral announcement of a one-year cessation of testing. This would put the Soviets on the defensive and win support in the UN General Assembly. This idea was on Stassen's mind as well, given the right political circumstances; however, Gromyko's July 12 call for an immediate cessation of atomic and hydrogen bomb tests was hardly the right circumstance. While the State Department draft won Dulles's approval on August 29, it never went beyond that stage. The State Department's rejection of Stassen's "Atoms for Peace" police force reflected a more accurate judgment of the administration's position on nuclear testing. Murphy replied to Stassen that, "while a proposal along the lines you suggest has merit, we must defer it for the time being."[44]

Although little progress was made on disarmament in the summer of 1956, the UN Disarmament Commission remained in session. The Soviets continued to advance proposals that asked the United States and Britain to refrain from nuclear testing. The Soviets had the implicit support of the commission when it approved the Peruvian delegate's recommendation, by a vote of ten to one, to instruct the five-member Subcommittee on Disarmament to reconsider the many proposals submitted during its spring sessions.[45]

A major explanation for this relative inaction was the upcoming presidential election in the United States. If the nation itself was distracted by politics in the summer of 1956, no political figure was more distant from his diplomatic obligations than Harold Stassen. His behavior seemingly defied easy explanation as he engaged in a one-man campaign to dislodge Vice President Nixon from his position as a candidate for reelection. His staff was uncomfortable with this effort.

Stassen was fortunate in that, over the years, he had assembled a group of able advisers and colleagues, some of whom occupied important positions on his various staffs. The most prominent member was Robert E. Matteson, a close personal friend who had served formally as the FOA's director of research and reports and subsequently as staff director of Stassen's special staff. Informally, Matteson had been Stassen's alter ego since his years as governor. Almost as important to Stassen's career was Amos J. Peaslee, Eisenhower's ambassador to Australia until February 1956 and then deputy special assistant to the president. A wealthy international lawyer from New Jersey, Peaslee had been an enthusiastic supporter of Stassen's 1948 presidential campaign. The former boy governor's intellectual and organizational qualities had attracted followers to his cause, and some of them became influential members of his team. Stassen, to his credit and advantage, listened to their advice on most matters, but not when it conflicted with his ambitions. Was this unwillingness due to an overwhelming self-confidence in his future, as Matteson sensed, or was it, as his biographers suggest, an inability to think introspectively?[46] It is also worth considering whether he believed—accurately or not—that he acted with the approval of the president. In any event, against the judgment of his friends, Stassen plunged into a hopeless campaign to unseat Nixon.

The Nixon Fiasco

Stassen's actions against Nixon were apparently based on long-standing grievances between the two politicians. They had met in 1944 during World War II, when both were serving as naval officers in the Solomon Islands. Nixon—six years Stassen's junior—professed that he had been favorably impressed by the chief aide to Admiral Halsey. Stassen claimed he had no recollection of the brief meeting. They shared a youthful belief in the need to liberalize the Republican Party, and both endorsed the other's campaigns—Nixon's for Congress in 1946 and the Senate in 1950, and Stassen's for the Republican presidential candidacy in 1948.[47]

But friction arose in 1952 when Nixon became the vice presidential candidate. Nixon never forgave Stassen for urging him to quit after the exposure of a Nixon campaign fund from wealthy contributors. Nixon, in turn, helped block Stassen's aspirations to be undersecretary of state in the Eisenhower administration when the vice president supported fellow Californian Herbert Hoover Jr. for that post.[48] In any event, it was unlikely that Dulles would have accepted Stassen as his undersecretary under any circumstances.

Was mutual estrangement a sufficient reason to explain Stassen's apparently impulsive effort to dump Nixon in 1956 in favor of a more suitable candidate? And given his personal history, there was only one obvious candidate: himself. But he could hardly present this alternative to the president or to the Republican Party. He thus made a point of excluding himself as Nixon's replacement.

Eisenhower's ileitis attack in June 1956, only two months before the Republican convention in Philadelphia, was a reminder of the critical role of the vice president if the president became incapacitated. It energized Stassen to act on what a Nixon biographer called a "plot" to replace Nixon with Governor Christian Herter of Massachusetts. When Republican Party chairman Leonard Hall asked Herter to nominate Nixon, he knew that "something was wrong" when the Massachusetts governor asked for time to think about it.[49]

Herter was a liberal Republican, with political views that Stassen and Eisenhower could appreciate. As a former diplomat, he was experienced in foreign relations and might have been a natural candidate to oppose Nixon, except for some obvious reasons. Among them were age—sixty-one—and physical infirmities—severe arthritis. But most notable was a lack of interest in serving as vice president, although he was flattered by the attention. Stassen's proposal of Herter was based in part on Nixon's association with Senator McCarthy, which had damaged his reputation in the liberal wing of the party. Moreover, as Stassen observed to reporters, the Gallup poll showed that with Nixon on the ticket, the Republicans would suffer a 6 percent loss in the general election. While this would not affect Eisenhower's reelection, it might have resonance in the congressional races.[50] What Stassen did not discuss was his recognition that an elderly Vice President Herter would not be a rival for the presidency in 1960.

The former Minnesota governor did not rest his case solely on opinion polls. He asserted that Nixon had "evident weakness" among labor, minority groups, and independent voters. Stassen also benefited from McCarthy's denunciation of him "as one of the most contemptible politicians of our era . . . possessed of an overpowering ambition to become President."[51] McCarthy may not have been far from the mark about Stassen's ambitions, but his antagonism two years after his censure by the Senate only served to raise Stassen's reputation among liberal Republicans.

That members of the Republican establishment, particularly party chairman Hall and Eisenhower's press secretary James Hagerty, were solidly behind Nixon did not deter Stassen. He believed that only Eisenhower could stop him from advancing his plan to install Herter in place of Nixon. He was mistaken; congressional Republicans solidly supported the vice president. Stassen never had the backing of more than a few liberal Republicans, and even they quickly retreated in the face of the party's opposition. Former Massachusetts governor Robert F. Bradford, who, according to Stassen, had encouraged the "dump Nixon" movement, denied ever writing to or talking with Stassen about the Nixon candidacy. Bradford wondered whether Stassen had confused him with his son, who had worked in Stassen's anti-Nixon headquarters.[52]

There were elements of absurdity in Stassen's attempt to oust Nixon. With Eisenhower in Panama at the Inter-American Conference, Stassen wrote to Nixon and expressed his "long and continuing personal friendly feelings toward you," yet he hoped Nixon would join him in supporting Herter for the vice presidency. This language indicates that Stassen was either hypocritical or delusional, and in light of his egoism, the latter seems more likely. Whatever excitement Herter experienced at his anointment by Stassen was quickly extinguished when Hall held out the possibility of an undersecretary of state position if he agreed to nominate Nixon. Given Herter's preferences, he accepted the invitation, regardless of whether the State Department post ever materialized. To avoid any further doubts, Hall pressed Nixon to tell the president that he wanted to stay in office. There was no question, as Hall made clear, that dropping Nixon from the ticket would disrupt party unity.[53]

Despite the lack of support from any corner of the Republican Party, Stassen persisted in his quixotic campaign right up to the opening of the convention. On the dubious assumption that Eisenhower remained on his side, he kept Herter's name in contention long after Herter himself had agreed to nominate Nixon on the convention floor. The situation created by Stassen may have caused a brief sensation, as convention chairman Joseph Martin (R-MA) remarked, but Stassen himself was an embarrassing joke by the time the party met in San Francisco. Stassen did not recognize either the embarrassment he created or the laughingstock he had become. He was convinced that new polls, which were never released, showed the wisdom of his choice of Herter. Even when Herter agreed to renominate the vice president, Stassen was undeterred. Nixon could hardly believe it when Stassen claimed that Herter's decision "was itself a confirmation of his [Stassen's] very strong standing in the party."[54]

Finally recognizing the inevitability of Nixon's renomination, Stassen asked Martin if he could second the nomination. He had no qualms about saying that he had always been a team player. Although the maximum number of seconding speeches had already been allotted, the chairman allowed Stassen two minutes for the sake of party harmony. Stassen rambled on for twelve minutes.[55]

The reactions of the two principals involved in Stassen's gambit—Nixon and Eisenhower—are worth noting. The vice president displayed the same reserve he had shown in September 1955 when the president suffered a heart attack. Nixon took pains not to appear too ready to assume presidential duties. Similarly, he took no public offense at Stassen's brash attempts to take his office from him. He commented to the United Press on July 29 that "any individual within a political party has a right to express his views on candidates." And, he added, "a healthy dispute" never proved harmful to a political campaign. Even in his memoirs, Nixon was restrained in his judgment of his adversary: "Many supporters urged me to shrug off Stassen's effort as a clownish and transparent power play. But I knew that Stassen was a clever man, and except when blinded by ambition, a very able one."[56] If Nixon's restraint was an act, it was successful. He did not come across as feeling unfairly attacked by his former friend. It was good politics. He expressed no objection to the concept of an open convention, since he knew he had the backing of the Republican establishment. He let Hall and Hagerty take up his cause. Whatever resentment he may have felt over Eisenhower's treatment of him was not exposed to the public.

The role of the president in this travesty was more complicated. He could have stopped Stassen in his tracks at any time but chose not to. Granted that Eisenhower's temperament disposed him to allow the party to determine the choice of a nominee, but he had given so many indications of his dissatisfaction with his vice president that a less determined man than Nixon would have taken the hint. Eisenhower had considered Robert B. Anderson, a former Democrat from Texas, to be a suitable candidate for the office, but Anderson was not interested. The president then urged Nixon to take a cabinet position. Dulles was securely positioned at the State Department, but Nixon could have Defense after Wilson retired. Nixon, however, recognized that there was no better position for a politician than serving as vice president under an old man with a heart condition. He did not take the bait, even when Ike reminded him that no vice president since Martin Van Buren had been elected president.[57] How the president responded to the Stassen initiative should have been an indication of his ambivalence toward Nixon's renomination. Eisenhower gave Stassen a leave of absence to drum up support for Herter. Stassen was free to promote his campaign against Nixon, as long as he did not do so as a member of the cabinet. After the election, speechwriter Emmett Hughes noted that Ike did not regret Stassen's campaign to remove Nixon from the Republican ticket: "I've watched Dick a long time," the president said, "and he just hasn't grown."[58]

It is obvious that Eisenhower had no enthusiasm for retaining Nixon, but he deferred to the will of his party. The vice president's popularity in right-wing circles of the Republican Party allowed him to ignore the president's signals. As for the Stassen intervention, Eisenhower suggested in his memoirs that it added some excitement to what might have been a dull affair.[59] In fact, he seemed to enjoy the theater it created.

Resuming His Post

Although the president identified Stassen pejoratively as a professional politician, he continued to value his adviser's many abilities. Three weeks before the Republican convention in San Francisco, Stassen told the press that he would return to his role as presidential assistant on disarmament, regardless of whether Nixon was renominated. After a four-week leave of absence, he was back at his White House duties immediately after the convention adjourned.[60] Stassen submitted his resignation after the election, but press secretary Hagerty made it clear that this action was nothing more than a traditional gesture extended to reelected presidents.[61] This sequence of events could not have taken place if the president had lost confidence in his adviser. Stassen had every right to assume that he would continue in his post, secure in the backing of the president.

When he returned to his office, it was as if the Nixon interlude had never happened. During his absence, Amos Peaslee had stepped in with confidence as his surrogate. The State Department's apparent dismissal of Stassen's proposals was not the final word on the subject. Speaking for Dulles, Murphy acknowledged that "there may be political considerations that would make it advisable for the US to take the initiative with regard to nuclear weapons." Not least of these were Soviet demands for discontinuing nuclear tests, whether or not there was a general agreement on disarmament in place. The British, French, and Canadians agreed and suggested that the UN Security Council take up the question of suspending nuclear tests. World opinion strongly favored this approach, as the public was becoming increasingly aware of the hazards of radiation. Accordingly, the secretary of state was supporting a draft that would have the United States abstain from testing nuclear weapons for at least a year. But, as noted, it was just a draft.[62]

The special assistant, however, lost no time in pushing Secretary Wilson to develop methods to measure reductions in armaments and military expenditures. He was heartened by Bulganin's willingness to reach a partial agreement without waiting for a resolution of the entire disarmament issue. After blaming the United States for failing to respond to the USSR's reasonable initiatives to reduce armaments, the Soviet premier admitted that, "in view of the existence of a genuine desire of all parties concerned to come to an agreement on the problem of disarmament, there is the possibility of reaching an agreement—if not on this entire problem, at least on some of the parts, i.e., the reduction of conventional armaments, prohibition of atomic weapons, reduction of military budgets, etc."[63]

A month later, Bulganin repeated his recommendation for a partial solution, with a specific reference to nuclear weapons tests: "Until the necessary agreement on the prohibition of atomic weapons is attained, it would, in our opinion be desirable to reach agreement at this time on at least the first step toward the solution of the problem of atomic weapons—the prohibition of testing atomic and hydrogen weapons."[64] Stassen might not concur with his priorities, but he could endorse Bulganin's statement on September 11 that "agreement on any individual problem or partial proposal should not be made contingent on agreement of the disarmament problem as a whole."[65]

The tenor of this correspondence should have confirmed the wisdom of the recommendations Stassen had been making for the past year. Instead, the United States was sidetracked by the exigencies of a heated presidential election that was entering its last phase and by the concurrent Suez crisis, which exacerbated differences with both the British and French allies and the Soviet adversary. On the eve of the election, the British and French, along with the Israelis, invaded Egypt, despite the opposition of the White House. At the same time, the USSR ousted Hungary's dissident Communist government by force, taking advantage of a split among the NATO allies. These diversions inevitably poisoned relations between the two superpowers and undermined Stassen's optimism.

Departing from the friendly tone of his earlier exchanges with Bulganin, Eisenhower laced into the Soviet premier on October 21 and accused him of a series of offenses, beginning with a note, sent in the midst of the presidential election campaign, that seemed to endorse his opponent's position on nuclear testing. The letter had been made public before it could be translated. In addition, Eisenhower charged that Bulganin's statement with respect to the secretary of state "is not only unwarranted, but is personally offensive to me." He added, "You seem to impugn my own sincerity."[66]

After this heated response to Bulganin's letter of October 17, the president backed off a little, saying he would not instruct the secretary of state to return the letter to the Soviet embassy. He made this concession not because he was "tolerant of these departures from accepted international practice" but because he still hoped that direct communication could serve the cause of peace. This outburst expressed Eisenhower's impatience with the USSR's repeated insistence "that all plans for disarmament be based on simple voluntary agreements. Now, as always this plan allows for no safeguards, no control, no inspection."[67]

Expectations of progress in limiting nuclear tests were further dashed by the Democratic candidate for the presidency, Adlai Stevenson. He had expressed his opposition to all nuclear testing in April 1956; then in October he promised to end all H-bomb testing if he were elected president. One consequence of these challenges was Stassen's need to distance himself from Stevenson's position to maintain credibility in his party. This might explain his vigorous attack on the Democrat's position as untenable and his announcement on August 24 that nuclear tests must continue.[68]

In this environment, Secretary Dulles, who had kept a low profile during the Nixon fiasco, raised the stakes to reinforce his hard line on disarmament. As his position became more acceptable to Eisenhower, Stassen's stock inevitably declined. Dulles managed to defer any response to Bulganin until further study on disarmament had been conducted in association with the British, French, and Canadian governments. Dulles had no shortage of allies in thwarting Stassen's initiatives, including the president at this time.[69] So the year ended with no progress on the partial steps toward arms limitation that Stassen had been advocating since taking office.

7

1957—Stassen's Gaffe?

In March 1957 a second round of meetings of the UN Subcommittee on Disarmament began in London. Although there were changes in the cast of characters among the five powers represented, Stassen remained the chief US delegate and exhibited the same exuberant optimism he had displayed since his appointment. On the eve of resumption of the London talks, Stassen outlined to Dulles his program of progressive aerial inspection zones, first in Europe and the Bering Strait and then expanding to cover the entire Soviet bloc. To confirm his plans, he not only repeated these steps to Eisenhower two days later but also added a draft of a treaty that incorporated the major points of US policy. The president's response was to agree that the draft treaty could be used "for illustrative purposes on a personal basis," but not as the official stance. Ambiguous though Eisenhower was, his reply was sufficient for Stassen to pursue his program in his own independent way.[1]

Stassen's assumption that he had the continuing confidence of the president seems unreasonable, based on his behavior in 1956. His caper over Nixon's vice presidency ended in failure and brought to the fore the many reservations even his closest friends had about his temperament and judgment, particularly when his own ambitions were involved.

Stassen Downgraded?

Stassen was aware in the winter of 1957 that currents in Washington were not flowing his way, as evidenced by the rumor that he would resign his position in the White House and seek the Republican nomination for governor of Pennsylvania in 1958. There was some substance to the rumor: he told his wife in May 1957, "We can hunt together for a site you like. If Pennsylvania develops as the course we wish to take. It continues to be, as far as I am concerned, a matter of keeping alternatives open."[2] After his awkward encounter with the Soviet delegate to the UN Subcommittee on Disarmament in May 1957 (described later), the rumor reappeared in October 1957.[3]

It should have been impossible for Stassen to miss a key signal from the White House when his disarmament duties were shifted to the State Department on March 1, 1957. The experience could not have been more humiliating. As his friend and disciple Robert Matteson observed, his staff was "tossed out of the White House executive office building and pushed into an old house across the street. He was not only moved out of the White House but given a temporary office behind the State Department a mile from his staff. His authority was reduced by putting him under Mr. Dulles. Many a man has walked out of government for far less."[4]

If Dulles could have had his way, Stassen would have been fired immediately. Dulles suggested to the president that Stassen be assigned an embassy position in Scandinavia or the Netherlands, where he would lose his position as disarmament adviser. But Eisenhower still valued Stassen's abilities and his arms-control aspirations. Respecting Dulles's sensibilities, he decided instead to place Stassen in the State Department under the secretary's supervision. Knowing Stassen as he did, Dulles did not consider this a satisfactory arrangement, but he laid down some ground rules, asserting that Stassen would no longer attend regular cabinet and National Security Council meetings. Not surprisingly, Stassen replied that the president wanted him at these meetings to express a liberal (i.e., the president's) viewpoint. Dulles had to be satisfied with a demand for Stassen's complete loyalty to the State Department, whether or not he agreed with its policies. Specifically, he was not to communicate with the press on his own authority. However, he would keep his role as special assistant to the president on disarmament.[5]

Whatever qualms Dulles had about his new subordinate, he could take satisfaction in the reduced status of the special assistant and, by implication, his own elevated role in the disarmament process. At the meeting of the NSC on March 6, 1957, where Stassen presented his aspirations in negotiations with the Soviets, Dulles warned him that if policy matters other than those approved by the NSC were the subject of discussion, they must be pursued with great caution to avoid the possibility of appearing to make any US commitment to its allies. If such views were advanced, they had to be made on a purely personal basis unless the State Department had provided approval in advance. The NSC itself made a point of emphasizing that "draft provisions for a treaty and statute were for illustrative and planning purposes and were not submitted as proposals for action by the Council and approval the President at this time."[6]

None of these caveats made an impression on Stassen in his capacity as chief US delegate to the UN Subcommittee on Disarmament. He interpreted the president's careful endorsement of his mission as freedom to pursue the objectives he had outlined without interference from his superior, the secretary of state. Even though Stassen stated that his initiatives were personal and unofficial, it was predictable that members of the subcommittee, chanceries of the NATO allies, and Soviet adversaries would regard the words of the senior US official at the London meetings as the voice of the government. It is also unlikely that Dulles actually believed that Stassen would become a docile member of his team.

Although Stassen understood that he had many enemies in the administration who were pleased with the downgrading of his office, as always, looked at the positive side of his situation. The inveterate optimist saw glimpses of light in Bulganin's correspondence with Eisenhower, and he intended to take advantage of any opening he found. Stassen had originally believed that a test ban should be embedded in a complete disarmament package. But if this objective was out of reach, Bulganin presented the alternative of aerial inspections of preselected areas.[7] Could this be a wedge that opened the way to a more ambitious program?

Prelude to the London Talks

Bulganin's alternative was the substance of Stassen's proposals to Dulles and Eisenhower at the NSC meeting in March 1957. They reflected his optimism about the progress he could make with the Soviets. As noted, Eisenhower's response was guarded but positive, while Dulles seemed to regard Stassen's statements as evidence of acquiescence in his inferior status in the Eisenhower administration. If so, it was a miscalculation on the part of the secretary of state.

But the administration's reception of his proposals was not the only source of his confidence as he prepared for the resumption of negotiations on disarmament. He seized on Bulganin's agreement in January 1957 to cosponsor a US resolution, based on past proposals (including Open Skies), calling for a reconvening of the UN Disarmament Subcommittee. The resolution was passed on January 25, 1957.[8]

These signals offered enough encouragement to propel Stassen in the direction he sought. He had reason to believe that his incremental approach impacted Soviet reactions. Two Soviet representatives at the United Nations, Vasilii V. Kuznetsov and Akadii A. Sobolev, asked Lodge and Stassen four questions that suggested their willingness to accommodate US positions: (1) Would the United States clarify Eisenhower's Geneva proposals with respect to progressive inspection? (2) In reducing the level of armed forces to 2.5 million, how much air inspection would be needed? (3) What was the US opinion on the 1.5 million final level and on Soviet proposals for a one-third reduction in Germany, notably in Warsaw Pact and NATO Pact territory? (4) What was the US reaction to the Soviet suggestion of a special session of the UN General Assembly to examine proposals concerning the prohibition of nuclear weapons?[9]

Stassen's reactions, solicited by Lodge, were positive. He was willing to display flexibility whenever possible. Although the United States wanted to implement Eisenhower's Geneva proposal in its entirety, he was not insisting that this was the only path. The United States would certainly consider alternative ways of achieving a credible inspection system, as long as it included aerial inspection. Reducing the 2.5 million force level would improve the climate of negotiations, but steps toward this goal would involve European armaments and the question of German reunification, which were outside the scope of these discussions. The Soviets did not extract support from either Stassen or Lodge for calling a special session of the UN General Assembly. This should come only after an agreement on its substance by the principal powers. Kuznetzov made it clear that the Soviets preferred to begin negotiations by prohibiting nuclear tests, without reference to how that prohibition would be enforced. Stassen preferred not to look at the caveats. In his judgment, these issues could lead to a sound opening step as long as adequate inspections were included.[10]

Stassen's hopes of achieving positive movement on disarmament impelled him to raise with Dulles the possibility of withdrawing US troops from Germany and imposing a sharp limitation on German armament in exchange for reunification. Dulles silenced him by relating the problem of German reunification to the status of the satellite countries. Only if they were truly independent could the United States consider troop withdrawals from Europe. When Stassen asked if their independence would come about if Soviet forces were withdrawn from their territory, the secretary pointed to Czechoslovakia, which was still under Soviet control even though no Soviet troops were stationed there. He likened the problem to "disarmament 'controls'—full of practical complexities."[11] Here was an example of Dulles treating Stassen not as a rival but as a naïf.

The secretary's skepticism rested on more than his personal differences with Stassen or his visceral distrust of Soviet behavior. He had to consider the reactions of allies, an aspect of foreign policy that often eluded Stassen. Britain was on the verge of major nuclear tests that would take place in May. To change course and precipitously endorse even a modest suspension of nuclear tests might serve as an opening gambit with the Soviets, but it could blight Anglo-American relations. When Eisenhower and Prime Minister Macmillan met in Bermuda in March 1957, the British were assured that "continued nuclear testing is required, certainly for the present."[12]

Stassen was prepared to ignore setbacks, since he felt that world opinion was working in his favor. He believed that a suspension of nuclear testing could be separated from the general question of disarmament. This was Stassen's position but certainly not Dulles's. Asked if such separation were possible, the secretary of state said it would be "rather difficult." When Stassen presented his staff's draft of provisions for a disarmament treaty to the NSC on March 6, Dulles was certain that "Governor Stassen would be the first person to agree that such a presentation . . . was merely an illustrative exposition." The Soviets would not accept Stassen's plan because his approach to the progressive installation of an inspection system would be perceived as too favorable to the United States. "So, while Governor Stassen's plan was interesting and useful, it was not [at] all likely to eventuate in the near future as a reality."[13]

This was a gentler dismissal of Stassen's proposal than the secretary of state might have delivered. Undoubtedly, Dulles's reaction would have been more negative had the tide of world opinion not been so strongly in favor of suspending nuclear tests. The alarm Adlai Stevenson had spread during the 1956 presidential campaign continued to have resonance in the United States. In Europe the sentiment was even more pronounced.

Norway, agitated by heavy radioactive fallout from Soviet tests in the fall of 1956, proposed an agreement whereby all tests would be announced in advance, permitting international observation. Responding to these pressures, Lodge offered a five-part disarmament program to the UN General Assembly on January 14, 1957. It called for an end of the production of nuclear weapons under strict international supervision, followed by a treaty to eliminate "all nuclear test explosions." Pro forma reductions in conventional forces were included as a version of Eisenhower's Open Skies.[14]

Stassen rightly interpreted Lodge's initiative as an endorsement of his steps toward a nuclear test ban. Colonel Andrew J. Goodpaster, Eisenhower's staff secretary, reported Stassen's support of a resolution "that would give continued consideration of the plan of Mr. Eisenhower . . . for exchanging military blueprints and mutual aerial inspection and the plan of Mr. Bulganin . . . for establishing control posts at strategic centers." Lodge regarded the UN Political Committee's subsequent vote to refer all disarmament proposals to the subcommittee as a Stassen success.

The resolution, adopted unanimously on February 14, 1957, surprisingly buried all proposals for ceasing H-bomb tests, despite the favorable mood at the United Nations for ending such tests. But the resolution included affirmative mention of Eisenhower's Open Skies plan. "This is the first Russian vote," Lodge informed the president, "in any way friendly to 'open sky.'" For this achievement he gave full credit to Stassen's role, and his remarks were more appreciative than Goodpaster's: "The fact that Harold Stassen was able to give me prompt decisions made all the difference and I wish to pay tribute to the results he has achieved in developing a positive United States position which enables us really to take the initiative—something which was impossible under the old state of affairs."[15]

Whatever disappointment Stassen felt when his office was placed in the State Department was offset by the conviction that he was on the right path to nudging the Soviets toward the US outlook on disarmament. He was certainly aware that successful negotiations would have a favorable bearing on his prospects for the presidency in 1960. He left for London with the usual ambiguous blessing of the president. The US stance on disarmament remained unresolved but sufficiently malleable to permit him the freedom he had always exercised in the past. Eisenhower was prepared to continue to explore any Soviet openings that could be found, although the caveat was clear: Stassen's proposals would be illustrative and personal and would not bear the imprimatur of the NSC.

The new Soviet interest in a major diplomatic effort toward arms control appeared to be based largely on ongoing worries about the future of a rearmed Germany in NATO, along with concerns about the loyalty of the Warsaw bloc raised by the Polish and Hungarian uprisings in 1956. These worries could account for the concessions implicit in Bulganin's November 17, 1956, letter to Eisenhower. From the Soviet perspective, Stassen was the perfect vehicle to exploit schisms within the Western alliance. His passion for an agreement on disarmament could be manipulated to Soviet advantage, which seemed all the more possible in light of his willingness to accept a suspension of nuclear testing—a Soviet priority.

The UN Subcommittee on Disarmament—Round 2

The State Department's instructions on procedures for the London meetings of the UN Subcommittee on Disarmament reflected less confidence about the USSR's change of heart than Stassen felt. He hoped to test "whether the unanimous General Assembly Resolution of February 14 presents new hope of progress." In essence, the resolution welcomed the various proposals on disarmament submitted by UN members. Dulles had no expectation of any serious changes. He was mainly concerned about Stassen straying from his instructions. Stassen was worried that the Soviets would try to dominate the proceedings at the beginning of the session, giving the press a distorted view of Western plans. Therefore, it was suggested that the subcommittee first consider disarmament under topical headings so that the Soviet Union "does not seize the ball at the outset."[16]

The presence of Valerian Zorin, the new head of the Soviet delegation, helped alleviate Stassen's concerns. Former ambassador to Czechoslovakia and deputy prime minister of the Soviet Union, Zorin was an influential figure in the Kremlin. Even more than his colleagues, he seemed anxious to pursue a relationship with Stassen, prefigured by Khrushchev's warmth during the Soviet reception at Claridge's in April 1956. It was equally obvious that Stassen appreciated the relationship, as he related to Dulles: "The first two weeks of this session have been quite different than the preceding subcommittee series. There has been a lack of recriminations from the Soviets and a more sensible approach to procedures than before." He made a point of telling his wife that the first week of meetings had been conducted in "a businesslike manner."[17]

Stassen's communications with the secretary of state indicate no sense that he was now occupying an inferior status or displaying deference to established State Department positions. Stassen appreciated his ongoing leadership on the subcommittee, and the information he provided Dulles indicated a continuation of his freewheeling activities, with no worries about their consequences in the State Department. He told Dulles about extensive talks with George Brown, the minister of defense in the shadow cabinet of the Labour Party, which was moving in the direction of the Eisenhower administration on nuclear testing policy. He did not intend to share details with the secretary of state: "His consultation with me, for his own sake, should be kept confidential."[18]

He had an opportunity to present his views face-to-face to Dulles, Strauss, and representatives from the US Information Agency, CIA, and Department of Defense. The occasion was a meeting at the State Department on April 20, when Stassen was in Washington over the Easter break. Stassen recommended, without contradiction from the secretary of state, that US foreign policy objectives should be a limited first-stage agreement that did not involve an unacceptable price in return. He believed the Soviets had indicated a willingness to accept a limited moratorium on nuclear testing if complete cessation could not be achieved. There was a sense of urgency, he asserted, because France would be ready to test its weapons in two years. Stassen envisioned only a modest risk in his twelve-month suspension proposal while a nuclear inspection system was being installed. Dulles was worried that the "fourth country" (France) would continue its preparations. Stassen disagreed, based on the assumption that France would wait to see how a moratorium worked with the three nuclear powers.[19]

Stassen and his team were prepared to meet objections from all quarters of the Eisenhower administration. He rejected criticism from Lewis Strauss of the Atomic Energy Commission (AEC) that the cessation of nuclear testing would mean the end of US weapons development, since scientists would drift away from the laboratories. Stassen assured him that under his proposed system, the laboratories would remain open. He also assured the Defense representative that the first steps would include conventional reductions and provisions for the transfer of nuclear materials to peaceful uses. When Secretary Dulles examined Stassen's proposal of a 10 percent reduction in nuclear delivery systems, he asked how it would be possible to decide how much 10 percent amounted to, since the Soviets had not provided any information about their total arms. Stassen quickly replied that the figure would be determined from the report on the armaments blueprint, which was due within the third month after the effective date of the treaty and would be verified during the remaining nine months of the year. He went on to identify concerns the United States shared with the Soviet Union, including a rearmed and "uncontrolled Germany" and nuclear weapons in the hands of "irresponsible powers."[20] Stassen not only anticipated these queries from his cabinet colleagues but also implied that he had no problem classifying the Soviet Union as a "responsible" power.

None of these Easter-break exchanges was supposed go beyond discussions at this early stage. Certainly, that is how Dulles, Strauss, and Major General Herbert B. Lopez, assistant to the secretary of defense for atomic energy, considered the meeting with Stassen. But Stassen's perspective differed from that of his colleagues. His fertile brain sought to cover all contingencies. He could envision little incentive for any country to violate a first-step agreement if one could be reached: "The risks of detection would far outweigh whatever advantage could be gained." He looked ahead to a second stage, after Zorin returned from his consultations in the Kremlin. Although Stassen repeatedly said these were only preliminary drafts of working papers, this was a cover for the more ambitious plans he had in mind.[21]

In a free-ranging conversation with the president during the same week, Stassen observed that the Soviets were showing more seriousness than they had in the past about grappling with nuclear disarmament. And he felt he was winning arguments with Zorin. The Soviet delegate seemed prepared, he told the president, to make his country's proposal of complete elimination of nuclear weapons "separable" from other aspects of disarmament. Zorin even accepted Stassen's refusal to have foreign bases abolished. When Eisenhower asked whether the Soviets showed indications of being ready to accept inspection, he responded that "they have indicated willingness to give a good deal on this issue but seem genuinely worried as to whether they could sustain their regime under such circumstances." Stassen sounded smug when he told Eisenhower that if the Soviets laid aside earlier unacceptable proposals, "we might be prepared to agree initially on less than complete air inspection throughout their country, so long as there is an undertaking to expand progressively the geographical area to be inspected."[22]

Dulles remained skeptical of Stassen's initiatives and did not quite believe his initial disclaimer that "the obstacles are, of course, very great and the odds continue to be adverse." He never forgot Stassen's propensity for going off on his own, despite his apparent acceptance of his new position under the State Department's authority. When Stassen spoke with the president on April 23 about daily meetings with his own delegation, a noon meeting of Western countries, and private bilateral meetings "from time to time as seems appropriate," he raised eyebrows in the cabinet. Dulles claimed that he wanted to hear Stassen's "ideas about any modifications in his existing instructions," but he appeared to take comfort in the knowledge that no changes could be made before the NSC and the president considered them.[23]

Stassen, true to form, ignored Dulles's caveats. It was his relationship with Zorin that buttressed his optimism. The head of the Soviet delegation had indicated earlier in the month that his government had "carefully reconsidered" US proposals. As evidence of his seriousness, he asked if the Senate would ratify an agreement once it was reached. Stassen told him, "If the President and Secretary Dulles considered that the agreement was sound, and approved it, they would be able to gain the necessary support of the people and the Senate."[24]

This was precisely the Soviet attitude Stassen was counting on. He anticipated that the next step would be completion of the inspection arrangements. He acknowledged that if Zorin returned from Moscow with "an obstinate stand on any collateral issue, this will be sufficient signal that they will not reach an agreement." But this was not his prognosis in April 1957.[25]

Significant as his relationship with Zorin was, the key to progress in ending nuclear testing and advancing mutual nuclear disarmament was where Eisenhower stood on the issue and how much he trusted his special representative. The president was fully aware of the direction Stassen was heading, more so than his secretary of state. Stassen cautiously raised the possibility of a twelve-month moratorium on testing, conditioned on the stoppage of nuclear production for weapons purposes. Eisenhower was receptive but foresaw obstacles in the cabinet. In fact, he thought the United States "might be the hardest to convince on the limiting of tests." He felt US scientists were "fascinated" by the potential outcomes offered by testing. He was also concerned about the reactions of allies, which did not occupy a central role in Stassen's calculations. If Stassen were to succeed, the president judged that unlimited inspections were "almost essential to any disarmament agreement."[26]

The president's mind-set in the spring of 1957 was inevitably influenced by the increasing tempo of opposition to nuclear testing. The firm advocacy of testing by the Atomic Energy Commission and much of the military, backed less vocally by Dulles, had an impact as well. In addition, at a meeting with Eisenhower in Bermuda in March, Britain had confirmed its intention to test an H-bomb in May. Moreover, the AEC had announced in January a series of tests at the Nevada proving grounds scheduled for late spring and early summer. The president's support for ongoing nuclear testing was hardly wholehearted. He hoped to undo the negative publicity from resistance to a test ban by announcing publicly that the tests would be observed by independent international officials. He promised that the fallout would be reduced to a minimum.[27]

Eisenhower's reassuring words to the AEC were not enough to slow the momentum toward a nuclear ban. When Albert Schweitzer, the world-renowned physician and philosopher, lent his name to the antinuclear cause, it carried enormous weight. As Schweitzer told Norman Cousins, editor of the influential *Saturday Review of Literature,* "All people are involved, therefore the matter transcends the military interests of the testing nations. It is clearly in the human interest that the tests be stopped." Schweitzer's appeal encouraged US Nobel Prize winner Linus Pauling to mobilize American scientists behind the ban-the-bomb project. Congressional hearings only added fuel to the fire of opposition. The Gallup poll reflected a change in US sentiment. When asked in April whether the United States should cease testing if all other nations did so as well, 63 percent of respondents said yes, 28 percent said no, and 8 percent had no opinion. But just six months before, 56 percent had opposed a test ban; the danger of nuclear fallout was beginning to penetrate the nation's consciousness.[28]

That Eisenhower recognized this rising opposition to nuclear testing was obvious. It was a major factor in his support for Stassen's initiatives, especially his proposal of a moratorium on testing. Although Dulles remained as doubtful as ever about the possibility of reaching a genuine agreement with the Soviets, he did not take the lead in opposing Stassen's goal of halting nuclear tests. Arguably, it was not necessary. Zorin's amiable exchanges with Stassen notwithstanding, there was a familiar deadlock at the five-nation subcommittee meeting in May. Stassen's call for an agreement to stop the production of all nuclear weapons as a precondition to a test ban was countered by the Soviets' demand for an immediate and unconditional cessation of all tests. Their aide-mémoire also insisted on "a solemn obligation not to use for military purposes atomic or hydrogen bombs of any type." Given the imbalance in conventional weaponry, this requirement could have been a deal breaker had Zorin's instructions not included an even larger inspection zone in the USSR than the United States had proposed. Optimistic as usual, Stassen saw this concession as a positive step toward nuclear disarmament.[29]

In a letter to Dulles on May 5, Stassen indicated that he regarded the aide-mémoire as a negotiating document that provided opportunities for the United States to advance its priorities. He said he had ideas about how to proceed but would like to go over "both the substance of such a partial agreement and the negotiating method." He was at least giving lip service to his new role in the State Department, but it was clear that his initiatives in promoting a partial test ban for twelve months would set the parameters of his discussions with the secretary of state.[30]

Stassen's apparent accommodation to the Soviets understandably set off alarm bells in the Pentagon and the AEC. Was he exceeding his authority by pushing ahead with plans for a partial ban on testing? Admiral Arthur M. Radford, chairman of the Joint Chiefs of Staff, certainly thought so. His response could not have been more explicit: "We cannot trust the Russians on this or anything. The Communists have broken their word with every country with which they ever had an agreement."[31] Radford's allies in the AEC and the Pentagon did their best to bolster support for continued nuclear testing, but it was too late for them to slow the momentum against it.

Dulles, well aware of popular sentiment and the president's predilections, was fearful of just how far Stassen's partial agreement with the Soviet Union would go. When Dulles asked him "to indicate in concrete terms the elements of the partial agreement which he thought would be acceptable to us and have some chance of achievement," Stassen replied that, "upon the effective date of the partial agreement (estimated as July, 1958) all signators would be committed to a twelve-month moratorium on nuclear tests." Additionally, they would be obligated to "cooperate in the design of an agreed inspection system to verify the nuclear materials cut-off commitment." The wave of world opposition to nuclear testing had given Stassen more confidence in his plan than the circumstances warranted.[32]

Stassen's initiatives seemed to leave little room for Dulles to maneuver. The secretary could hope for delays in April arising from the need to consult the Senate about the boldness of the proposals. Seeking flaws to exploit, he could concentrate on the political impossibility of Europeans accepting nuclear-free testing zones without their approval. Moreover, a plan that split the United States, leaving some areas subject to Soviet overflights while others were not, would have no chance of ratification.[33]

If Dulles seemed unable to cope with Stassen's bold maneuvers at this point, an explanation lies in the president's position in support of Stassen's proposals. Radford's outburst had infuriated Eisenhower. In a press conference on May 22, he expressed his hope for successful London talks and warned his countrymen against being "recalcitrant "or "picatunish" about arms control: "We ought to have an open mind and make it possible for others, if they are reasonable, logical men, to meet us half way so we can make these agreements." When it became obvious that neither Radford nor Strauss shared his openness to change, the president demanded: "Something has to be done. We cannot just drift along or give up. This is a question of survival and we must put our minds at it until we can find some way of making progress. Now that's all there is to it." Stassen listened and took to heart Eisenhower's obvious sympathy with his approach.[34]

He had Dulles's attention. When Stassen suggested that he return to Washington to talk with the secretary about implementing the partial agreement that might result from Zorin's instructions from the Kremlin on April 26, Dulles advised against it. He said an abrupt return to Washington "would give rise to undesirable optimistic speculation." Instead, he urged more preparatory work and recommended that details of any partial agreement be sent to the State Department. "After it has been studied then you could, if it still seems desirable, return in person."[35] Though he expressed his feelings more diplomatically, the secretary of state was no less dismissive of Stassen's proposals than his colleagues in the Pentagon and the AEC had been.

The flurry of correspondence between Stassen and the State Department in April and May disclosed his impatience for action. He claimed he had consulted with the principal allies on the subcommittee and won their informal concurrence with his ideas. Zorin's responses, he assured them, provided a clear view of the kind of partial agreement that would be acceptable to France, West Germany, and other key nonnuclear countries and still serve US objectives without exacting an excessive price. He wanted Dulles's authorization to tell Zorin that if the subcommittee agreed to the draft of partial measures, as a first step, the foreign ministers could sign the agreement and then, "if fruitful work appeared possible," establish negotiating groups to seek solutions to the inevitable political problems. "Early action is needed to assure the Soviets that we are serious in these negotiations for partial agreement despite speeches from Pentagon leaders that fed Russia suspicions about U.S. intentions." He might have added that Soviet suspicions were reinforced by their knowledge of the AEC's and Pentagon's opposition to ending nuclear tests.[36]

In Stassen's mind, however, none of these problems presented obstacles that could not be overcome. If the Senate could not tolerate Soviet inspection of specific zones in the United States, Stassen would confine the affected areas to more remote parts of the nation such as Alaska and the Aleutians, to be matched by the Kamchatka Peninsula and the Kurile Islands on the Soviet side—all north of the Arctic Circle. He understood as well the special fear of West Germany that exposing its territory to Soviet inspection would promote not disarmament but insecurity. Adenauer made this clear during a visit to Washington in May. Stassen also anticipated similar if less urgent reservations from other NATO allies. Dulles responded, "We must see if our allies would permit our going alone with Russia, and whether the Soviets would do so without a prior solution to the European problem." He emphasized that Stassen should talk with the three Western powers to agree on a common approach with Zorin.[37]

Although agreement with the allies was an unlikely prospect, Stassen was excited by what he took to be free rein to exploit the administration's willingness to entertain a nuclear test ban with the Soviet Union. It would obviously involve the NATO allies, and he was eager to present the new position to the British and French immediately. He was confident that the allies would go along without serious reservations. All he had to do was win agreement among the four powers in London and then give the NATO members in Paris a background briefing.[38]

Stassen's staff was less sanguine about managing relations with the NATO allies. They felt that NATO Secretary-General Paul-Henri Spaak and the North Atlantic Council were "not educated" on the issues involved and demanded an unreasonable length of time to deliberate before granting their approval. C. H. Owsley expressed the annoyance of his staff colleagues when they rejected Belgium's insistence on "fuller knowledge and participation in negotiations." He suggested that Stassen "gently remind [the Belgians] that the Sub Committee was set up as [a] small body which could more effectively seek solution[s] of disarmament question[s]."[39]

Dulles, too, was doubtful about the ease of dealing with the allies. Both the British and the French had nuclear ambitions that would be impacted by the new developments. As for German reactions, Stassen brushed aside potential problems by suggesting "the possibility of NATO setting up a side negotiating group in London." Germany, he knew, "was considering sending a man to their London Embassy." He assured Dulles that if other nations did that, "it would be a way of coordinating." Moreover, he was convinced that Adenauer "had come close to our position that German reunification was not a prerequisite to a first step in disarmament."[40]

That this was Adenauer's position was arguable. Dulles was aware of the danger inherent in reducing pressure on the Soviets with respect to German reunification. The thrust of Stassen's negotiations was to undermine the rationale of the US military buildup in Germany. And while the Germans appeared to accept the first stage of a nuclear test ban, they stressed that it was a long way from a final resolution of the nuclear problem. It was obvious that Stassen underestimated German fears that the proposed European inspection zone would lead to the eventual demilitarization of Europe. Eisenhower soothed the German chancellor on May 28 during Adenauer's visit to Washington, saying that the United States would take "no action on any matter in which one of our allies is concerned without permission of that ally." According to historian David Tal, this gave Adenauer a de facto veto over American policy on nuclear testing. Dulles further complicated the issue by promising Adenauer that no system of inspection and control in Europe would be applied until German unification had been secured.[41] Stassen was not privy to this information.

Stassen's staff director Robert Matteson was amazed by the successes he achieved in April and May 1957: "Despite the opposition of almost all of the top advisers to the President, Stassen had succeeded in building a psychological atmosphere at home and abroad that seemed to be moving the US and U.S.S.R. towards agreement." The president himself was caught up in the mood of this moment, expressing at his April 17 press conference his confidence in Stassen's belief that "the atmosphere is better and there is more indication that we are really, all of us, trying to get some kind of a reasonable answer than we have been in the past."[42]

It was a bravura performance by the former Minnesota governor. "The sheer boldness and imaginativeness, of his approach," Matteson gushed, "had left Stassen's opposition flat-footed and almost speechless. In one month's time Stassen had written into the official UN record personal ideas which went beyond anything authorized as US policy. And governments were responding to the ideas as if they were US policy."[43] Eisenhower's imprimatur was largely responsible for the atmosphere that fostered his freewheeling ways—not that the president specifically endorsed each step, since he was left in the dark on the nuances of the negotiations. Ultimately, Stassen's hubris would lead to his departure from the administration.

Stassen's Blunder

Stassen knew that his negotiating proposal was a working paper that could not be taken as government policy until approved by the president and the National Security Council. He had heard these warnings many times before and thought he could ignore them. As for the NATO allies, he recognized that they had to be brought up to date on the status and control of armaments.[44] These precautions did not faze Stassen. He was confident about his powers of persuasion and felt he was on the cusp of a major triumph that would serve both the nation's interests and his own presidential prospects for 1960.

Nevertheless, Stassen knew that he still had enemies in the government and that Dulles's apparent willingness to give him leeway had distinct limits. As so often in the past, Stassen gave his detractors sufficient ammunition to derail his plans. To forestall any disruption of his progress, he pushed ahead too quickly, only to find himself out on a limb. His presumption of an informal alliance with Zorin, whom he saw as his counterpart in the Kremlin, led him to tell Zorin that the decisions made in Washington would accelerate the path toward a partial disarmament agreement. The Soviets would be informed of the details as soon as the NATO allies had been consulted. When Zorin replied that his delegation should not be the last to know, Stassen not only reassured him but also asked for a day-long meeting between the US and Soviet delegations on May 31. In typical Stassen fashion, he acted on his own authority. To further cement his relations with Zorin, he gave the Soviet delegate the same informal memorandum provided to the Western delegations, outlining the new US policy decisions reached at the White House on May 25.[45]

Junior Soviet diplomat Arkady N. Shevchenko, who served with the Soviet Mission to the United Nations in 1957, confirmed the direction Zorin was signaling, He suggested that the Soviet posture on disarmament changed considerably at this time, largely due to the leadership of Nikita Khrushchev, and a number of substantial concessions to the West were made. He was convinced that Khrushchev was making a genuine effort to reach an accord with the United States "on at least some measures for limiting the arms race, and that he was moving our country in the right direction." Shevchenko felt that Khrushchev "was making an effort to change the country's direction in the face of resistance from those die-hard conservatives who resisted any change of the old order."[46] If Shevchenko's reflections are credible, Stassen's timing in approaching Zorin seemed serendipitous.

It did not turn out that way. Stassen did not anticipate the storm of criticism that would descend on him for sharing the memorandum with Zorin. He had paid no attention to Undersecretary of State Herter's May 30 cable: "I trust we shall receive promptly the revised basic paper incorporating May 25 decisions which you discussed with the Secretary on Sunday. President expects this to be agreed by interested agencies here and then submitted to him before you undertake detailed negotiations based on the revised policy."[47]

Stassen's response seemed to signal full compliance: "US Del[egation] will continue to confine its activities to informal explorations and informal indications of potential; movement, drawing out the Soviets, and will not . . . undertake detailed negotiations based on the revised policy at this time." He chose not to see any impropriety in his informal communications with Zorin. The key term for him was "informal," which he considered permissive enough to take the action he did. In fact, his reply to Herter was serenely optimistic: "We are well advanced on the initial informal consultations and are pursuing them actively with the governments concerned. Preliminary reactions as favorable as could be expected."[48] Apparently, it did not occur to him that his "informal" talks with the Soviets would be taken as settled US policy.

The essence of Stassen's memorandum to Zorin was the president's authorization to resume negotiations for a partial agreement as a sound first step toward disarmament. The US delegation "is further authorized to meet half-way on a reasonable basis the positions and proposals of the other members of the Subcommittee including the USSR's." It is worth noting that he did not concede any basic principles of the US position. The United States, he underscored, is "not willing to completely renounce the use of nuclear weapons and finds unacceptable the Soviet proposal for such a complete prohibition of use. . . . Thus, the United States will not agree to a partial agreement which includes such a clause or such a declaration." On the critical issue of nuclear tests, the US delegation would consider a temporary cessation of tests, provided the USSR considered cessation of the manufacture of fissionable material for nuclear weapons.[49]

There was little in his lengthy presentation that contravened US intentions, as developed a week earlier in Washington. He had the willing imprimatur of the president and the less enthusiastic backing of the secretary of state. What might be read between the lines was another matter. Would the Kremlin detect in Stassen's zeal for accommodation a weakness that could be exploited in subsequent negotiations?

This was not a question that deterred him. He focused on the partial agreements that could be used as confidence-building measures and lead to further progress at the negotiating table. To achieve this goal, he was glad to demonstrate his understanding of Soviet sensitivities. For example: "with respect to the inspection system, the United States Delegation further comments to the Soviet Delegation that it does not contemplate an inspection system so onerous as amounts to the management control of the entire atomic economies of our respective countries." And the US proposal also agreed with the Soviets about the dangers of a fourth power acquiring nuclear weapons: "all signatories who had not previously produced nuclear weapons would as of the effective date of the treaty voluntarily . . . renounce the manufacture, possession, or acquisition of nuclear weapons."[50]

The Impact

Stassen exceeded his authority no matter how cogently he explained the US problems with the Soviet response to his proposals. He violated the clear instructions of the State Department and the formal admonition from the president about consultation. The French rightfully complained that he gave an important new proposition on disarmament to the Soviets before any real consultation with the NATO allies. The lack of appropriate consultation with the allies had long been a concern of the State Department. NATO Secretary-General Spaak was especially disturbed that the memo to Zorin had been sent just a few days after Stassen and Moch had assured the North Atlantic Council that the time had come for it to prepare a Western position on a "European-Russian inspection zone."[51] In this context, the Stassen memo to Zorin came as a shock, since it had been dispatched without NATO approval.

Stung by what he considered unwarranted criticism, Stassen fired off an indignant response to Undersecretary of State Christian Herter. He denied that any new proposals to other states had been initiated, with the obvious exception of the British, French, and Canadian delegations on the subcommittee. They had been consulted on the outlines, as had the North Atlantic Council at its session in Paris. He justified the timing of his actions. Had he "further delayed any talk with the Soviet delegation there was danger of a complete breakdown in the atmosphere and the potential for a careful and constructive negotiation in line with the new US decisions might have been lost." He dismissed British and French fears that the Soviets would use the memorandum for propaganda purposes: "The paper has been carefully drafted so as to contain more propaganda advantage to the US than to the USSR."[52]

As for exposing his views to Zorin without consulting the allies, he protested in his report on the four-powers meeting on June 3 that "he had no intention of discussing the informal talking paper in subcommittee at any time." If the Soviets would not respect a "talking paper it would mean they were not really interested in reaching an agreement." But if they were interested, "it was important that they [had] not misunderstood [the] US position." A few days later, he reverted to his optimistic prognosis, noting that Zorin's reactions to the informal memorandum suggested that the Soviets had moved toward the US position on nuclear testing and on the wider application of aerial inspections, even if they remain dissatisfied with the US refusal to reduce troops in NATO and Warsaw Pact countries.[53]

His rationalizations did not appease the allies. The French government expressed its unhappiness with Stassen's action immediately. Jules Moch, the prickly French representative on the subcommittee, was miffed, according to Herve Alphand, France's ambassador to the United States, because Stassen had said nothing to him about his intention to send the memorandum to Zorin. Alphand objected to Stassen presenting "objectionable" new ideas to Zorin, such as the aerial inspection of Europe, to which neither France nor Germany had agreed. The French foreign ministry was sufficiently upset to consider instructing Moch not to attend future meetings of the subcommittee, or if he did attend, "he would remain completely silent." Arguably, the nub of the problem for France was its government's conviction that "there was no such thing as a personal approach to the Soviets who would exploit any statement or document as having official meaning." Actually, France's response turned out to be mild compared with Germany's.[54]

Chancellor Adenauer was livid when he heard that Stassen had given Zorin a paper that he considered a sellout to the Russians. The Americans, he feared, were "prepared to give away all of their bases" for the sake of an agreement with the Soviets. The US consul general in Bonn, Elim O'Shaughnessy, did his best to calm the chancellor, claiming he had no knowledge of such a paper being given to Zorin. More importantly, he repeated Dulles's assurances that the United States would stand by the recent commitments made in Washington concerning phase one of the negotiations. Adenauer was supposedly comforted by this knowledge and believed it, he told O'Shaughnessy, "only because of his strong faith and trust" in Dulles.[55]

Adenauer was not fully satisfied and continued to refer to the "Stassen paper," which he knew was bound to leak to the press, implying that US policy was one thing privately and another publicly. He worried that the German public would assume their country had been duped, which would have a disastrous effect on his upcoming electoral campaign. Dulles quickly disowned Stassen's memorandum to Zorin: "It was unauthorized and unknown to us in Washington. It exceeded his authority and as soon as the President and I learned of it we instructed Mr. Stassen to inform Mr. Zorin that it was not authorized or approved by the President or me and that its return was requested. Mr. Stassen has done this and tells us that he has Mr. Zorin's agreement to treat the memorandum as nonexistent." Dulles had already rebuked Stassen in much the same words the day before.[56]

Of all the allies who were disturbed over Stassen's memorandum, the British reaction most alarmed Eisenhower. Prime Minister Harold Macmillan felt betrayed. Stassen's action "was particularly inept," allowing the Disarmament Subcommittee "to develop a kind of life of its own without sufficient control from the Governments concerned." As he wrote to Eisenhower, "I would not be straight with you if I tried to disguise a certain feeling of distress that we were not told in advance that this document was to be given to the Russians. . . . A cynical critic might say that, at the end of the process which they envisage, two great nuclear powers would remain: the United Kingdom would be prevented from developing the nuclear strength which she is just beginning to acquire." He concluded his complaint with a reminder that whatever the final agreement, the United States had promised that "the United Kingdom's nuclear needs would not be prejudiced."[57]

In his apology to Macmillan, the president stated how "disappointed" he had been to learn of these developments, which "took place without any knowledge or authorization of any of us here in Washington." He was contrite when he assured Macmillan that "the cooperative spirit so obviously present at the Bermuda Conference is something I regard as of the greatest value as between our two countries and I shall do my best to preserve it and live by it." He went on to recognize that "once the Soviets have a piece of paper in their hands from the Head of the United States Delegation, it puts you and our other allies in an awkward position, one that is not easy to address, but we shall do what we can."[58]

To his friend John Hay Whitney, the US ambassador to Britain,

Eisenhower said he was "wholly on Harold Macmillan's side—in fact I was more than angry. I dictated a telegram to Harold Macmillan which expressed my feelings in no uncertain terms." Dulles toned it down, however, explaining that the furor was already dying down. "Nevertheless," Eisenhower admitted, "it is going to be hard for me to forgive a man for what I believe to be, at this moment, one of the most stupid things anyone on a diplomatic mission could possibly commit."[59]

Despite the president's distress over this gaffe, he did not fire Stassen. Eisenhower acknowledged that he had "not heard the other side of the story but on the face of things, it looks like he was more than clumsy." The extent of Stassen's punishment was Dulles's report to Macmillan that, "with Presidential authority, I have had a very thorough review of disarmament procedures with Governor Stassen and that the President and I feel confident that there will be no repetition of unauthorized proceedings or uncoordinated submissions to Soviets of US position papers."[60] This was hardly more than a slap on the wrist.

Certainly, Stassen did not behave as if he had been thoroughly chastised. Under ordinary circumstances, Stassen would not be disturbed by harsh tones of criticism, which would just pass over his head. He dutifully asked Zorin to return the informal draft, without ever acknowledging his gaffe in presenting it to the Soviet diplomat.

Dulles informed the president in a telephone conversation that Stassen appeared "very humble and contrite," and he vowed that no such lapse would happen again. To secure this promise, the secretary of state had Julius C. Holmes, a seasoned diplomat and special assistant to the secretary of state for European affairs, monitor Stassen's behavior in his capacity as Stassen's deputy. Any disagreement between the two would be referred to the State Department before any action was taken. Eisenhower seemed relieved when Stassen accepted Holmes as his guardian.[61]

Given the many failed efforts to restrain Stassen, the question remains: why did the Eisenhower administration keep him in office? No matter how much humility he displayed about his errors, there was nothing in his past behavior to indicate that he would become a loyal subordinate to Dulles. Just two days before the telephone conversation between the secretary of state and the president, Stassen was still trying to explain away his actions. He insisted to Dulles, "My endeavor during these past two weeks was to bring the NATO Council into negotiations without causing a breakoff with the Soviet Union, and to do so carefully within my instructions on both procedure and substance. . . . The discussion with the Soviet Delegation took place only after the other three Western delegations had been consulted on all points." Nothing in the discussion with the Soviets, he asserted, gave them any reason to believe that any new commitments would be unfavorable to NATO or to West Germany. Stassen concluded his letter to Dulles with the comment that both Macmillan and Adenauer had "been given erroneous briefings on the contents of the US talking paper." He was now convinced that "they will both support our position [at] the London talks when they correctly understand it."[62]

There was no sense of contrition in this communication, nor any hint of misjudgment on his part. He confidently expected to continue his leadership of the US delegation at future meetings of the UN Subcommittee on Disarmament. Eisenhower and Dulles may have perceived humility in Stassen on June 11, but there is scant evidence that he took their rebukes seriously.

It is worth asking how far Stassen really departed from the agreed-on US position in May that misled both the allies and the Soviet adversary. It was more the tone than the actual message that aroused his opponents. Eisenhower's readiness to forgive was understandable. He shared with his special assistant a wish to de-escalate the Cold War and implement disarmament measures, no matter how limited the means to accomplish this vital end. He might have expressed embarrassment over Stassen's impulsive behavior, especially as it complicated relations with the NATO allies, but this did not change his conviction that Stassen was the appropriate person to move negotiations with the Soviets toward a satisfactory conclusion.

Dulles was less forgiving. His feud with Stassen was too long-standing for him to believe in a conversion experience. He could take satisfaction in the harsh scoldings both he and the president had delivered. Dulles's rebuke, unlike Eisenhower's, was intended to humiliate his rival, and the president noted that if Stassen had received such a message, he would have resigned. Stassen's most intimate associate, Robert Matteson, was bemused by Dulles's seeming unwillingness to fire him. Matteson assumed that "every day that goes by he wishes that he had taken the bit in the teeth and done it then."[63]

Stassen kept his job because the president appreciated the talents he brought to his office and chose not to remove him. There were other factors that affected the secretary of state as well as the president. Public opinion at home and abroad was growing rapidly in favor of ending nuclear testing, beyond the exhortations of the scientific community. Dulles himself began to see the usefulness of continued negotiations. Consequently, Stassen remained at his post in London.

8

The Long Anticlimax, June 1957–February 1958

If Matteson was correct in his speculation that Dulles was waiting for Stassen "to step over the line he has drawn so that he can lower the boom," Dulles had a long wait ahead. Not until February 14, 1958, did Stassen step down and leave the Eisenhower administration. Rumors circulated about the president's dissatisfaction with Stassen's conduct in London. This was obvious when Peter Lisagor of the *Chicago Daily News* asked Eisenhower on June 19, 1957, if reports that Stassen had been reprimanded for exceeding his authority at the London disarmament talks had limited his effectiveness as a diplomat. The president's defensive response seemed to confirm the rumors: "Well, first of all, let's get one thing clear. He was not reprimanded. . . . He may have been rushing too fast." That Eisenhower softened his statement with praise for Stassen's dedication to his job did little to stop the rumors.[1]

Stassen's tin ear with respect to his position ensured that he would not anticipate the objections to his communications with Zorin. He reported to his wife, Esther, on June 1 that he flew to Paris for a NATO session and then back to London for more talks. There was no sense of a personal crisis in this letter. His concern for his wife's health may have been a reason for avoiding the controversy, but based on the pattern of his life, it is more likely that he had already dismissed the issue as no longer important and was concentrating on the more pressing reasons for postponing a formal submission of his revised recommendations on arms control. He explained to Esther the need for new direct consultations with key NATO allies.[2] When the State Department produced a paper on June 11, it centered on a partial agreement with no conditions that were unacceptable to the Russians.[3] Despite the furor he had raised in Washington and among the allies, Stassen appeared to have won his argument. No wonder that throughout June he exuded a sense of optimism and assumed that only procedural difficulties stood in the way of completing a deal with the Soviets. As he told Esther, negative press commentary, "usually so inaccurate and anxious to breed controversy[,] blocked completion of the slow but steady progress" he was making.[4]

Back at his post in London, he behaved as if the warnings and rebukes had never been issued. At a dinner on June 19 with Macmillan and Eden, he had no qualms about assuring his British hosts that he was speaking for the administration in saying that "US policy had at no time contemplated that nuclear testing would be stopped tonight; that a temporary suspension would only begin upon the ratification of a treaty." He foresaw nothing that would stop the British from proceeding with their nuclear plans.[5]

He continued with his sunny expectations of support from Britain and other NATO allies when he reported to the president on July 1 that "much was accomplished in accordance with the effective and welcome instructions from Secretary Dulles." No details of Dulles's reactions to Stassen's conversations were included in this letter, but the assumption was that the secretary of state was in tune with its confident tone. Stassen admitted "that new obstacles may arise or some barriers that are now being lowered may suddenly stiffen, but as of today it looks as if, with free world backing, we are entering the phase of careful and thorough formal presentation to the USSR. I will not endeavor to anticipate their response."[6] But despite this disclaimer about foreknowledge of Soviet reactions, he was optimistic about the outcome.

Stassen's team shared his optimism The first preliminary draft of a working paper on June 15 "welcomed the acceptance by the delegation of the USSR of the necessity of inspection posts to be located within the territory of the USSR, US, [and] UK" for the control and detection of nuclear testing. Consequently, "the four [Western] delegations accept in principle the proposal for a temporary suspension of nuclear testing as a . . . first step of disarmament."[7]

This illusion of optimism should have been exposed on July 28, when Dulles personally took over negotiations in London. If Stassen did not recognize the change, it may have been because the proposals the secretary carried with him were not substantially different from his own. The United States, Dulles declared, was prepared to accept inspection of all its territory in North America and asked the same from the Soviets. If they were not prepared to follow suit, he proposed a less ambitious Arctic zone where the United States and the USSR adjoined.[8]

This approach seemed to conform with Stassen's first steps, offering hope for subsequent gains. Where it differed was with regard to the suspension of nuclear testing. Dulles agreed with the reservations expressed by physicists Lawrence and Teller. He then told Stassen that their opinions had also made a deep impression on the president: "since then he has had serious mental reservations as to the correctness of our proposal to suspend testing."[9]

At a meeting of the subcommittee on July 8, the Soviet delegate confirmed Dulles's skepticism about Soviet intentions. While asserting that the subcommittee was on the threshold of an agreement, Zorin's position was essentially unchanged: he opposed the linkage of test suspension to the cessation of production, along with its complicated inspection system. He complained that the discussions in London were proceeding too slowly and that the United States had not responded satisfactorily to Soviet initiatives.[10]

Andrei Gromyko, Soviet foreign minister since February 1957, underscored his country's dissatisfaction. When US Ambassador to the Soviet Union Llewellyn E. Thompson talked with him on July 12, Gromyko complained that the London talks were moving much too slowly. The Soviet proposals had been submitted on June 7, yet "the US delegation had responded to them only in part and had not dealt with them fundamentally." The Soviet foreign minister felt that his country had made a major concession by allowing aerial inspections without receiving appropriate compensation. Thompson, however, came away with the impression that the issue of inspection and control continued to stand in the way of progress.[11]

It was in the context of this renewed deadlock that Dulles decided that negotiations had reached the stage where his presence in London would not only advance the disarmament process but also convince the allies that the United States continued to have their interests in mind.[12] If Stassen had his way, he would have continued to meet with Zorin, hoping for an eventual breakthrough. But his was a losing battle. The secretary of state controlled US policy in every particular. Implicit in his decision to take charge in London was the upstaging of Stassen as head of the

US delegation, an action that the president's assistant had no choice but to accept. Stassen took refuge in his belief that the president essentially backed his approach to disarmament. He was further encouraged by the conviction of the Supreme Allied Commander in Europe, General Lauris Norstad, that a system of nuclear inspection in Europe would protect the allies from a surprise air or ground attack. Minimally, the general believed that Germany, Poland, and Czechoslovakia should be included in ground inspections, and he would prefer the aerial inspection zone to extend to the Urals—all with NATO's endorsement.[13]

During one of his few opportunities to confer with Zorin, Stassen's zeal for accommodation was manifested in his statement that suspension of testing would go into effect on the same day as the treaty, without waiting to establish a control system. But he added the expectation that both sides would quickly install an inspection system to monitor the suspension of testing. Stassen left the meeting satisfied that it had been conducted in a businesslike manner with a serious tone that promised results.[14]

His colleagues on the delegation were wary of Zorin, suspecting that he was "looking for soft spots in [the] US position in order to get on with [the] Soviets' basic mission of separating out tests by paper agreement."[15] Stassen may have been surprised by Zorin's new hostile tone in July, but he was not put off by it. He was always able to see the silver lining. His repetitive advice to the administration was to keep the negotiating process in place no matter how high the obstacles seemed to be.

Terminating the London Negotiations

The spirit of accommodation, however, did not appear either in the formal US paper on disarmament or in the Soviet response at the end of August. In fact, the US proposal, overseen by Dulles, was a repudiation of many of the first-step proposals Stassen had initiated and the president had approved. Dulles's paper, in essence, was a declaration of all or nothing. Any agreement would have to recognize that all the provisions were inseparable. The suspension of nuclear testing was dependent not only on a cutoff of the manufacture nuclear weapons but also on the whole package of conditions, including reductions in the size of the armed forces, safeguards against surprise attacks, and an inspection system to verify the suspension of testing. Particular emphasis was placed on the requirement for inspection of a significant part of the Soviet Union, as well as countries in the Warsaw bloc. This was one of the points the Soviets had never accepted in the past.[16]

Stassen usually took for granted the allies' willingness to follow the US lead; Dulles did not. He was more sensitive to the aspirations and fears of the NATO allies. He was particularly concerned about Britain's nuclear capabilities and that country's worry that the United States would compromise those capabilities in dealing with the USSR. Macmillan's visceral reaction to Stassen's initiatives reflected his anxiety. Similarly, Moch wanted no agreement that would interfere with France's entry into the nuclear club. Above all, the Western proposals submitted to the UN Disarmament Subcommittee in August displayed the secretary of state's belief that the Soviets could not be trusted to abide by any agreement.

The August 29 document should have made the secretary of state's views abundantly clear to Stassen. It did not. He still hoped that, after the Soviets' inevitable rejection of the US position (resulting in the end of the London negotiations), the Soviets would offer new concessions.[17]

The Soviet response was negative and unbending. On the connection between nuclear test suspension and the cutoff of production, Zorin claimed that the Soviet stockpile was significantly smaller than America's, so the USSR would be at a disadvantage if it accepted the US demands.[18]

This caveat was not at the heart of Soviet objections, however. The Soviet pronouncement on disarmament talks—issued two days before the US paper, but with knowledge of the Western position—blamed the United States unequivocally for the failure of the London talks and implicitly blamed Stassen as head of the US delegation. The Soviet statement of August 27 asserted that the UN subcommittee, under the control of the United States and its allies, had rejected a reasonable, comprehensive program for disarmament that called for the complete prohibition of atomic and hydrogen weapons.

Zorin was especially upset by NATO's decision to place atomic weapons at the disposal of a number of Western European members of the bloc, including West Germany. In brief, his position was that whereas the Soviet delegates had been consistent in their efforts to promote disarmament, the United States and its allies had "been consistently increasing the production of all types of armaments, and particularly of mean[s] of mass destruction, such as atomic and hydrogen weapons."[19] Such was the litany of obstacles, the Soviets insisted, originating in the United States.

The Soviet statement was a surprising ad hominem attack on Stassen as leader of the US delegation. Given the seemingly close relationship that had developed between Zorin and Stassen, at least from the latter's perspective, the language terminating the London talks was harsh: "So far, the work of the United Nations Commission and its Sub-Committee has failed to yield positive results. There is no truth to the assertions of those who are now trying to give world public opinion the impression that the disarmament [talks] that have been going on in London for five months, at this session of the Sub-committee, have made satisfactory progress. In all this time the Sub-Committee has not advanced one inch towards the solution of the problems referred to it." Zorin went on to accuse "ruling circles of the Western powers of playing a double game": to deceive the public, they "are camouflaging military preparations under talks about disarmament and trying to create the impression that some genuine effort is being made in the United Nations Sub-Committee, whereas in fact the Sub-Committee is marking time."[20] Since US behavior in the subcommittee had frustrated Soviet disarmament proposals, Zorin recommended that "disarmament questions could be discussed in the United Nations not by five countries alone, but also by other states having a vital interest in the settlement of the problem of disarmament."[21]

Stassen's Last Efforts

If Stassen recognized that the Soviets viewed him as their primary antagonist, it was not reflected in his reactions. He dismissed the Soviet criticism, just as he had the criticisms from his colleagues. On the eve of his departure from the Eisenhower administration, pundit Arthur Krock labeled Stassen the "'asbestos man' in his special suit of asbestos, on a deck that everyone told him was burning beneath him."[22] If Stassen could withstand the Nixon debacle of 1956 and the Zorin embarrassment of 1957, he had no reason to believe he could not go on as he had in the past.

He was mistaken in assuming that he could undo the all-or-nothing approach of the August 29 position that terminated the London meetings of the UN Subcommittee on Disarmament. Failing to appreciate his loss of status in the administration, he plunged ahead with an informal proposal to the secretary of state on September 23 that could satisfy the Soviets. It was much like Zorin's July approach. There would be a two-year suspension of nuclear weapons testing, without reference to a cutoff in the production of fissionable material. He also omitted the installation of an inspection system to ensure compliance with the test ban.[23]

Dulles quickly responded, even though it was hardly necessary. The Defense Department expressed all his objections. Most objectionable to Dulles was abandonment of the principle of inseparability of all components in the nuclear de-escalation process—the heart of his August 29 paper. To further cloud Stassen's case, the Joint Chiefs were quick to note that his recommendations were in consonance with the Soviet resolutions on the suspension of nuclear tests introduced to the UN General Assembly on September 20, hinting that Stassen was a Soviet agent.[24]

Not surprisingly, these dissents did not stop Stassen from making a vigorous argument for the immediate cessation of testing without obtaining agreement on any of the red lines required by the August 29 statement. This was, he insisted a "historic moment" that should not be wasted. He believed that the consensus of UN members supported his position, and he could take satisfaction in knowing that the US ambassador to the United Nations, Henry Cabot Lodge, agreed. He professed that the Soviet acceptance of inspection posts that included a portion of the northwestern United States and western Canada, along with approximately the same number of square miles of Soviet territory, signaled an opening up of the Soviet Union.[25]

Stassen did not win approval from the secretary of state, but the president expressed support for restarting talks. He thought "it might be of interest to try to ascertain as to whether in fact the Soviets would 'open up' and to what degree, this to be done without any implication that we would accept testing without cut-off or inspection against surprise attack or the other features of our program."[26]

The president's opaque response buoyed Stassen's hopes, but the weight of the opposition from every other corner of the administration assured his defeat. Eisenhower deferred to the opposition. Dulles used this opportunity to urge the president to part with Stassen. "I have come reluctantly to the conclusion," he wrote in a memo to the president on September 28, "that Harold feels that we should seek some sort of agreement with the Russians on almost any terms—on their terms if necessary." Such an approach to disarmament, Dulles continued, was dangerous for the allies as well as for the United States. Just how "reluctant" Dulles was to raise this issue with Eisenhower can be judged by his conclusion that "Harold recognizes that the difference of our viewpoint is perhaps irreconcilable."[27] Nevertheless, the president chose not to act on Dulles's advice at this time.

While Dulles the lawyer was usually careful not to insult Stassen in his communications with Eisenhower, he was more candid when addressing him directly. Recklessly, Stassen challenged Dulles in December, reprimanding him for announcing to the press that his informal May 31 memorandum to Zorin had not been authorized. Dulles curtly replied, "What I said, however, could have been no surprise to you." He referred to the cable of June 4, which explicitly stated that there were certain aspects of the memorandum that the government could not accept: "Under these circumstances, I could hardly have answered affirmatively the question of 'whether this memorandum was representative of the views of the American government.'"[28]

There could have been no sharper reminder of Stassen's loss of status than this reference to his May 31 gaffe. Once again, Stassen chose to ignore the implication that he was persona non grata in Washington, relying on Eisenhower's vague backing. Two weeks later, at the National Security Council meeting on January 6, 1958, he repeated his recommendations for revising the decisions of August 29. He sounded confident that the Soviet Union would also find his recommendations workable. While he was specific in his advocacy of inspection stations in the United States and USSR, he purposely left other contentious issues, such as cessation of the production of nuclear weapons, to subsequent negotiations.[29]

There was essentially nothing new in these proposals. Dulles then recorded his objection to every particular, from the certain dissent of the NATO allies, who would be opposed to any test suspension, to the protests of West Coast congressmen, who would oppose opening their districts to Soviet inspection while the rest of the country was exempt. Dulles's dissent was familiar and unnecessary by this time. He, the Pentagon, and the Atomic Energy Commission had won the president over to their side. Eisenhower pondered alternatives. He recognized the validity of Stassen's concern about world public opinion but leaned toward the judgments of those scientists who distrusted Soviet intentions. The NSC recorded the president's decision to adhere to the proposals Dulles had set out on August 29.[30]

End of the Journey

At last, Stassen's place in the Eisenhower administration was coming to an end. It was a messy exit as he ignored the many hints about his impending departure emanating from the White House. On February 1, 1958, he could not have avoided the headline in the *New York Times,* "President Ready to Drop Stassen as an Assistant," followed by James Reston's report that the president was prepared to accept his resignation and to request it if necessary.

This was not the understanding Stassen took away from a meeting with the president a week later. He stated that he had not been asked to resign. Nevertheless, he did so on February 15, ostensibly to announce his candidacy for the Republican nomination as governor of Pennsylvania.[31]

It is tempting to conclude that Stassen's egoism and his ambition to be at the center of power accounted for his insensitivity and his unwillingness to accept the success of his enemies in thwarting his plan to reduce tensions with the Soviet Union. He met every rebuff with renewed energy and continued to submit proposals that he knew were unwelcome among all his colleagues, with the exception of Ambassador Lodge.

But was he as detached from reality as the record suggests? If so, he would not have laid the groundwork for engaging in Pennsylvania politics as early as February 1957, when his interest in that state's governor's race was leaked to the *New York Times*. This alternative took an even more serious turn when he advised his wife to look for a Pennsylvania location after selling his home in Washington. His intentions as the year ended were not secret, and his enemies were not silent about his ambitions. Representative James P. Fulton (R-PA) was annoyed enough to ask Dulles in January 1958 to make Stassen choose between keeping his job as presidential assistant and running for governor of Pennsylvania.[32]

Stassen's quixotic Pennsylvania ventures, as doomed as his presidential aspirations had been, do not explain why he clung so long to his position as presidential adviser. A reasonable answer may be found in his passion to mitigate the dangers of the Cold War. Toward this end, he was always able to marshal evidence, in his methodical way, to justify his opinions, believing that his ideas were more sensible than those of his adversaries. Even as he left Washington, he could not refrain from submitting two articles to the *New York Times* urging a trial agreement with the Soviet Union and suspending nuclear tests for two years under a rigid inspection system. It was a variation of the many "first steps" he had been urging since his appointment as special assistant. He followed this up with a detailed proposal for a summit, similar to the one in Geneva in 1955. He suggested the United Nations as the venue, with six nations drawn from both blocs. Republican and Democratic senators would be involved as well, and UN Secretary-General Dag Hammarskjöld was his choice to chair the sessions.[33]

Were these articles a signal that he was ready to return to Washington if called? This was not a plea for his old job but notice that he was ready to implement his ideas as president if the opportunity arose. And if such an invitation were not forthcoming, his six subsequent attempts to win the Republican nomination—ending with the 1992 campaign when he was eighty-five years old—suggest that he was willing to create his own opportunities. His presidential aspirations were unrealistic, but putting ego aside, what remained was the liberal Republican who had emerged from World War II determined to serve his party and his country, following a path that derived from his experience as one of the fathers of the UN Charter. His belief in his destiny may have been unjustified, but a steadfast conviction that it was possible to live in a world free from the menace of a nuclear bomb resonated throughout his long life.

Conclusions and Reflections

Given the consistent failures in Harold Stassen's long pursuit of the presidency, it is difficult to find space for his pursuit of an accord with the Soviet Union that would de-escalate the Cold War. His transparent ambitions stood in the way of an appreciation for his positive contributions to American policy during his four years in the Eisenhower administration. One remembers his quixotic and self-defeating attempt to remove Richard Nixon from the vice presidency in 1956, his alienation from almost all his colleagues in the Eisenhower cabinet, his losing feud with Secretary of State Dulles, and—not incidentally—his bad luck in seeing his recommendations fall victim to presidential campaign politics in 1956 and to the implications of *Sputnik* for Soviet-American relations in 1957.

The problems emerging from his presence in the Eisenhower administration were exacerbated by his generation-long effort to keep himself in the public limelight after his resignation from the White House in 1958. His attempt to win the Republican nomination for governor of Pennsylvania—an effort to transform himself into a Pennsylvanian, based on his experience ten years before as president of the University of Pennsylvania—failed badly; he antagonized the Republican establishment in the state. Failure only spurred him on over the next forty-four years. He threw his hat into the presidential ring in 1964, 1968, 1980, 1984, 1988, and 1992. Counting his three earlier attempts in 1944, 1948, and 1952, he tried to win the nomination nine times. Only in 1948 was it a genuine possibility. When he was not looking toward the presidency, he turned to the governorship of Pennsylvania, his adopted state, in 1958 and 1966 and to the governorship of Minnesota in 1982, after returning to his home state. In Minnesota he ran for a US Senate seat in 1978 and again in 1994, when he was eighty-seven years old. He had even tried to become the mayor of Philadelphia in 1959. None of these ventures came close to success. There was one slight exception: he was Minnesota's Republican candidate for Congress in 1986 but lost the election to his Democratic opponent in November.

In spite of this record, Stassen cannot merely be dismissed as the "perennial" candidate. Rather, he seemed to fit the definition of insanity: repeating the same mistakes while expecting different results. Even Robert Matteson, who was usually more outspoken about Stassen's virtues than his defects, was frustrated by his vendetta against Nixon in 1956 and attributed the problem to Stassen's inability to see himself as others saw him.[1]

Those closest to him were aware of the folly of his ambitions, but this did not prevent Stassen from attracting a number of devoted followers at an early age and keeping them over the years as supporters and allies in his political odyssey. An example of the loyalty he inspired may be found in the career of Amos J. Peaslee, a successful Republican lawyer and committed internationalist who was attracted to Stassen's strong championship of the United Nations. In addition to being a key figure in Stassen's 1948 and 1962 campaigns, he edited a collection of Stassen's speeches in 1951 when the former governor tried again for the Republican nomination. Peaslee's prestige in the Republican Party won him an ambassadorship to Australia and then service with Stassen as deputy special assistant to Eisenhower in 1956–1957.

The enthusiasm among young Republicans for the liberal governor of Minnesota in the 1940s did not wane, despite his abortive campaigns. Stassen's progressive views on labor and the United Nations and his ability to articulate his positions effectively assured him of a loyal staff during his tenure in the Mutual Security Agency in 1953–1955 and in the White House and State Department in 1955–1958. His aides were no longer young or even radical by then, but they had become effective members of his team. The extensive correspondence and commentaries from his staff disclose how supportive they were of Stassen in his capacity as the president's assistant on disarmament. They rarely addressed him informally: no one referred to him as "Harold"; "Governor" seems to be as informal as they could manage. But there was a warmth in their appreciation of both his talents and his objectives. No serious friction surfaced in Stassen's communications with his aides. So harmonious was the relationship that one simple request—asking an aide not to sit behind any delegate other than a US member—was treated as a rebuke, but not by Stassen. The guilty aide apologized, asserting that he had been trapped when a latecomer took the American delegate's seat while he was delivering a note to the British delegate.[2]

Although relations with his staff are well documented in the Stassen collection at the Minnesota Historical Society, another important element of his life—his religious sensibilities—are rarely displayed in his professional correspondence. Not that his connections with the religious community were absent from the public record. They were present in abundance. A lifelong member of the American Baptist Convention, he demonstrated his commitment to civil rights by joining Martin Luther King Jr. in his 1963 march to Washington. He sought and achieved high offices in church affairs beyond his own denomination. Opposed to the Vietnam War, he was a prominent member of the US delegation to the Inter-Religious Committee for Peace that visited Vietnam in 1968.

His religious convictions were most clearly displayed in his correspondence with his wife, son, and daughter. His prayers for his wife's health were heartfelt. An affectionate tone permeated his correspondence, especially during his long periods abroad in the 1950s. Particularly revealing was an exchange between Stassen and his son, Glen, who asked for his father's blessing on his choice of a wife. Glen assured him that his fiancée was a faithful Baptist and would be a suitable partner for a young man entering the clergy.[3] Glen later became a professor of Christian ethics at Fuller Theological Seminary in Pasadena, California.

Although a mix of the personal with the professional is rarely found in his writings, Stassen's goals for the country reflected that combination. The ultimate objective of his diplomacy was to de-escalate and end the Cold War with the Soviet Union, based on the reasonable assumption that the rivalry surrounding nuclear weapons had the capacity to destroy the world. He believed he knew the means to achieve this goal and had the capacity to bring it to fruition.

It was World War II that compelled Stassen to move from his progressive concerns for labor relations and efficient government to the larger world scene. President Roosevelt provided the first platform for him to learn about and participate in US foreign policy as a delegate to the San Francisco Conference on the United Nations Charter. On leave from his naval duties in 1945, he displayed the kind of leadership that marked all his activities, charting a course for the United States that equated the objectives of the United Nations with those of the United States.

Even if he had not been at the center of the movement out of isolationism, his identification with Republican internationalism likely would have marked him as a leader. That he saw himself as a key player in the transition of US foreign policy was an indication of his future as a leading figure in US politics. The United Nations became a lodestar in Stassen's career, even as he recognized its limitations. His concern about the Soviets' abuse of the veto power in the UN Security Council, which he expressed at the San Francisco Conference, anticipated future difficulties between the Soviet Union and the Western democracies.

While Stassen's opposition to communism caused his misstep in the fateful debate with Dewey in 1948, it did not define his future relations with Soviet leaders or his expectations of collaboration with the Soviets in arms-control negotiations. Once again, his ego was involved. In 1946 he announced his candidacy for the Republican presidential nomination, and in 1947 he embarked on a fact-finding tour of Europe to polish his credentials. Visiting Moscow on the eve of a meeting of foreign ministers, he managed to have an extensive conversation with Stalin about the differences in their respective nations' economic systems. It was a cordial meeting that allowed him to proclaim the virtues of a free democracy over communism. At the same time, it gave him excessive visibility at a time when Secretary of State George Marshall should have monopolized the attention of the American press. That the Soviet leader would spend time with an American politician who held no office was a boost to Stassen's self-esteem and a sign that he could speak openly with and perhaps influence the Communist leader.

This conception of himself as a communicator with the other side resurfaced ten years later. Andrei Gromyko, then the Soviet ambassador to Britain, had no record of warm friendships with American politicians, yet he purposely brought Stassen together with Nikita Khrushchev at a reception at the French embassy in April 1956. It is likely that Gromyko saw in the president's assistant someone whose openness to negotiations might serve Soviet interests. Certainly, Khrushchev himself went out of his way to display cordiality, even intimacy, in his dealings with Stassen. He also told Charles Bohlen, the US ambassador to France, that Stassen was a much more effective diplomat than Secretary of State Dulles. Stassen accepted this praise as evidence of the importance of personal connections in diplomatic negotiations. His hopes for a breakthrough were enhanced by the informal connections he made with Valentin Zorin, his counterpart as head of the Soviet delegation in London. That he exaggerated his influence with the Soviets did not dampen his enthusiasm for securing Soviet collaboration in his quest for nuclear de-escalation.

If Stassen misjudged his relationship with the Kremlin, he also failed to identify exactly where he stood with President Eisenhower in the 1950s. He never lost faith in the linkage between his own conception of the Cold War and Eisenhower's. This confluence in their outlooks was still strong in his mind a generation later when he wrote his account of life in the Eisenhower administration. In *Eisenhower: Turning the World toward Peace* Stassen underscored his bond with the president. They were both dedicated to a liberal new order embodied in the United Nations, as well as a conservative means of achieving it. An incremental approach accompanied by sensitivity to fiscal obligations was a common denominator.

There was some substance to this evaluation. Eisenhower undoubtedly wanted Stassen to serve as his surrogate in a cabinet dominated by strong personalities with harsh judgments of the Soviet Union, most notably John Foster Dulles. Yet Eisenhower was always aware that Stassen's ambitions affected and weakened his judgment. As he told Matteson in an interview in 1964, "Mr. Stassen was very imaginative—a tireless worker with great energy—but he had difficulty working as a team."[4] When he had to choose between his secretary of peace and the secretary of state, Eisenhower usually chose the latter, even when he felt that Stassen was closer to the path he wanted to follow.

Eisenhower has been credited with a "hidden hand" presidency, and his treatment of Stassen and Dulles confirms this judgment.[5] He often left advisers in the dark, playing on their fears and aspirations. Alternatively, he kept them guessing about his own intentions, which may have been a result of indecision on his part. His hand was always well hidden, even from himself, to the discomfort of Stassen and, to a lesser degree, the secretary of state. Dulles was more aware of Eisenhower's occasional ambivalence than Stassen was, and he could usually use it to his advantage.

Stassen's advice on leaving office in February 1958 was a variation of the themes he had been propounding since entering public life. It included listening to signals from the Soviet Union and acting on them to reduce the tensions that could result in a nuclear catastrophe. He was always ready with detailed approaches, most notably, suspending nuclear tests for a specific time and holding a summit gathering at a suitable venue, such as UN headquarters in New York. Relaxing pressure rather than increasing pressure, as Dulles would have it, was his key to future relations with the Communist superpower. His eventual hope, much like George Kennan's, was to expose the inner contradictions of communism and to assume that the benefits of democratic capitalism would transform the USSR.

Writing at the National War College a decade later, Matteson, Stassen's closest adviser, judged: "The fact that the Dulles policy won out resulted in the loss of a great opportunity in the spring and summer of 1957. That opportunity was to break the 11 years of East-West deadlock in the disarmament negotiation by accepting a final offer to suspend nuclear tests for two or three years under an agreed inspection system."[6] Matteson, like Stassen, was more optimistic about the future of arms control than circumstances warranted. Neither took sufficient account of the power of the opposition in Eisenhower's cabinet or the implications of external events. Public opinion in the West strongly supported the steps Stassen advocated, but the Soviet success with *Sputnik* in the fall of 1957 and the United States' resulting vulnerability to intercontinental ballistic missile attacks inevitably stiffened the Soviet embrace of nuclear weapons, undermining the developing rapprochement Stassen had championed. It would take more than a generation for the Cold War to end and the Soviet empire to implode. Stassen lived to see this outcome.

Stassen's pursuit of nuclear disarmament was one that Eisenhower shared. It reflected an aspiration that emerged from World War II—a liberal American foreign policy centered on a new world order, exemplified by the United Nations. Its goals remain an essential part of America's conception of its place in the world, even though it has never been fully implemented. But the idea of taking modest steps toward a freer and more orderly world endures. Stassen's vision of a future free from fear of a nuclear holocaust has not been realized. But the optimism he personified has not yet been extinguished.

Acknowledgments

My thanks to the staff of the Minnesota Historical Society in St. Paul, the Dwight D. Eisenhower Library in Abilene, Kansas, and the Library of Congress for facilitating my access to the papers of Harold E. Stassen, John Foster Dulles, and Robert A. Taft. As so often in my past efforts, Steve Rearden has been an indispensable commentator on my work. For this volume, Phil Cantelon's close reading and wise advice made an invaluable contribution. Not least among the those who supported this project is Allison Webster, executive assistant to the director of the press, who has been a constant source of encouragement over the last several years.

Notes

1. The Preparatory Years, 1938–1945

1. Alec Kirby, David G. Dalin, and John F. Rothmann, *Harold Stassen: The Life and Perennial Candidacy of the Liberal Progressive Republican* (Jefferson, NC: McFarland, 2013), 7.

2. John Gunther, "Young Man Going Somewhere," *Harper's,* January 1946, 12, quoted in Kirby et al., *Stassen,* 8.

3. Kirby et al., *Stassen,* 8.

4. Ibid., 9.

5. Ibid., 7.

6. Ibid., 12.

7. *Time,* October 17, 1938, 13.

8. Marshall Houts, introduction to Harold Stassen and Marshall Houts, *Eisenhower: Turning the World toward Peace* (St. Paul, MN: Merrill/Magnus, 1990), ix.

9. Ibid.

10. Bernard Weintraub, "The 1938 Nomination?" *Esquire,* August 1937, 99.

11. Erwin D. Canham, "Young Men on Elephants," *Christian Science Monitor,* December 1, 1938, 1.

12. Howard V. Williams, "Harold Stassen: Fake Liberal," *New Republic,* June 5, 1944, 759; *Time,* May 15, 1939, 20.

13. For Brayman's informal account of Stassen's off-the-record Gridiron speech, see Kirby et al., *Stassen,* 24–26.

14. Ibid., 26.

15. Ibid., 25.

16. *New York Times,* December 16, 1939, 9.

17. Steve Neal, *Dark Horse: A Biography of Wendell Willkie* (Garden City, NY: Doubleday, 1984), 72.

18. Ibid., 73.

19. Richard Norton Smith, *Thomas E. Dewey and His Times* (New York: Simon & Schuster, 1982), 308–10.

20. Mary Earhart Dillon, *Wendell Willkie, 1892–1944* (Philadelphia: J. P. Lippincott, 1952), 148.

21. Joseph Barnes, *Willkie* (New York: Simon & Schuster, 1952), 182; Kirby et al., *Stassen,* 16.

22. Arthur Krock, *Memoirs: Sixty Years on the Firing Line* (New York: Funk & Wagnalls, 1968), 194.

23. Dillon, *Wendell Willkie,* 163; Donald R. McCoy, *Landon of Kansas* (Lincoln: University of Nebraska Press, 1966), 444.

24. Quoted in Neal, *Dark Horse,* 100.

25. *New York Times,* June 23, 1940, 2; Neal, *Dark Horse,* 214.

26. The text of Stassen's keynote speech appeared in *New York Times,* June 25, 1940, 16. Mencken quoted in Neal, *Dark Horse,* 100.

27. "Washington Notes," *New Republic,* May 13, 1940, 638.

28. *New York Times,* June 25, 1940, 17.

29. Dillon, *Wendell Willkie,* 333.

30. Ibid.

31. Kirby et al., *Stassen,* 21.

32. Quoted in ibid., 18, from the December 13, 1941, edition of the *Nation.* Republican isolationists Taft and Vandenberg, as well as Willkie and Stassen, spoke about the "Future of the Republican Party." As the editors pointed out, their remarks were prepared before December 7.

33. *New York Times,* October 17, 1940, 12; April 4, 1942, 10. Although their departure for military service was noted, there were no special commentaries about the military careers of Representative Lyndon B. Johnson (D-TX) and Senator Henry Cabot Lodge (R-MA).

34. Ibid., August 11, 1941, 4; August 31, 1941, 21.

35. Ibid., June 23, 1942, 15; June 24, 1942, 14; November 29, 1942, 59; December 18, 1942, 12; August 31, 1941, 21.

36. Ibid., January 9, 1943; March 9, 1943, 4.

37. *Saturday Evening Post,* May 23, 1943, quoted in Kirby et al., *Stassen,* 37.

38. *New York Times,* April 1, 1944, 2.

39. Richard H. Rovere, "Stassen of Minnesota," *Nation,* June 3, 1944, 645–48.

40. *New York Times,* April 11, 1943, sec. VII, 1.

41. Dillon, *Wendell Willkie,* 332.

42. *New York Times,* April 17, 1944, 18.

43. Ibid., March 11, 1944, 1; Arthur H. Vandenberg Jr., ed., *The Private Papers of Senator Vandenberg* (Boston: Houghton Mifflin, 1952), 84–86.

44. Gunther, "Young Man Going Somewhere," 18.

45. *New York Times,* March 8, 1945, 11.

46. Harold Stassen, oral history interview by Richard D. McKinzie, June 26, 1973, Harry S. Truman Library, quoted in Kirby et al., *Stassen,* 2–8.

47. *New York Times,* May 1, 1945, 14.

48. Quoted in Kirby et al., *Stassen,* 29.

49. Vandenberg diary, May 5, 1945, Bentley Historical Library, University of Michigan.

50. Minutes of the First Meeting of the US Delegation in Washington, March 13, 1945, in *Foreign Relations of the United States, 1945,* vol. 1 (Washington, DC: Government Printing Office, 1968), 116 (hereafter cited as *FRUS 1945*).

51. Minutes of the Twenty-First Meeting of the US Delegation to the San Fran-

cisco Conference, April 27, 1945, ibid., 478; Minutes of the Thirty-First Meeting of the US Delegation, May 7, 1945, ibid., 621; Memorandum of Conversation, sub: Veto Power of Permanent Members of the Security Council, box 123, Harold Stassen Papers, Minnesota Historical Society, St. Paul.

52. Minutes of the Eleventh Meeting (Executive Session) of the US Delegation, April 17, 1945, in *FRUS 1945,* 317.

53. Memorandum of Conversation, May 23, 1945: Meeting with Fadhil, Director General, Foreign Affairs, of Iraq, box 123, Stassen Papers; Meeting with Emir Faisal, Saudi Arabia Foreign Minister, ibid.; Minutes of the Fifty-Sixth Meeting of the US Delegation, May 28, 1945, in *FRUS 1945,* 1950.

54. Memorandum of Conversation, May 18, 1945, box 123, Stassen Papers; Minutes of the Fifty-Ninth Meeting of the US Delegation, May 1, 1945, in *FRUS 1945,* 1003.

55. Memorandum of Conversation with Gen. Romulo, May 25, 1945, box 123, Stassen Papers; Minutes of the Forty-Fifth Meeting of the US Delegation, May 18, 1945, in *FRUS 1945,* 792–93.

56. Minutes of the Twelfth Meeting of the US Delegation, April 18, 1945, ibid., 334; Minutes of the Seventy-Third Meeting of the US Delegation, June 16, 1945, ibid., 1305; Minutes of the Fourteenth Meeting of the US Delegation, April 14, 1945, ibid., 376.

57. Minutes of the Thirty-Seventh Meeting of the US delegation, May 11, 1945, ibid., 668.

2. Toward the 1948 Debacle

1. *New York Times,* July 3, 1945, 1.

2. Ibid., July 6, 1945, 1, 11.

3. Ibid.

4. Ibid., May 1, 1945, 24; May 4, 1945, 13.

5. "United Nations Charter Revision," in *Vital Speeches of the Day,* January 15, 1948, 213.

6. Ibid.

7. Minutes of the Twelfth Meeting of the US Delegation to the San Francisco Conference, April 18, 1945, in *FRUS 1945,* 331; Minutes of the Thirty-First Meeting of the US Delegation, May 7, 1945, ibid., 618, 624.

8. "United Nations Charter Revision," in *Vital Speeches of the Day,* 234.

9. Inventory, box 125, Stassen Papers.

10. Draft chapter for a new UN Charter, seven booklets in three folders, including "Restructuring Suggested for the United Nations Organization" (1995), ibid.

11. Kirby et al., *Stassen,* 30; Harold Stassen, *United Nations: A Working Paper for Restructuring* (Minneapolis: Lerner, 1991).

12. Stassen, *United Nations,* ii, 55–57, 43–47, 33–42. The proposals are listed in Kirby et al., *Stassen,* 30, 21.

13. *New York Times,* November 9, 1945, 4.

14. Ibid. Henry D. Smyth, "Atomic Energy for Military Purposes," was released on August 12, just six days after the bombing of Hiroshima. Stassen was too hasty in his dismissal of the report. Its author won the scientific community's support for international control of the atomic bomb.

15. *New York Times,* November 9, 1945, 4.

16. Ibid.

17. Ibid., December 15, 1945, 4.

18. Acheson-Lilienthal Report on the International Control of Atomic Energy, March 16, 1946, Department of State Publication 2498. See Gary B. Ostrower, *The United Nations and the United States, 1945–1995* (New York: Twayne, 1998), 46.

19. Richard D. Hewlett and Oscar Anderson, *A History of the United States Atomic Energy Commission,* vol. 1, *The New World, 1939–1946* (University Park: Pennsylvania State University Press, 1962), 579; Proposals by the Representative of the US to the UN Atomic Energy Commission (Baruch), June 14, 1946, Department of State Publication 2560.

20. Joseph Alsop and Stewart Alsop, "One Man Bandwagon," *Saturday Evening Post,* September 7, 1946, 14–15.

21. *New York Times,* March 24, 1947, 18.

22. *Time,* March 25, 1946, 21.

23. Kirby et al., *Stassen,* 37–38.

24. Ibid., 38.

25. *Newsweek,* July 24, 1946, 28; *Washington Post,* December 18, 1946, 1, 16.

26. *Washington Post,* December 17, 1946, 3.

27. *New York Times,* February 13, 1947, 2.

28. Harold Stassen, "Marshall Plan: Europe's Only Alternative to Communism," delivered at the New York Chamber of Commerce, September 17, 1947, in *Vital Speeches of the Day,* October 15, 1947, 20–23; *New York Times,* August 12, 1947, 1.

29. *New York Times,* January 31, 1947, 22.

30. Ibid., January 12, 1947, 9.

31. Ibid.

32. Ibid., February 8, 1947; Walter Davenport, "Stassen's Political Gamble," *Collier's,* May 4, 1946, 16, 17.

33. Taft to Charles D. Hilles, May 21, 1945, in *The Papers of Robert A. Taft,* 4 vols., ed. Clarence E. Wunderlin Jr. et al. (Kent, OH: Kent State University Press, 2003), 3:46; Taft to David S. Ingalls, April 29, 1946, ibid., 126.

34. Taft speech at Steubenville (Ohio) Grant High School, April 22, 1948, ibid., 426.

35. Ibid.

36. *New York Times,* March 25, 1947, 3.

37. *Washington Post,* February 28, 1947, 15.

38. Kirby et al., *Stassen,* 47; Harold Stassen, *Where I Stand* (Garden City, NY: Doubleday, 1947), 13.

39. Stassen, *Where I Stand,* 15.

40. Quoted in Kirby et al., *Stassen,* 47; *New York Times,* April 15, 1947, 1.

41. *New York Times,* April 15, 1947, 1.

42. Ibid., May 22, 1947, 9.

43. Address at the Annual Community Celebration, Jefferson, Iowa, May 22, 1947, in *Man Was Meant to Be Free: Selected Statements of Governor Harold E. Stassen, 1940–1951,* ed. Amos J. Peaslee (New York: Doubleday, 1951), 137.

44. *New York Times,* April 11, 1947, 11.

45. Milburn P. Akers, "What Are Stassen's Chances?" *Nation,* June 29, 1946, 778.

46. *New York Times,* November 16, 1945, sec. VII, 7.

47. Stassen, *Where I Stand,* 65–68.

48. Ibid., 72–127.

49. Fred Smith, "Does Stassen Have a Chance?" *Saturday Review of Literature,* November 15, 1947, 9.

50. James Reston, *Saturday Review of Literature,* November 15, 1947, 9–10.

51. For details of Stassen's campaign in New Hampshire, Wisconsin, Nebraska, Ohio, and Oregon, see Kirby et al., *Stassen,* chaps. 5–10.

52. Ibid., 51–52.

53. Smith, *Dewey,* 487.

54. Ibid., 486.

55. Ibid., 488; Kirby et al., *Stassen,* 69.

56. Kirby et al., *Stassen,* 81.

57. Ibid., 86; Memo for Sen. Taft from Thomas G. Shroyer, Chief Counsel, Joint Committee on Labor Management Relations, "Stassen's Labor Record," 96, Robert A. Taft Papers, Library of Congress.

58. Stassen's address at Memorial Hall, Dayton, Ohio, April 21, 1948, in Kirby et al., *Stassen,* 89.

59. Kirby et al., *Stassen,* 92–93.

60. Press release of Senator Taft's address before the Cleveland City Club, May 1, 1948, Taft Papers.

61. Kirby et al., *Stassen,* 93.

62. Ibid., 105; Smith, *Dewey,* 488 (see 492–94 for background).

63. Robert E. Matteson, *Harold Stassen: His Career, the Man, and the 1957 Arms Control Negotiations* (Inver Grove Heights, MN: Desk Top, 1991), 15.

64. Harold Stassen," Should the Communist Party in the United States Be Outlawed? May 17, 1948, in *Vital Speeches of the Day,* June 1, 1948, 483.

65. Dewey's response, ibid., 486.

66. "Stassen Upsurge Halted by Dewey," *Life,* May 31, 1948, 32–33.

67. Smith, *Dewey,* 499; Burger quoted in Matteson, *Stassen,* 16.

3. The Eisenhower Solution, 1948–1952

1. *New York Times,* July 13, 1948, 29; Kirby et al., *Stassen,* 107.

2. *New York Times,* August 2, 1948, 13; Kirby et al., *Stassen,* 108.

3. Quoted in *New York Times,* July 30, 1948, 21.
4. Kirby et al., *Stassen,* 108, citing *Philadelphia Inquirer,* July 2, 1948, 1.
5. *New York Times,* August 5, 1948.
6. Editorial, *New York Times,* July 30, 1948.
7. *Daily Pennsylvanian,* December 3, 1948; Kirby et al., *Stassen,* 110.
8. Kirby et al., *Stassen,* 119–21.
9. Ibid., 121–22.
10. *New York Times,* January 7, 1951, 74; Kirby et al., *Stassen,* 120.
11. Kirby et al., *Stassen,* 111.
12. Ibid., 113.
13. *New York Times,* November 12, 1949, 4.
14. Harold Ickes, "Harold E. McStassen," *New Republic,* October 22, 1951, 15; Willard Shelton, *Nation*, October 21, 1951, 321.
15. *New York Times,* October 26, 1950, 15; Arthur J. Graham, "The Sad Case of Harold Stassen," *New Republic,* November 6, 1950, 32.
16. *New York Times,* December 8, 1950, 3.
17. Ibid., October 5, 1949, 3.
18. Ibid., February 19, 1950, 19.
19. Ibid.
20. Ibid., March 4, 1951, 6.
21. Ibid., January 17, 1952, 12.
22. Ibid., November 20, 1951, 6; November 21, 1951, 6.
23. Ibid., December 9, 1948, 40.
24. Ibid.
25. Ibid., May 2, 1950, sec. IV, 2E; May 6, 1950, 8; May 18, 1950, 15.
26. Ibid., October 31, 1950, 23.
27. Kirby et al., *Stassen,* 115.
28. Ibid., 128.
29. Quoted in ibid.
30. *New York Times,* August 16, 1950, 3.
31. Ibid., January 16, 1951, 12.
32. *Newsweek,* September 17, 1951, 27; *New York Times,* October 5, 1950, 1, 9.
33. Stassen to Stalin, October 1, 1950, in Peaslee, *Man Was Meant to Be Free,* 345.
34. *New York Times,* October 21, 1950, 18.
35. Ibid., October 30, 1950, 9.
36. Ibid., March 22, 1951, 14.
37. Ibid., April 25, 1951, 14; April 28, 1951, 1.
38. Kirby et al., *Stassen,* 121.
39. Stassen and Houts, *Eisenhower,* 1, 3. In his diary entry on December 15, 1951, Eisenhower confirmed Stassen's account of their meeting on December 12. Robert H. Ferrell, ed., *The Eisenhower Diaries* (New York: W. W. Norton, 1991), 207.

40. Stassen and Houts, *Eisenhower,* 13.
41. Ibid., 12, 14.
42. Kirby et al., *Stassen,* 124–25; *New York Times,* November 13, 1949, sec. IV, 7.
43. *New York Times,* October 30, 1950, 9; September 17, 1950, 46.
44. Ibid., October 22, 1950, sec. IV, 3; August 17, 1950, 7; April 2, 1951, 29.
45. Kirby et al., *Stassen,* 29, 126.
46. Ibid., 127.
47. *New York Times,* December 28, 1951, 1.
48. Ibid., December 28, 1951, 6; January 7, 1952, sec. I, 3; Kirby et al., *Stassen,* 127.
49. *New York Times,* December 28, 1951, 8.
50. Ibid., January 29, 1952, 7.
51. "A New Up-to-Date American Foreign Policy," February 28, 1952, in *Vital Speeches of the Day,* March 15, 1952, 327–29.
52. *New York Times,* April 19, 1952, 16; July 2, 1952, 20.
53. Taft to Hugh A. Butler, December 28, 1951, in *Papers of Taft,* 4:331.
54. Taft to Renfro Creager, January 8, 1949, ibid., 6–7.
55. James T. Patterson, *Mr. Republican: A Biography of Robert A. Taft* (Boston: Houghton Mifflin, 1972), 526; Statement on Primary Election Victories, in *Papers of Taft,* 4:366.
56. Statement on Primary Election Victories, in *Papers of Taft,* 4:367; Patterson, *Mr. Republican,* 526; *New York Times,* April 25, 1952, 13; ibid., January 18, 1952, 56.
57. *New York Times,* January 19, 1952, 8.
58. Ibid.
59. Jean Edward Smith, *Eisenhower in War and Peace* (New York: Random House, 2012), 506–7.
60. *New York Times,* January 4, 1952, 11.
61. Ibid., February 5, 1952, 21.
62. Ibid., January 4, 1952, 14; January 14, 1952, 9.
63. Ibid., January 19, 1952, 9; Kirby et al., *Stassen,* 132–34.
64. *New York Times,* April 25, 1952, 14.
65. Ibid., July 2, 1952, 14.
66. Ibid., 19.
67. Quoted in Kirby et al., *Stassen,* 146.
68. Stassen and Houts, *Eisenhower,* 36.
69. Krock, *Memoirs,* 269.
70. *New York Times,* June 12, 1952, 8.
71. Stassen and Houts, *Eisenhower,* 44.
72. Ibid., 59–69, 54–57.

4. The Mutual Security Agency and Foreign Operations Administration, 1953–1955

1. *New York Times,* July 14, 1952, 4.
2. Ibid., November 22, 1952, 1.

3. Stassen and Houts, *Eisenhower,* 104.
4. Quoted in ibid., 107–8.
5. Quoted in *New York Times,* November 22, 1952, 11.
6. Ibid., 22.
7. Ibid., November 23, 1952, sec. IV, 3.
8. Ibid., December 3, 1952, 4.
9. Ernest K. Lindley, "Stassen's Role in Foreign Aid," *Newsweek,* December 8, 1952, 2.
10. Ibid.
11. Nomination of Harold Stassen, Hearing before the Senate Committee on Foreign Relations, 83rd Cong., 1st sess., January 21, 1953, 3–4.
12. Ibid., 17; *New York Times,* January 28, 1953, 1.
13. *New York Times,* January 28, 1953, 3.
14. Stassen to Dulles, November 26, 1952; Dulles to Stassen, November 29, 1952, Select Correspondence and Other Materials, box 76, John Foster Dulles Papers (photocopies), Library of Congress.
15. Stassen and Houts, *Eisenhower,* 124.
16. Quoted in Stephen E. Ambrose, *Eisenhower, the President* (New York: Simon & Schuster, 1984), 119.
17. *New York Times,* February 10, 1953, 1, 3; Kirby et al., *Stassen,* 153.
18. Kirby et al., *Stassen,* 153.
19. Ambrose, *Eisenhower,* 49; Dwight D. Eisenhower, *The White House Years: Mandate for Change, 1953–1956* (Garden City, NY: Doubleday, 1963), 140, 141; Kirby et al., *Stassen,* 153.
20. Stassen and Houts, *Eisenhower,* 144.
21. Dulles to Stassen, February 16, 1953, March 16, 1954, box 76, Dulles Papers; Emmett Hughes, *The Ordeal of Power: A Political Memoir of the Eisenhower Years* (New York: Atheneum, 1963), 69.
22. Dulles to Stassen, March 18, 1954, box 76, Dulles Papers.
23. Dulles to Stassen, April 3, 1954, ibid.
24. Stassen to Dulles, April 3, 1954, ibid.
25. Stassen to Dulles, April 6, 1954, ibid.
26. Ibid.
27. Stassen and Houts, *Eisenhower,* 248.
28. Thomas C. Reeves, *The Life and Times of Joe McCarthy* (New York: Stein & Day, 1982), 145; Harold Ickes, "Harold E. McStassen," *New Republic,* October 22, 1951, 121; Stassen and Houts, *Eisenhower,* 244.
29. *New York Times,* March 31, 1953, 1.
30. Quoted in ibid., 18.
31. Ibid.
32. Stassen and Houts, *Eisenhower,* 249.
33. Ibid., 249–50.
34. Quoted in *New York Times,* June 1, 1953, 4.

35. Ibid., April 27, 1953, 18.
36. Quoted in Kirby et al., *Stassen,* 150.
37. Ibid., 154, 155.
38. Quoted in *New York Times,* February 23, 1953, 19.
39. Ibid., May 6, 1953, 1; May 7, 1953, 1.
40. Ibid., July 26, 1953, 1.
41. Ibid., November 18, 1953, 1.
42. Ibid., April 7, 1954, 1.
43. Ibid., December 10, 1954, 21.
44. Ibid., December 15, 1954, 21, 2.
45. Lawrence S. Kaplan, "The United States, NATO, and the Third World Issues in Historical Perspective," in *East-West Rivalry in the Third World,* ed. Robert W. Clawson (Wilmington, DE: SR, 1984), 3.
46. Stassen and Houts, *Eisenhower,* 149.
47. Harold E. Stassen, *Report to the President on the Foreign Operations Administration, January 1953–June 1955,* June 30, 1955, 14, National Archives and Records Administration.
48. *New York Times,* December 21, 1953, 2.
49. Special Message to Congress on the Organization of the Executive Branch for the Conduct of Foreign Affairs, June 1, 1953, in *Public Papers of the Presidents—Eisenhower, 1953* (Washington, DC: Government Printing Office, 1954), 344.
50. Ibid., 342, 343.
51. Ibid., 344, 345.
52. Memorandum on the Organization of the Executive Branch for the Conduct of Foreign Affairs, June 1, 1953, ibid., 351.
53. Draft, March 21: State Department Recommended Text: Memorandum for the President on Foreign Affairs Organization, box 76, Dulles Papers.
54. Memorandum on Organization of Executive Branch, June 1, 1953, in *Public Papers of the Presidents—Eisenhower, 1953,* 351.
55. Special Message to Congress, June 1, 1953, ibid., 344.
56. Letter to Secretary Dulles Regarding Transfer of the Affairs of the Foreign Operations Administration to the Department of State, April 17, 1955, in *Public Papers of the Presidents—Eisenhower, 1955* (Washington, DC: Government Printing Office, 1956), 399–401.
57. Quoted in Burton I. Kaufman, *Trade and Aid: Eisenhower's Foreign Economic Policy, 1953–1961* (Baltimore: Johns Hopkins University Press, 1982), 54.
58. Ibid., 52.
59. *New York Times,* August 1, 1956, 22.

5. Special Assistant for Disarmament, 1955–1958

1. Address before the UN General Assembly on Peaceful Uses of Atomic Energy, December 8, 1953, in *Public Papers of the Presidents—Eisenhower, 1953,* 820–21.

2. Thomas Soapes, "A Cold Warrior Seeks Peace: Eisenhower's Strategy for Nuclear Disarmament," *Diplomatic History* 4 (Winter 1980): 657–70.

3. Quoted in Kirby et al., *Stassen,* 164.

4. David Tal, *The American Nuclear Disarmament Dilemma, 1945–1963* (Syracuse, NY: Syracuse University Press, 2008), 67.

5. Kirby et al., *Stassen,* 164–65.

6. Stassen, *Report to the President on the Foreign Operations Administration,* 18–19.

7. *New York Times,* March 20, 1955, 1; Statement by the President Announcing the Appointment of Harold Stassen as Special Assistant to the President for Disarmament Studies, March 19, 1955, in *Public Papers of the Presidents—Eisenhower, 1955,* 343–44.

8. *New York Times,* March 19, 1955, 3.

9. Quoted in Sherman Adams, *Firsthand Report: The Story of the Eisenhower Administration* (New York: Harper & Brothers, 1961), 177.

10. *New York Times,* March 20, 1955, 1.

11. Stassen and Houts, *Eisenhower,* 304–5. Stassen pointed out that the media picked up the term "Secretary of Peace" when Eisenhower used it at the press conference following his appointment.

12. Ibid., 286–87.

13. Quoted in Kirby et al., *Stassen,* 166.

14. Quoted in H. W. Brands Jr., *Cold Warriors: Eisenhower's Generation and American Foreign Policy* (New York: Columbia University Press, 1988), 141.

15. Department of State, *Disarmament: The Intensified Effort, 1955–1958* (Washington, DC, 1958), 10.

16. Robert A. Divine, *Eisenhower and the Cold War* (New York: Oxford University Press, 1981), 117.

17. Harold Stassen, "A Progress Report on Proposed Policy for the United States on the Question of Disarmament," May 26, 1955, in *Foreign Relations of the United States, 1955–1957,* vol. 20, *Regulations of Armaments; Atomic Energy* (Washington, DC: Government Printing Office, 1990), 97 (hereafter cited as *FRUS 1955–1957*).

18. Richard Norton Smith, *On His Own Terms: A Life of Nelson Rockefeller* (New York: Random House, 2014), 235.

19. Ibid., 240; Divine, *Eisenhower and the Cold War,* 118–19; Interview with Rockefeller, December 16, 1964, box 3, Robert E. Matteson Papers, Minnesota Historical Society, St. Paul.

20. Stassen and Houts, *Eisenhower,* 295.

21. Ibid., 296.

22. His speechwriter Emmett Hughes recalled Eisenhower saying about Dulles: "There's only one man I know who has seen *more* of the world, talked with more people and *knows* more than he does—and that's *me.* Hughes, *Ordeal of Power,* 251.

23. Brands, *Cold Warriors,* 142–43.

24. Dulles, Memorandum of Conversation with Stassen, May 20, 1955, in Stassen and Houts, *Eisenhower,* 304.

25. Brands, *Cold Warriors,* 143.

26. Stassen, "Progress Report," May 26, 1955, in *FRUS 1955–1957,* 93.

27. Ibid., 101, 107.

28. Stassen and Houts, *Eisenhower,* 300–301; Kirby et al., *Stassen,* 168–69.

29. Dulles, Memorandum for the President, June 10, 1955, Subject: Congressional Representation at Geneva Conference, box 11, Dulles Papers.

30. Memorandum from Lewis L. Strauss, Chairman, Atomic Energy Commission, to the Secretary of State, June 16, 1955; Strauss to Undersecretary of State Herbert Hoover Jr., June 26, 1955, Correspondence, 1954–1957, White House Office, Office of the Special Assistant for Disarmament, box 25, Dwight D. Eisenhower Library, Abilene, KS.

31. Radio and TV Address to the American People Prior to Departure for the Big Four Conference at Geneva, July 15, 1955, in *Public Papers of the Presidents—Eisenhower, 1955,* 606.

32. Stassen and Houts, *Eisenhower,* 322, 324.

33. Eisenhower to Nixon, October 19, 1955, box 76, Dulles Papers.

34. Stassen and Houts, *Eisenhower,* 325.

35. Ibid., 335.

36. Dulles, Draft Memorandum on Limitation of Armament, June 29, 1955, in *FRUS 1955–1957,* 141; Dulles Memorandum: A Meeting in My Office, Wednesday, June 29, 1955, 3 to 6 PM, ibid., 143.

37. Memorandum of Discussion at the 253rd Meeting of the NSC, June 30, 1955, ibid., 155; Editorial Note, ibid., 163.

38. Stassen and Houts, *Eisenhower,* 339.

39. Eisenhower, *White House Years,* 529.

40. Bulganin to Eisenhower, August 10, 1955, Chronological Correspondence Series, Dulles Papers, thanking him for photographs taken at the Geneva Conference, typifies the friendly tone of his correspondence. Dulles, Memorandum for the President, July 26, 1955, ibid., reflects his reservations, based on Bulganin's assertion that West Germany's membership in NATO ruled out unification.

41. Charles E. Bohlen, *Witness to History, 1929–1969* (New York: W. W. Norton, 1973), 384.

42. Ibid., 476; Eisenhower, *White House Years,* 530.

43. Kirby et al., *Stassen,* 169; Divine, *Eisenhower and the Cold War,* 118; Stassen and Houts, *Eisenhower,* 330–31.

44. Editorial Note, in *FRUS 1955–1957,* 166.

45. Dulles to Deputy Representative on the United Nations Disarmament Commission, August 15, 1955, ibid., 172.

46. Brands, *Cold Warriors,* 145; Tal, *American Nuclear Disarmament Dilemma,* 84–85.

47. Stassen to Secretary of Defense Wilson, August 15, 1955, in *FRUS 1955–1957,* 172–73.

48. Memorandum of Conversation, Department of State, August 25, 1955, Sub-

ject: Advance Consultation on Meetings of UN Subcommittee on Disarmament—Stassen, Striganov (Soviet Embassy), et al., ibid., 185–87.

49. Wilson to Stassen, August 27, 1955, ibid., 190–91; Memorandum of Conversation—Dulles, Lodge, Stassen—Council of Foreign Relations, New York, August 26, 1955, ibid., 191–92.

50. Dulles to Stassen, September 1, 1955, ibid., 194–96.

51. Stassen to Acting Secretary of State (Hoover), September 13, 1955, ibid., 196–97.

52. Memorandum of Conversation, Department of State, September 19, 1955, Subject: President's Proposal in Disarmament Subcommittee—Dulles, Stassen, et al., ibid., 200–201.

53. *New York Times,* September 17, 1955, 53.

54. Memorandum of Conversation, September 19, 1955, in *FRUS 1955–1957,* 202; Editorial Note, ibid., 203.

55. Memorandum of Discussion at the 261st Meeting of the NSC, October 13, 1955: Report by the Special Assistant to the President on Disarmament, ibid., 215, 217–18.

56. Lodge to Dulles, October 26, 1955, ibid., 223.

57. Stassen's Progress Report, November 1, 1955: Proposed Policy of the United States on the Question of Disarmament (NSC Action 1419), ibid., 227, 231.

58. Ibid., 228–29.

59. Dulles to Stassen, December 11, 1955, ibid., 240–41.

60. Memorandum of Discussion at the 271st Meeting of the NSC, December 22, 1955, ibid., 253.

61. Ibid.

62. Ibid., 252–54.

63. Ibid.; Brands, *Cold Warriors,* 145; Tal, *American Nuclear Disarmament Dilemma,* 85.

64. Memorandum of Discussion, December 22, 1955, in *FRUS 1955–1957,* 253.

65. Brands, *Cold Warriors,* 14.

66. *New York Times,* November 17, 1955, 1.

67. Memorandum of Discussion, December 22, 1955, in *FRUS 1955–1957,* 254–55.

68. *New York Times,* December 17, 1955, 9.

6. The Illusion of Progress, 1956

1. Report of the President's Special Assistant to the NSC, undated, in *FRUS 1955–1957,* 261. The UN General Assembly resolution confirming the US approach passed by a vote of fifty-six to seven.

2. Ibid.; Secretary of State to President's Special Assistant, January 26, 1956, ibid., 287.

3. Memorandum of Discussion at the 274th Meeting of the NSC, January 26, 1956, ibid., 291–92.

4. Ibid., 295.

5. Ibid., 296–97, 298.

6. Ibid., 299–300.

7. Ibid., 301.

8. Ibid., 298, 301, 304.

9. Record of Actions Taken at the 275th Meeting of the NSC, February 7, 1956, in *FRUS 1955–1957,* 329.

10. President to Secretary of State, January 23, 1956, ibid., 272; Secretary of State to the President's Special Representative, February 7, 1956, ibid., 332; President to His Special Assistant, March 10, 1956, ibid., 355.

11. Ibid.

12. Eisenhower, *White House Years,* 519.

13. President to His Special Assistant, March 10, 1956, in *FRUS 1955–1957,* 358.

14. Robert A. Divine, *Blowing in the Wind: The Nuclear Test Debate, 1954–1960* (New York: Oxford University Press, 1978), 67–68.

15. Telegram from Department of State to Embassy in the United Kingdom, April 14, 1956, in *FRUS 1955–1957,* 376; Tal, *American Nuclear Disarmament Dilemma,* 89.

16. Tal, *American Nuclear Disarmament Dilemma,* 90.

17. Ibid., 90–91.

18. Ibid., 95.

19. Telegram from Embassy in the United Kingdom to Department of State, April 25, 1956, in *FRUS 1955–1957,* 379.

20. Chancellor Adenauer to Secretary of State Dulles, March 13, 1956, ibid., 359.

21. Telegram from Department of State to Embassy in the United Kingdom, April 16, 1956, ibid., 376. See Ronald J. Granieri, *The Ambivalent Alliance: Konrad Adenauer, the CDU/CSU and the West, 1949–1966* (New York: Berghahn Books, 2003), 86–88.

22. Officer in Charge, Office of UN Political and Security Affairs (Meyers), to Assistant Secretary of State for International Affairs (Wilcox), April 16, 1956, in *FRUS 1955–1957,* 373–74.

23. Telegram from Secretary of State to US Delegation to UN Disarmament Subcommittee, March 30, 1956, National Archives and Records Administration, Record Group 59, 330.13/3056.

24. Telegram from Embassy in the United Kingdom to Department of State, April 25, 1956, in *FRUS 1955–1957,* 378–80.

25. Telegram from Embassy in the United Kingdom to Department of State, April 26, 1956, ibid., 385–86.

26. Telegram from Embassy in the United Kingdom to Department of State, April 25, 1956, ibid., 379–80.

27. Divine, *Blowing in the Wind,* 69.

28. Tal, *American Nuclear Disarmament Dilemma,* 95.

29. *New York Times,* April 22, 1956, 1; Stevenson, speech to American Society of Newspaper Editors, April 21, 1956, in *The Papers of Adlai Stevenson: Toward a New America, 1955–1957,* ed. Walter Johnson (Boston: Houghton Mifflin, 1976), 115–18.

30. Editorial Note, in *FRUS 1955–1957,* 392–93.

31. Memorandum of Discussion at the 284th Meeting of the NSC, May 10, 1956, ibid., 393.

32. Ibid., 394.

33. Ibid., 396.

34. Ibid.

35. *New York Times,* May 5, 1956, 5.

36. Memorandum of Conversation at the 284th Meeting of the NSC, May 10, 1956, in *FRUS 1955–1957,* 398–400.

37. *New York Times,* June 1, 1956, 1; May 20, 1956, sec. IV, E3.

38. Ibid., May 15, 1956, 8.

39. Ibid., May 19, 1956, 1, 4.

40. Brands, *Cold Warriors,*151; *New York Times,* May 19, 1956, 4.

41. Divine, *Blowing in the Wind,* 69.

42. Memorandum from the President's Special Assistant to the President, July 20, 1956, in *FRUS 1955–1957,* 410–11.

43. Undersecretary of State Murphy to the President's Deputy Special Assistant Peaslee, August 16, 1956, ibid., 416–17; President's Special Assistant (Anderson) to the President's Deputy Special Assistant (Peaslee), August 24, 1956, ibid., 418–19; Murphy to Peaslee, August, 18, 1956, ibid., 418. Peaslee served in Stassen's place while he was on leave to advance his bid for the Republican vice presidential nomination.

44. Murphy to Stassen, August 31, 1956, ibid., 419–21.

45. *New York Times,* July 17, 1956, 1, 3.

46. Kirby et al., *Stassen,* 176–77.

47. Ibid., 170.

48. Ibid., 172.

49. Quoted in Jeffrey Frank, *Ike and Dick: Portrait of a Strange Political Marriage* (New York: Simon & Schuster, 2013), 136.

50. *New York Times,* July 24, 1956, 9.

51. Ibid., August 7, 1956, 16; August 5, 1956, 16.

52. Ibid., August 21, 1956, 14.

53. Frank, *Ike and Dick,* 131; R. Alton Lee, *Dwight D. Eisenhower: Soldier and Statesman* (Chicago: Nelson-Hall, 1981), 246.

54. Richard M. Nixon, *RN: The Memoirs of Richard Nixon* (New York: Grosset & Dunlap, 1978), 175.

55. Joe Martin, *My First Fifty Years in Politics* (New York: McGraw-Hill, 1960), 172.

56. *New York Times,* July 30, 1956, 1; Nixon, *RN,* 174.

57. Lee, *Dwight D. Eisenhower,* 245.

58. Dwight D. Eisenhower, *Waging Peace, 1956–1961* (New York: Doubleday, 1965), 10; Hughes, *Ordeal of Power,* 173. Irwin Gellman, *The President and the Apprentice: Eisenhower and Nixon, 1952–1961* (New Haven, CT: Yale University Press, 2015), dissented from this view, noting that Eisenhower entrusted Nixon with crucial issues and gave him more authority than that held by any of his predecessors in the office of vice president.

59. Eisenhower, *Waging Peace,* 10.

60. *New York Times,* August 7, 1956, 16; August 29, 1956, 17.

61. Ibid., November 10, 1956, 38.

62. Murphy to Stassen: Draft Announcement, August 31, 1956, in *FRUS 1955–1957,* 421–22.

63. Stassen to Wilson, September 7, 1956, ibid., 422–23; Soviet Premier (Bulganin) to President Eisenhower, September 11, 1956, Department of State Publication 7008, in *Documents on Disarmament, 1945–1969,* 2 vols. (Washington, DC: Government Printing Office, 1969), 1:691.

64. Bulganin to Eisenhower Regarding Nuclear Weapons Test, October 17, 1956, ibid., 695.

65. Bulganin to Eisenhower, September 11, 1956, ibid., 691.

66. Eisenhower to Bulganin, October 21, 1956, ibid., 697. The president was referring to Bulganin's assertion that Dulles "does not hesitate to make direct attacks against the Soviet Union and its peace-loving policy" (ibid., 694).

67. Eisenhower to Bulganin, October 21, 1956, ibid., 697; Statement by President Eisenhower Regarding Nuclear Tests, October 23, 1956, ibid., 701.

68. Stevenson, speech to American Society of Newspaper Editors, April 21, 1956, in *Papers of Adlai Stevenson,* 115–18; Stassen to Emmett J. Hughes, October 15, 1956, in *FRUS 1955–1957,* 436; *New York Times,* October 24, 1956.

69. Brands, *Cold Warriors,* 153; Memorandum from Secretary of State to the President, October 4, 1956, in *FRUS 1955–1957,* 433. The specific subject of the memo was Bulganin's correspondence. Although Eisenhower's intention was primarily to criticize the Soviet actions against Hungary in October, he also expressed disappointment over the Soviets' rejection of his Geneva proposals; see Eisenhower to Bulganin, December 31, 1956, in *Documents on Disarmament,* 1:729–30.

7. 1957—Stassen's Gaffe?

1. Quoted in Matteson, *Stassen,* 31.

2. *New York Times,* February 14, 1957, 17; Stassen to Esther Stassen, May 11, 1957, box 160, Stassen Papers.

3. *New York Times,* October 28, 1957, 19.

4. Matteson, *Stassen,* 33.

5. Brands, *Cold Warriors,* 153ff.

6. Memorandum of Discussion at the 315th Meeting of the NSC, March 6, 1957, in *FRUS 1955–1957,* 460, 462.

7. Soviet Premier (Bulganin) to President Eisenhower, November17, 1956, enclosing Declaration of the Soviet Government Concerning the Question of Disarmament and Reduction of International Tension, November 17, 1956, in *Documents on Disarmament,* 1:720.

8. Tal, *American Nuclear Disarmament Dilemma,* 96.

9. Telegram from Mission to the United Nations to Department of State, January 17, 1957, in *FRUS 1955–1957,* 449–51; Soviet draft resolution proposing a special session of the UN General Assembly, January 24, 1957, in *Documents on Disarmament,* 1:728.

10. Telegram from Mission to the United Nations to Department of State, January 17, 1957, in *FRUS 1955–1957,* 449–51.

11. Memorandum of Conversation between Secretary of State and President's Special Assistant (Stassen), January 20, 1957, ibid., 453.

12. Joint Statement with Prime Minister Macmillan following Bermuda Conference, March 24, 1957, in *Public Papers of the Presidents—Eisenhower, 1957* (Washington, DC: Government Printing Office, 1958), 211–12.

13. Memorandum of Discussion at the 315th Meeting of the NSC, March 6, 1957, in *FRUS 1955–1957,* 458.

14. Divine, *Blowing in the Wind,* 113–14.

15. Representative at the United Nations (Lodge) to the President, January 26, 1957, in *FRUS 1955–1957,* 454–55.

16. General Assembly Resolution 1011, February 14, 1957, in *Documents on Disarmament,* 2:747; Draft Position Paper for Discussion with Western Four: Procedures to Be Followed in Disarmament Sub-Committee, London, 1957, March 6, 1957—White House Office, Office of the Special Assistant for Disarmament (Harold Stassen), Records 1955–1958, box 25, Correspondence, 1954–1957, Dwight D. Eisenhower Library, Abilene, KS.

17. Stassen to Secretary of State, Memorandum of Discussion at the 315th Meeting of the NSC, March 6, 1947, in *FRUS 1955–1957,* 468; Stassen to Esther Stassen, March 24, 1957, box 160, Stassen Papers. Stassen might have been less enthusiastic about the arrival of Zorin had he known that Zorin was a KGB officer involved in the Prague coup in 1948. See William R. Harris, "March Crisis 1948, Act II," Joint Chiefs of Staff records, declassified NND 847003.

18. Stassen to Secretary of State, April 2, 1957, in *FRUS 1955–1957,* 468.

19. Memorandum of Conversation, Department of State, April 20, 1957, ibid., 476.

20. Ibid., 476–77, 478–79, 480–81.

21. Ibid., 481–82.

22. Memorandum of a Conference with the President, Augusta, Georgia, April 23, 1957, ibid., 486–87.

23. Ibid., 489; Brands, *Cold Warriors,* 156; Memorandum of Conversation, Department of State, April 20, 1957, in *FRUS 1955–1957,* 480.

24. Memorandum of Conversation, April 23, 1957, in *FRUS 1955–1957,* 490.

25. Ibid.

26. Ibid., 489.

27. Divine, *Blowing in the Wind,* 115, 118.

28. Ibid., 121, 125–26, 139.

29. Ibid., 143; Soviet Memorandum Submitted to the Disarmament Subcommittee: Implementation of Partial Disarmament Measures, April 30, 1957, in *Documents on Disarmament,* 2:786, 784–85.

30. Stassen to Secretary of State, May 5, 1957, in *FRUS 1955–1957,* 499.

31. Quoted in Divine, *Blowing in the Wind,* 144.

32. Francis O. Wilcox to Undersecretary of State: Highlights of Mr. Stassen's Disarmament Proposal of May 9, May 10, 1957, National Archives and Records Administration, Record Group 59, 600.0012/5-1057.

33. Oral Record of Meeting in Secretary's Office with Senior Officials, May 14, 1957, Mr. Stassen's Disarmament Proposal, ibid., 600.0012/5-1457.

34. Press conference, May 22, 1957, in *Public Papers of the Presidents—Eisenhower, 1957,* 405; Adams, *Firsthand Report,* 326.

35. Telegram 7854, Dulles to London, May 8, 1957, National Archives and Records Administration, Record Group 59, 330.13/5-85, in *FRUS 1955–1957,* 500n.

36. Telegram from Embassy in the United Kingdom to Department of State, May 9, 1957—Eyes Only for the Secretary from Stassen, in *FRUS 1955–1957,* 503.

37. Editorial Note, ibid., 551; Memorandum of Conversation, Dulles Residence, with Stassen and C. Burke Elbrick, Assistant Secretary of State for European Affairs, May 26, 1957, ibid., 556–57.

38. Ibid., 557.

39. London Arms Control Negotiations: Harold Stassen and Staff, March to December 1957, box 160, Stassen Papers.

40. Memorandum of Conversation, Dulles Residence, May 26, 1957, in *FRUS 1955–1957,* 557.

41. Memorandum of Conversation, Eisenhower and Dulles, May 28, 1947, National Archives and Records Administration, Record Group 59, 6000.0012/5-2887; Tal, *American Nuclear Disarmament Dilemma,* 100.

42. Matteson, *Stassen,* 38–39; Press Conference, April 17, 1957, in *Public Papers of the Presidents—Eisenhower, 1957,* 285–86.

43. Matteson, *Stassen,* 38–39.

44. Telegram from Office of the Permanent Representative at NATO to Department of State, May 29, 1957, in *FRUS 1955–1957,* 564–65.

45. Memorandum from Delegation to the Subcommittee of the UN Disarmament Commission to Secretary of State, May 31, 1957, ibid., 566–72; Informal Memorandum from Stassen to Zorin, May 31, 1957, ibid., 574–83; Editorial Note, ibid., 572–73; Matteson, *Stassen,* 44.

46. Arkady N. Shevchenko, *Breaking with Moscow* (New York: Alfred A. Knopf,

1985), 85–86. In 1978 Shevchenko, then undersecretary-general of the United Nations, defected to the United States.

47. Telegram from Department of State to Embassy in the United Kingdom, Acting Secretary of State to Stassen, May 30, 1957, in *FRUS 1955–1957,* 565.

48. Stassen to Department of State, May 31, 1957, in Editorial Note, ibid., 572–73.

49. Informal Memorandum from Stassen to Zorin, May 31, 1957, ibid., 574, 576–78.

50. Ibid., 579.

51. Telegram from Office of the Permanent Representative to NATO to Department of State [George W. Perkins], June 2, 1957, ibid., 585. At a party given by British Ambassador Gladwyn Jebb for British Minister of Defense Duncan Sandys, Spaak expressed his displeasure about the memo.

52. Telegram from Embassy in the United Kingdom to Department of State [Stassen to Herter], June 2, 1957, ibid., 584.

53. Telegram from Embassy in the United Kingdom to Department of State, Report of Four Powers Meeting, June 4, 1957, ibid., 584; Request for Instructions, June 7, 1957, ibid., 609–10.

54. Memorandum of Conversation, Department of State, Subject: Stassen Memorandum to Zorin, June 3, 1957, ibid., 588–89.

55. Telegram from Embassy in the Federal Republic of Germany to Department of State, June 5, 1957, ibid., 604–5.

56. Ibid., 605; Adenauer to Dulles, June 5, 1957, ibid., 607–8; Dulles to Adenauer, June 5, 1957, ibid., 608–9.

57. Editorial Note, ibid., 589–90; Harold Macmillan, *Riding the Storm* (London: Macmillan, 1971), 301–2.

58. Telegram from Department of State to Embassy in the United Kingdom, Eisenhower to Macmillan, June 4, 1957, in *FRUS 1955–1957,* 597–98. "Disappointed" was substituted for "astonished and chagrined," as advised by Dulles.

59. President to Ambassador in the United Kingdom, June 11, 1957, ibid., 616.

60. Dulles drafted the telegram to Macmillan, assuring him that Stassen would not repeat his mistake in the future. Ibid., 616n3.

61. Memorandum of Telephone Conversation between President and Secretary of State, June 11, 1957, ibid., 618.

62. President's Special Assistant (Stassen) to Secretary of State, June 9, 1957, ibid., 612.

63. Brands, *Cold Warriors,* 158; Kirby et al., *Stassen,* 193.

8. The Long Anticlimax, June 1957–February 1958

1. Quoted in Kirby et al., *Stassen,* 193; President's News Conference, June 19, 1957, in *Public Papers of the Presidents—Eisenhower, 1957,* 115.

2. Stassen to Esther Stassen, June 1, 1957, Personal Papers—Stassen-Esther Correspondence, box 160, Stassen Papers.

3. US Position on First Phase of Disarmament, June 11, 1957, in *FRUS 1955–1957,* 620ff.

4. Stassen to Esther Stassen, June 27, 1957, box 160, Stassen Papers.

5. Telegram from Stassen to the Secretary, June 20, 1957, in *FRUS 1955–1957,* 633.

6. Stassen to the President, July 1, 1957, ibid., 644–45.

7. First Preliminary Draft, Working Paper, June 15, 1957, London Arms Control Negotiations, Harold Stassen and Staff, March to December 1957, box 160, Stassen Papers.

8. Dulles Radio and Television Report to the Nation, July 22, 1957, *Department of State Bulletin,* August 12, 1957, 267–82.

9. Telegram from Secretary to Stassen, July 1, 1957, in *FRUS 1955–1957,* 649.

10. US Del Disarmament No. 389, Subject: 132nd Meeting Subcommittee, July 8, 1957, ibid., 652–53.

11. Telegram from Embassy in the Soviet Union to Department of State, July 12, 1957, ibid., 655–56.

12. Editorial Note, ibid., 664–65.

13. Tal, *American Nuclear Disarmament Dilemma,* 111.

14. Telegram from Whitney to Secretary of State, July 8, 1957, National Archives and Records Administration, Record Group 59, 330.13/7-857; US Del Disarmament No. 534, Paris for Embassy and USRO [US Mission to NATO and Regional Organizations], Subject: US-USSR Bilateral, August 22, 1957, in *FRUS 1955–1957,* 710–13.

15. Harold Stassen and Staff, March to December 1957, box 160, Stassen Papers.

16. Western Working Paper Submitted to the Disarmament Subcommittee, August 29, 1957, in *Documents on Disarmament,* 2:868ff; Bernhard G. Bechhoefer, *Postwar Negotiations for Arms Control* (Washington, DC: Brookings Institution, 1961), 409.

17. Tal, *American Nuclear Disarmament Dilemma,* 114.

18. Telegram from Barbour, American Embassy, London, August 29, 1957, National Archives and Records Administration, Record Group 59, 330.13/8-2957.

19. Soviet Statement on the Disarmament Talks, August 27, 1957, in *Documents on Disarmament,* 2:849.

20. Ibid., 849–50.

21. Ibid., 868.

22. *New York Times,* February 4, 1958, 28.

23. Brands, *Cold Warriors,* 158–59.

24. Memorandum from Secretary of State to Stassen, September 27, 1957, in *FRUS 1955–1957,* 723–24; Deputy Secretary of Defense (Quarles) to Secretary of State, September 30, 1957, ibid., 726–28; Memorandum from Joint Chiefs of Staff to Wilson, September 30, 1957, ibid., 729.

25. Memorandum from Stassen to Dulles, October 7, 1957, ibid., 736; Memorandum of Conversation, White House, October 8, 1957, ibid., 739.

26. Memorandum of Conversation, White House, October 8, 1957, ibid., 740.

27. Memorandum from Dulles to the President, September 28, 1957, ibid., 726.

28. Stassen to Dulles, December 23, 1957, ibid., 781; Dulles to Stassen, December 24, 1957, ibid., 781–82.

29. Memorandum of Discussion at the 350th Meeting of the NSC, January 6, 1958, in *Foreign Relations of the United States, 1958–1960,* vol. 3 (Washington, DC: Government Printing Office, 1992), 533ff.

30. Ibid., 534–35, 538–41, 544.

31. *New York Times,* February 2, 1958, 1; February 8, 1958, 1; February 16, 1958, 1; Letter Accepting Resignation of Harold E. Stassen, February 16, 1958, in *Public Papers of the Presidents—Eisenhower, 1958* (Washington, DC: Government Printing Office, 1959), 138–39.

32. *New York Times,* February 14, 1957, 3; Stassen to Esther Stassen, May 11, 1957, box 160, Stassen Papers; *New York Times,* January 9, 1958.

33. *New York Times,* February 27, 1958, 1; February 28, 1958, 1.

Conclusions and Reflections

1. Kirby et al., *Stassen,* 176–77.

2. London Arms Control Negotiations: Harold Stassen and Staff, March to December 1957, box 160, Stassen Papers.

3. Personal Papers—Stassen-Esther Correspondence, February to December 1957, ibid.

4. Memorandum of Conversation, Gettysburg, Participants: Eisenhower and Matteson, Subject: Disarmament 1955–1958, November 24, 1964, box 1, Matteson Papers.

5. Fred Greenstein, *The Hidden-Hand Presidency: Eisenhower as a Leader* (New York: Basic Books, 1991).

6. Robert E. Matteson, "1955—A Watershed Year in the History of Disarmament Policy," National War College Paper, box 1, Matteson Papers.

Selected Bibliography

Archives

Bentley Historical Library, University of Michigan
  Arthur H. Vandenberg Papers
Dwight D. Eisenhower Library, Abilene, KS
Library of Congress
  John Foster Dulles Papers, Princeton University, microform copies
  Robert A. Taft Papers
Minnesota Historical Society, St. Paul
  Robert E. Matteson Papers
  Harold Stassen Papers
National Archives and Records Administration, College Park, MD

Books and Articles

Adams, Sherman. *Firsthand Report: The Story of the Eisenhower Administration.* New York: Harper & Brothers, 1961.

Alsop, Joseph, and Stewart Alsop. "One Man Bandwagon." *Saturday Evening Post,* September 7, 1946.

Ambrose, Stephen E. *Eisenhower, the President.* New York: Simon & Schuster, 1984.

Bechhoefer, Bernhard G. *Postwar Negotiations for Arms Control.* Washington, DC: Brookings Institution, 1961.

Bohlen, Charles E. *Witness to History, 1929–1969.* New York: W. W. Norton, 1973.

Brands, H. W., Jr. *Cold Warriors: Eisenhower's Generation and American Foreign Policy.* New York: Columbia University Press, 1988.

Canham, Erwin D. "Young Men on Elephants." *Christian Science Monitor,* December 1, 1938.

Divine, Robert A. *Blowing in the Wind: The Nuclear Test Ban Debate, 1954–1960.* New York: Oxford University Press, 1978.

Documents on Disarmament, 1945–1969. 2 vols. Washington, DC: Government Printing Office, 1969.

Eisenhower, Dwight D. *The White House Years: Mandate for Change, 1953–1956.* Garden City, NY: Doubleday, 1963.

Foreign Relations of the United States, 1955–1957. Vol. 20, *Regulations of Armaments; Atomic Energy.* Washington, DC: Government Printing Office, 1990.

Frank, Jeffrey. *Ike and Dick: Portrait of a Strange Political Marriage.* New York: Simon & Schuster, 2013.

Gellman, Irwin. *The President and the Apprentice: Eisenhower and Nixon, 1952–1961.* New Haven, CT: Yale University Press, 2015.

Gunther, John. "Young Man Going Somewhere." *Harper's,* January 1946.

Hewlett, Richard D., and Oscar Anderson. *A History of the United States Atomic Energy Commission.* Vol. 1, *The New World, 1939–1946.* University Park: Pennsylvania State University Press, 1962.

Hughes, Emmett. *The Ordeal of Power: A Political Memoir of the Eisenhower Years.* New York: Atheneum, 1963.

Kaufman, Burton I. *Trade and Aid: Eisenhower's Foreign Economic Policy, 1953–1961.* Baltimore: Johns Hopkins University Press, 1982.

Kirby, Alec, David G. Dalin, and John F. Rothmann. *Harold Stassen: The Life and Perennial Candidacy of the Liberal Progressive Republican.* Jefferson, NC: McFarland, 2013.

Krock, Arthur. *Memoirs: Sixty Years on the Firing Line.* New York: Funk & Wagnalls, 1968.

Lee, R. Alton. *Dwight D. Eisenhower: Soldier and Statesman.* Chicago: Nelson-Hall, 1981.

Lindley, Ernest K. "Stassen's Role in Foreign Aid." *Newsweek*, December 8, 1952.

Macmillan, Harold. *Riding the Storm.* London: Macmillan, 1971.

Martin, Joe. *My First Fifty Years in Politics.* New York: McGraw-Hill, 1960.

Matteson, Robert E. *Harold Stassen: His Career, the Man, and the 1957 Arms Control Negotiations.* Inver Grove Heights, MN: Desk Top, 1991.

Neal, Steve. *Dark Horse: A Biography of Wendell Willkie.* Garden City, NY: Doubleday, 1984.

Nixon, Richard M. *RN: The Memoirs of Richard Nixon.* New York: Grosset & Dunlap, 1978.

Ostrower, Gary B. *The United Nations and the United States, 1945–1995.* New York: Twayne, 1998.

Patterson, James T. *Mr. Republican: A Biography of Robert A. Taft.* Boston: Houghton Mifflin, 1972.

Peaslee, Amos J., ed. *Man Was Meant to Be Free: Selected Statements of Governor Harold E. Stassen, 1940–1951.* New York: Doubleday, 1951.

Public Papers of the Presidents—Eisenhower, 1953, 1955, 1957, 1958. Washington, DC: Government Printing Office, 1954–1959.

Rovere, Richard H. "Stassen of Minnesota." *Nation,* June 3, 1944.

Schevchenko, Arkady N. *Breaking with Moscow.* New York: Alfred A. Knopf, 1985.

Smith, Jean Edward. *Eisenhower in War and Peace.* New York: Random House, 2012.

Smith, Richard Norton. *On His Own Terms: A Life of Nelson Rockefeller.* New York: Random House, 2014.

———. *Thomas E. Dewey and His Times.* New York: Simon & Schuster, 1982.

Stassen, Harold. *United Nations: A Working Paper for Restructuring.* Minneapolis: Lerner, 1991.

———. *Where I Stand.* New York: Doubleday, 1947.

Stassen, Harold, and Marshall Houts. *Eisenhower: Turning the World toward Peace.* St. Paul, MN: Merrill/Magnus, 1990.

Taft, Robert A. *The Papers of Robert A. Taft.* 4 vols. Edited by Clarence E. Wunderlin Jr. et al. Kent, OH: Kent State University Press, 2003.

Tal, David. *The American Nuclear Disarmament Dilemma, 1945–1963.* Syracuse, NY: Syracuse University Press, 2008.

Weintraub, Bernard. "The 1938 Nomination." *Esquire,* August 1937.

Index

Page numbers in *italics* refer to photographs.

Studies in Conflict, Diplomacy, and Peace

Series Editors: George C. Herring, Andrew L. Johns, and Kathryn C. Statler

This series focuses on key moments of conflict, diplomacy, and peace from the eighteenth century to the present to explore their wider significance in the development of U.S. foreign relations. The series editors welcome new research in the form of original monographs, interpretive studies, biographies, and anthologies from historians, political scientists, journalists, and policymakers. A primary goal of the series is to examine the United States' engagement with the world, its evolving role in the international arena, and the ways in which the state, nonstate actors, individuals, and ideas have shaped and continue to influence history, both at home and abroad.

Books in the Series

Truman, Congress, and Korea: The Politics of America's First Undeclared War
Larry Blomstedt
The Gulf: The Bush Presidencies and the Middle East
Michael F. Cairo
Reagan and the World: Leadership and National Security, 1981–1989
Edited by Bradley Lynn Coleman and Kyle Longley

American Justice in Taiwan: The 1957 Riots and Cold War Foreign Policy
Stephen G. Craft
Diplomatic Games: Sport, Statecraft, and International Relations since 1945
Edited by Heather L. Dichter and Andrew L. Johns
Nothing Less Than War: A New History of America's Entry into World War I
Justus D. Doenecke
Aid under Fire: Nation Building and the Vietnam War
Jessica Elkind
Enemies to Allies: Cold War Germany and American Memory
Brian C. Etheridge
Grounded: The Case for Abolishing the United States Air Force
Robert M. Farley
The American South and the Vietnam War: Belligerence, Protest, and Agony in Dixie
Joseph A. Fry
Obama at War: Congress and the Imperial Presidency
Ryan C. Hendrickson
US Presidential Elections and Foreign Policy: Candidates, Campaigns, and Global Politics from FDR to Bill Clinton
Edited by Andrew Johnstone and Andrew Priest
The Conversion of Senator Arthur H. Vandenberg: From Isolation to International Engagement
Lawrence S. Kaplan
Harold Stassen: Eisenhower, the Cold War, and the Pursuit of Nuclear Disarmament
Lawrence S. Kaplan
Nixon's Back Channel to Moscow: Confidential Diplomacy and Détente
Richard A. Moss
Peacemakers: American Leadership and the End of Genocide in the Balkans
James W. Pardew
The Currents of War: A New History of American-Japanese Relations, 1899–1941
Sidney Pash
Eisenhower and Cambodia: Diplomacy, Covert Action, and the Origins of the Second Indochina War
William J. Rust
So Much to Lose: John F. Kennedy and American Policy in Laos
William J. Rust
Foreign Policy at the Periphery: The Shifting Margins of US International Relations since World War II
Edited by Bevan Sewell and Maria Ryan
Lincoln Gordon: Architect of Cold War Foreign Policy
Bruce L. R. Smith